PIONEERING AVIATION IN THE WEST

As told by the pioneers

Lloyd Bungey

with additional research and editing by
Arnold M. Feast
Jerry E. Vernon

Project co-ordinator: Rose Zalesky

ISBN 0-88839-271-0

Cataloguing in Publication Data
Bungey, Lloyd M., 1943-
Pioneering aviation in the West,
as told by the pioneers

ISBN 0-88839-271-0
1. Aeronautics—British Columbia—History—Anecdotes. I. Feast, Arnold M. II. Zalesky, Rose. III. Title.
TL523.B86 1991 629.13'009711 C91-091049-9

Edited by Harold M. Feast and Jerry E. Vernon
Co-ordinated by Rose Zalesky
Pioneer interviews by Lloyd Bungey and Kenneth I. Swartz
Photo research by Ingwold Wikene
Photo reproduction by Donald P. Olsen
All photographs courtesy of private owners and the Canadian Museum of Flight and Transportation collection. A special thanks to those who donated photos to help build the collection.
Much of the narrative material incorporated in this book was derived from the audio-visual records of personal interviews conducted by Museum personnel. This aspect was financially assisted by a grant from the 99's Award in Aviation and an employment grant from Employment and Immigration Canada. A production of The Senior's Wing, Canadian Museum of Flight and Transportation, 13527 Crescent Road, Surrey, B.C., V4A 2W1
Printed in Hong Kong

Published simultaneously in Canada and the United States by

HANCOCK HOUSE PUBLISHERS LTD.
19313 Zero Avenue, Surrey, B.C. V3S 5J9
HANCOCK HOUSE PUBLISHERS
1431 Harrison Avenue, Blaine, WA 98231

CONTENTS

Dedication

This book is dedicated to Arnold Feast, who took up the challenge to help complete the editing, help choose photos, and generally take the book to publication in spite of failing health. Sadly, he passed away before the book went to press.

For I dipt into the future, far as human eye could see
Saw the vision of the world, and all the wonders that would be
Saw the heavens fill with commerce, argosies of magic sails
Pilots of the purple twilight, dropping down with costly bales
Tennyson – From LOCKSLEY HALL

This futuristic monument to the future was a longtime landmark at Vancouver Airport. It was built by Sheet Metal Workers Union Local 280.

CMFT Collection #206.7
Arnold Feast collection

Introduction

When the Canadian Museum of Flight and Transportation commenced a series of interviews to record the reminiscences of various aviation pioneers in B.C. in 1985, it was the intention that the material would be used to supply the background facts for a book about the growth and development of aviation in British Columbia. As "Pioneer Profiles" developed, however, it became apparent that those interviewed were supplying more than just the background material, they were telling the story of B.C.'s aviation heritage. We have, therefore, chosen to have our "pioneers" relate much of the story for the reader.

With an industry as young as commercial aviation, the "pioneering" is a remarkably recent event; therefore it becomes necessary to consider some current developments as being of a pioneering nature. We have taken a very liberal view of who constitutes a "pioneer" in order to have as comprehensive a story as possible. Where pioneers were no longer available to directly tell their tale, we have looked to the written records of their contemporaries or sought those who could remember their activities.

Readers may notice the omission of sections devoted to some notable individuals and companies which have had a major impact on B.C. aviation, such as Russ Baker and Pacific Western Airlines, Grant McConachie and Canadian Pacific Airways, and Jim Spilsbury and Queen Charlotte Airlines. This is intentional since their stories have been adequately told by others. We sought to record the efforts of others involved in the aviation industry, the successes and the failures, so their struggles might not be forgotten.

Some of those, who relate their tales within these pages, have passed on to fly in more ethereal realms since being interviewed for our "Pioneer Profiles," but we have chosen to retain the use of present tense when referring to them, since their words are still alive on our tapes. This, then, is their legacy to us all.

The names of many pioneers are indelibly preserved on the Roll of Honour emblazoned on the wall of the Terminal building in Vancouver's International Airport. This volume is in tribute to them and the "others" recorded here, for they also served.

Some status changes, corporate names and structure have occurred over the five years that this book was written. In most cases, no attempt was made to update the information, and the text is as written at the time.

CMFT Collection #289.3 John Moutray collection

A Curtiss Pusher like this one was the first aeroplane to fly in B.C.

At Vancouver 1908
First plan seen in Vancour
we paid .50¢ to see if it fly and
this is as high as it got.

CMFT Collection #148.1 Art Seller collection

First powered flight in B.C. Charles K. Hamilton flew this Curtiss Pusher on March 25, 1910 from Minoru Park, Richmond, B.C. Note incorrect date written on photo.

1

EXHIBITION FLIGHTS AND EXPERIMENTS

The arrival of aviation in B.C.

The new phenomenon of manned flight in heavier-than-air flying machines was introduced to the B.C. public by a series of exhibition flyers who commenced visiting the area in 1910. These exhibitions were somewhat like travelling road shows with promoters making extravagant claims to attract thrill seekers and milk their purses of admission fees to the flying demonstrations. As each year passed, new serial novelties were required to whet the public appetite and keep the customers coming.

The first such pilot, however, required only a simple exhibition of flying to satisfy his audience. He was Charles K. Hamilton of California who brought his Curtiss-type pusher biplane to the Minoru Park racetrack in Richmond, B.C. on the Easter holiday weekend of 1910. The B.C. Electric Railway Company ran special trains to cater for the crowds drawn to the display.

On Friday, March 25, 1910, Hamilton became the first man to fly an aeroplane in B.C.:

> *With great courage and marvelous skill and a seagull's grace, aviator Charles K. Hamilton gave to the 3,500 spectators at Minoru Park, a daring and at times thrilling exhibition. . . . Ten minutes after his heavier than air machine soared on its first flight in graceful curves sweeping toward the grandstand, to the amazement of the crowd it suddenly swerved to the middle of the field and plunged to the earth.*

Hamilton landed safely but considerable damage was done to one of the planes while a tyre was ripped from one of the wheels. But here the aviator justified his reputation for courage of the kind seen only in men who play with the clouds. Making such repairs as he could within the period of the spectators' patience and his machine still incomplete, the engine was again started, the propeller again buzzed sending the coats of his assistants flying with the swift revolutions as they held his machine to the earth. Vaulting to his seat, Hamilton gave the front planes the slant that would catch the air and then like a giant seagull, the machine rose to the accompaniment of deafening cheers . . . everyone was satisfied."
(Daily Province, Vancouver, March 26, 1910)

There was no failure or accident in the flights made by aviator Hamilton at Minoru Park Saturday afternoon. The wind was still and the sky was bright, the only drawback being the somewhat low temperature which in the upper reaches of the atmosphere, to which he attained, was scarcely bearable. His most successful flight was one of about 20 miles to New Westminster following the course of the North arm of the Fraser River. He did this in 30 minutes, rising along the way to between 2,250 feet and 2,500 feet being forced to descend to a lower altitude owing to the intense cold. The flight was the occasion of keen interest. No-one was expecting that he intended to go so far. Spectators gathered in the grounds watched him soar out into the sky growing fainter and fainter until he became a speck. Then he disappeared entirely from view and some thought that because he could no longer be seen low on the horizon he must have descended to earth.

In some 10 minutes everyone was speculating as to where he could be and what had become of him. The nervous and pessimistic suggested an accident . . . 20 minutes after his departure a faint speck was discerned to the northeast where

> *he was last seen. . . . The aviator circled round the grounds, swooped down in front of the grandstand . . . and gracefully alighted amidst hearty applause of the onlookers. Everybody crowded around him and asked where he had been. "New Westminster" came the reply.*
>
> *Mr. Hamilton was shaking with cold and immediately supplied with a stimulant. Between the chattering of his teeth, he told a curious knot of spectators how he had followed the winding course of the north arm of the river, mounting to 2,500 feet and then finding the temperature too chilly descended to a lower altitude which he maintained until reaching New Westminster where he sank to within nearly a hundred feet off the ground. His arrival there caused considerable interest. The streetcars stopped while their occupants watched his evolutions. Turning just west of the bridge he began his homeward flight.*
>
> *Mr. Hamilton made two other flights on Saturday. . . . During the second which was described as a speed test against a motor car, the biplane was beaten.*
>
> (Daily Province, Vancouver, March 28, 1910)

On the following Monday, Hamilton made the final appearance of his three-day engagement. Again, a gimmick race was set up this time with racehorse Prince Brutus. A handicap distance of 3/8ths of a mile was conceded to the racehorse, but it was too great. The Curtiss biplane was catching up to Prince Brutus at the end of its mile flight but the racehorse was still ahead at the post.

Hamilton's flights at Minoru Park gained him the honour of being the first man to fly in B.C. His achievement was closely followed later in 1910 by William Wallace Gibson of Victoria, who, without formal training, built and flew an aircraft of his own design, from a farm near Mount Tolmie. Called a Twinplane because it had dual-wings – one set in front and one behind the pilot – it flew 200 feet at a height of twenty feet on September 8.

The trial was made over the Dean farm in the vicinity of Mount Tolmie. When he did alight, the severe concussion fractured the riding wheels of the Twinplane and further flights have been delayed for a day or two. . . .

In length the twin plane measures 54 feet with a width of eight feet, while the planes wings are positioned lengthwise on the craft and are controlled by a single lever which guides the course of the airship. The planes measure twenty feet each in length and are eight feet wide, supplemented with one hundred springs girded with wire which make the machine indestructible."
(Daily Colonist, Victoria, September 10, 1910.)

Gibson followed his Twinplane with a second original design, the Multiplane, in 1911, but financial problems and local skepticism led him to move his experiments to Ladner, then Kamloops and finally to Calgary where he ultimately ran out of money to support his endeavours.

The next touring exhibition to visit B.C., following Hamilton's successful 1910 exhibition, was the "Pacific Aviation Company," which brought two Curtiss biplanes and flyers Jack de Pries and the Manning Brothers to Minoru Park in 1911. The crowds were larger than the previous year but the show was less than satisfactory.

An immense crowd that was howling enthusiastically at 3 o'clock was conspicuously apathetic when at 4:45 de Pries and his Curtiss type biplane appeared, one hour and 45 minutes late. . . . de Pries ran the biplane along the ground 300 yards when it raised off the ground a foot and turning sharply rammed its nose into the fence on the left side of the track. Spectators scattered and some fell off the fence. . . . The machine was incapacitated. . . .

de Pries then trundled out the 40 HP Curtiss type biplane, the machine that Jack Manning had been advertised to fly, . . . after gliding 300 yards he rose to an altitude estimated at 250 feet sailing in a westerly direction over the

racetrack highboard fence. He alighted in the meadow back of the fence after a flight of 500 yards. This concluded the events of the first day of the 3 days meet.
(Daily Province, Vancouver, April 15, 1911)

On the Saturday, the paying public at the racetrack were just barely treated to the spectacle of flight and were poorly placed to witness the most exciting part of the action.

Starting at the commencement of the track, the aviator took to the air just before reaching the grandstand, rising gracefully to a height of a couple of hundred feet, taking the turn that followed the course three parts round and sailing away in the direction of Steveston. The flight was about 2 miles and from the park the machine appeared to alight easily. It was stated that it was the aviator's intention to alight there and then to sail back but the machine was badly damaged.
(Daily Province, Vancouver, April 17, 1911)

If Friday was bad and Saturday worse, then Monday was a total disaster, receiving scathing criticism.

Cold feet was a common complaint with the aviators at Minoru Park, yesterday. Aerial navigation, the dream of the prime romance of our boyhood days was nearly brought into vivid realization when Browning Manning of the Manning brothers, in an attempt to break the height record for aeroplanes, rose about four feet from the ground. Then, afraid that he really was going up, he altered his planes and made a quick return to terra firma, ran into a fence and damaged one of his wings, ending by nearly making a record of another kind—a mad rush from his machine as though it were haunted.

After an hour's weary wait, the machine was repaired and a second attempt was made. The result was as before. Through chattering teeth and knocking knees he (made his excuses) . . . adding that the spectators had seen enough for

their money. Altogether, it was the poorest of the three very disappointing, would be hair-raising, mid-air maneuvers.
(Daily Province, Vancouver, April 18, 1911)

With the professionals generating so much adverse publicity at Minoru Park, it is not surprising that the locally designed and built Templeton-McMullen biplane was completed without fanfare, taken out to Minoru Park and test flown very quietly during the first week of May 1911, before the information was discreetly leaked to the press.

Without laying any claim to being dare-devils of the air, two young Vancouver boys from West Fairview have just completed a biplane of the Curtiss type and, several days ago, the machine was given a trial spin at Minoru Park with results which are said to have been very satisfactory. William McMullen . . . and William Templeton are the two youthful aviators who have the honour of flying the first airship built in the city. The former is the actual driver of the aircraft, receiving the assistance of young Templeton in designing and building it.
(Daily Province, Vancouver, May 6,1911)

Although the Templeton-McMullen aircraft, the first aeroplane built in Vancouver, had been upstaged by the Twinplane of W. W. Gibson, for the honour of being the first such in B.C., the arrival on the Vancouver aviation scene of Bill Templeton was of some importance. In the 1920s, he was to become the chief proponent for the creation of a Vancouver Airport, convincing the Vancouver City Council of the need for such, selecting the site of the present Vancouver Airport, planning, building and managing it for the council. He was a visionary who foresaw, far better than most, the needs of the future.

Another Vancouver visionary, but one with a more immediate vision, was Billy Stark. The son of the owner of a chain of Vancouver shoe stores, Stark saw in aviation an escape from the dreary occupation of selling shoes and a

CMFT Collection #240.1 Jeri Lee collection

William "Billy" Stark, B.C.'s first licenced pilot.

chance for making his fortune. Obtaining Aero Club of America Certificate No. 110 at the Curtiss Flying School in San Diego, California, he returned home to Vancouver with a Curtiss pusher biplane for touring the country in a series of exhibitions.

After some informal flights at Minoru Park racetrack on April 13, 1912, he made three exhibition flights on April 29, followed by some passenger carrying flights on the following Wednesday, April 24. To the sports editor of the Daily Province, James T. Hewitt, goes the honour of being the first passenger to be carried in an aeroplane in B.C., while Stark's wife, Olive, has the distinction of being the first woman aeroplane passenger in Canada. Their flights were made, seated beside Stark on the wing of the biplane.

The Curtiss biplane is not built for that purpose and the passenger has to take a seat on the plane close to the engine and mix up with the wires that control the machine.
(Daily Province, Vancouver, April 26, 1912)

A further flying demonstration, scheduled to be held at Minoru Park on the last weekend in May was postponed due to inclement weather and held then at Hastings Park instead. There, Stark made two successful flights on Saturday May 4, followed by a less successful one.

A frightened cow which ran across the landing ground just as Billy Stark, the plucky Vancouver aviator, was planing to earth at Hastings park on Saturday was the cause of an accident which resulted in some slight damage to the machine and the injury of the aviator's assistants. Stark himself escaped unharmed. . . .

A herd of cows, grazing in the infield, took fright as he neared the ground and one of them ran directly in front of the machine. Seeing this the aviator tipped his machine and went up a short distance, only to discover that he was too near the trees, which rim the track, to clear them. Then, being past the cow he came down again. The machine was going at a terrific pace and, when it hit the ground, rebounded fully 10 feet before it settled down again and speeded for the fence which encircled the enclosure. Two assistants, J. Perry, the machinist, and J. Watson, an auto driver, grabbed the machine in an effort to stop it and suffered the unique experience of being run over by an aeroplane. Perry was bowled over on the ground and given a bad shaking up while Watson's left hand was badly torn by a wire. The machine refused to stop and crashed into the fence.

Stark saved himself by dropping from his seat about 20 feet from the fence, and allowed the machine to shoot over him.
(Daily Province, Vancouver, May 6, 1912)

The damage to Stark's machine was not serious, and, after making repairs, he commenced his planned tour of the province, appearing at Victoria, Chilliwack and Armstrong, amongst other locations during the following months.

Stark was not the only aviator to appear before the Vancouver crowds in 1912. Just two weeks after his appearance at the Hastings Exhibition grounds, Stark was upstaged by Americans Phil Parmelee and Clifford Turpin who, as an added attraction, had brought along a parachutist billed as, "Professor Morton." In providing the Hastings Park crowd with the spectacle of a parachute jump, on May 24, 1912, Morton also found his way into history as the first person to perform a parachute jump from an aeroplane over Canada.

1933. Vancouver. "Batman" Cecil MacKenzie made many successful parachute jumps.

CMFT Collection #259.31
Margery Morton collection

Morton took his position in the body of the aeroplane within touch of the canvas parachute attached to the bottom of the airship. Parmelee made off from a splendid start, again in the same direction he had followed on the first trip, but perhaps owing to the increase in weight, the airship did not rise very rapidly until it had gone out of the park grounds, continuing fairly low as it flew over the waters of the inlet. Those standing on the ground in the park were unable to follow it owing to the surrounding trees and failed to see the turn made. It was a minute and a half before either sound or sight of the airship again was noticed. Then it appeared well over North Vancouver heading east. Parmelee and his professorial passenger were now flying high and the machine followed up the course of the inlet until, with a wide sweep, it turned and retraced its course clear against the skyline over Lynn Valley. Shining like a huge white bat with two spread pinions, two circles were made in close quarters, then the expectant watchers saw the professor drop, and hundreds of sighs of relief went up when the parachute was seen to fill. Three minutes afterwards Parmelee brought the airship down light as a bird in front of the grandstand. But what had become of the professor?

No one knew until the aviator gave out the word that he had seen Morton get up and pick up his parachute. The shifting character of the wind had decided Parmelee to run no risk of being able to drop the parachutist short of the park grounds, so he let him go at a suitable place which happened to be over the mud flats at Seymour Creek. The height from which the drop took place was 1,800 feet. When Morton reached terra firma he was immediately surrounded by several hundreds of picnickers who were rather astonished at his sudden appearance amongst them. The daring parachutist was promptly conveyed to the shore and at four o'clock he appeared carrying his parachute, smiling and none the worse for his experience.
(Daily News Advertiser, Vancouver, May 25, 1912)

Later in 1912, James V. Martin visited Vancouver with a two-seat biplane of his own design. His flight at Minoru Park on August 10, during a lull between horse races, was terminated when the machine suffered engine failure on take off and ran into a fence.

Nelson, B.C. became a venue for a series of demonstration flights in September 1912 when the Nelson Exhibition Committee made a contract with Billy Stark for an appearance at the Nelson Exhibition. An accident in Portland, Oregon prevented Stark himself from fulfilling this obligation but he arranged for Walter Edwards, an American pilot, to perform in his stead. In spite of adverse conditions, Edwards made successful flights on September 24, 25, and 27.

The following year, 1913, saw yet another travelling aviation show, the Bennett Aero Company, entertain the Vancouver area public. By this time, the crowds needed more than just the usual dips, swerves and figure eights to attract them to the show. For crowd pleasers, Bennett, the manager, arranged for an altitude record attempt by John

CMFT Collection #601.5 George Fawkes collection

Alys McKey Bryant, American aviatrix who on July 31, 1913, in Vancouver, became the first woman to fly in Canada.

M. Bryant and a flight by an aviatrix, Alys McKey Bryant. For whatever it was worth, Bryant established a new Pacific Northwest altitude record of 5,100 feet, on Thursday, July 31, 1913. The flight by his wife, Alys, the same day was more significant, since it was the first flight in Canada made by a woman pilot.

Alys McKey had a short lived career in aviation. Bennett, foreseeing the advantages of having a woman pilot on his list of attractions, had recruited her in 1912 and arranged for her training. During this period, she had married the star of the show, John Bryant, but it was to be a short marriage. The week following their appearance in Vancouver, Mrs. Alys McKey Bryant became Canada's first aviation widow, when Bryant was killed in Canada's first fatal aircraft accident while making a flight over Victoria.

CMFT Collection #601.3 George Fawkes collection

Pioneer American airman John Milton Bryant killed in flying mishap at Victoria B.C. on August 7, 1913. Husband of Alys McKey Bryant.

The daring airman, after twice attempting to bring his machine into the wind and at the same time descend towards the harbour, whence he had arisen five minutes before, dashed down like a plummet as his craft became helpless. When the plane collapsed Bryant was between 350 and 400 feet from the earth. Bearing him securely attached to the seat, the machine fell almost perpendicularly, alighting upon the roof of the two-story structure at the northwest corner of Theatre Alley and Cormorant Street. With a crash that could be heard for several blocks, the Hydroplane dashed upon the roof. Bryant was underneath, the craft having overturned in its descent through the air.
(Daily Colonist, Victoria, August 8, 1913)

CMFT Collection #471.2 Henry E. Stevenson collection.

Nelson, B.C., July 14, 1914. Curtiss Pusher flown by Weldon Cooke .

This accident changed Mrs. Bryant's outlook on aviation and she left the airshow circuit and gave up flying.

In 1914, Billy Stark brought his Curtiss out of retirement and resumed flying, while an American, Weldon Cooke, brought a Curtiss-type seaplane to Nelson in July to fly from Kootenay Lake over the Nelson Carnival. A month later, on August 13, he made a flight from Okanagan Lake at the Kelowna Regatta.

With the outbreak of World War I on August 4, 1914, however, the days of the exhibition flights were numbered and flying soon took on a more serious nature.

CMFT Collection #471.1 Henry E. Stevenson collection

Curtiss Pusher biplane, 60-horsepower, water-cooled, 8-cylinder engine, was flown on September 24, 1912 by Walter Edwards in Nelson, B.C. from a 600-foot ball park which had an eight foot fence around the perimeter.

2

WORLD WAR I FRUSTRATIONS

An Aero Club, a flying school, two aircraft manufacturers, but no real progress

The outbreak of World War I in August 1914 provided the impetus needed to take aviation out of the realm of a carnival attraction and into a participant activity. Under the stimulus of war, B.C. gained its first Aero Club, its first commercial flying school and its first aircraft manufacturers, but all were shortlived.

In the spring of 1915, as the first reports of the activities of the Royal Flying Corps were being received, Billy Stark, Vancouver's pioneer aviator, met with a group to discuss the possibility of providing flight training for local volunteers. The upshot of this meeting was the formation of the Aero Club of B.C. which purchased Stark's old Curtiss pusher biplane for $2,500 and employed Stark as instructor. Twenty-seven people had agreed to contribute $100 each, but only twelve contributors actually joined. A public subscription was organized to obtain the extra funds needed.

"We had nothing decent to offer in exchange for contributions," says Cy Perkins, one of the original trainees. *"Normally, if you put money into something you expect to get a return for it. We could not even tell them that we were getting government support because at first we were not getting anything from them. We had to do a lot of things to get the public in favour of our idea.*

"We had a fund drive throughout the lower Fraser Valley and various people subscribed, some with small contribu-

tions and others with larger amounts. Some were individuals who had a few bucks to spare; others were big wholesalers. A lot came from business people."

Prominent among the club supporters and board of directors were: secretary, J. W. Pattison, J. H. Senkler, KC, W. E. Burns, H. O. Bell-Irving Sr., and Judge Schultz.

When sufficient funds had been obtained, Stark commenced training students at the Minoru Park racetrack, then moved to the Milligan Farm in Steveston near the Terra Nova Cannery where a larger field was available.

"Billy Stark took us up and flew us around sitting on the lower wing," says Perkins. *"It was small satisfaction for all the time spent and all the work that had been done."*

Selected students were trained by taxiing the machine down the field with the throttle travel limited to prevent take off power being applied. As the student gained skill, more power was allowed until finally flight was possible. In addition, Stark took the students into the air for flight experience.

Between September and November 1915, two members of the Aero Club of B.C., Murton Seymour and Philip Smith, completed their training and were accepted for the Royal Flying Corps, but in November, the muddy condition of the ground made use of the field impractical.

"The plane went to land in the field," recalls Cy Perkins, *"but it was so muddy that the plane tipped up and so twisted out of shape that it had to be realigned.*

"We had the Hoffar Brothers Boat Works rebuild it," wrote another member of the club, Vic Phillips, in 1971. *"They put pontoons under it to land on water. The club moved it to Deadman's Island beside Stanley Park for a while and later to Pitt Lake."*

This conversion to floatplane configuration enabled the club to continue operations into the winter months but the aircraft became water-logged and badly damaged following a collision with a drifting log while being used to give taxiing training to students.

By the end of 1915, the Aero Club of B.C. was unable to continue its training activities without obtaining new aircraft. Such a purchase demanded additional funding and a new organization, the B.C. Aviation School Limited, was set up to obtain the necessary money.

> *Determined to boost the flying game in Vancouver, and place this city on the map as a rival of United States flying centers such as San Diego, Cal., and San Antonio, Texas, a committee appointed by the executive of the B.C. Aviation School Limited, whose destinies are fathered to a great*

CMFT Collection #120.8 Margery Morton collection

In front of the Curtiss tandem in September, 1916, Coquitlam, B.C. stand members of the B.C. Aviation School, successor to the 1915 Aero Club. Right to left: N. B. Robbins, Gerry Hodgson, Charles Raynor, G. McRae, Arthur Allardyce, Phillip H. Smith, unknown, Cy Perkins, Robert Main, W. E. Damer, J. B. Crawford, Chad Chadwick; all graduates of the school.

extent by the Vancouver Aero Club, starts today to seek funds to place the science of aeronautics on a firm basis in this city. That the "made in B.C. aviator" will soon take his proper place along with other aviators of Great Britain and the Allies is the fond hope of a number of prominent business and professional men of Vancouver. Local members have set their faces towards the task of raising a sum of not less than $30,000 to further the ends of the aviation school.
(Daily Province, Vancouver, December 29, 1915.)

Jointly with the advent of B.C. Aviation School Limited, came an impressive list of new directors: Sir Charles Tupper; Honorable James Duff; H. H. Stevens, M.P.; C. H. Cowan, K.C.; G. C. Crux; T. F. Hamilton; G. E. MacDonald; and W. B. Burnside. J. W. Pattison continued to function as secretary.

This new Aviation School was a patriotic, nonprofit venture established to train pilots for the armed forces. To raise funds to support the war effort. Stock in the company was offered to the public. When the school's first flying machine became available, the aircraft was used to lead a military parade through Vancouver in an effort to draw attention to the school.

This aircraft, a Hamilton biplane patterned after a Curtiss tractor design, had been constructed in Vancouver by the Hamilton Aeroplane Co. Ltd., a subsidiary of the Seattle based Hamilton Aero Manufacturing Co. Using premises on Fourth Avenue, the company had commenced the construction of four aircraft designed by T. F. Hamilton. When the B.C. Aviation School Llimited was formed late in 1915, the company merged with the school in order to obtain a market for its aircraft.

A merger, which was effected with the Hamilton Aeroplane Company Limited, has placed at the disposal of the B.C. Aviation School Limited four machines of various *types now under construction at the factory of the Hamilton Company, and valued at $28,000. These air vessels will at once locally form the nucleus of the fleet which will be used under the guidance of the builders and instructors selected from the ranks of the Royal Flying Corps.*

Visitors at the plant of the Hamilton Company evince surprise that a branch of the service is as far advanced as it is and are correspondingly proud that this city should be so far advanced in the science of aeronautics.
(Daily Province, Vancouver, December 29, 1915.)

Helping the company to complete the aircraft were the enthusiastic members of the Aero Club of B.C.

"During the winter, we worked on the aircraft in an old factory in south Vancouver," reports J. L. Haight, who was also a member of the club, *"then moved in the spring to another factory near Coquitlam, where we completed the machine.*

"The field we were going to use was beside the Pitt River near the site of the present Pitt Meadows Airport, but there was a creek between the factory and the field. I engineered the construction of a bridge over the creek, using logs and timbers salvaged from the river.

"There were severe downdrafts around that field, and one of our group finally cracked up the aircraft when he hit some wires, and turned over in a wheat field; so we moved from there to Lulu Island."

Charlie Raynor's crash, from which he escaped relatively unscathed, was probably caused either by engine failure, or his own inexperience – it was never made fully clear. At an earlier date, August 27,1916, two charming and daring young ladies by the names of Margery Tunn and Edna Rayner had their first airplane ride in the same machine piloted by the steadier hand of instructor N. B. Robbins. The Pitt Meadows operation closed down after the loss of its sole machine.

Ready for my flight at
Coquitlam B.C. Aug 27th 1916
Mr Robbin in rear seat.
Jerry Hodgson in front.

CMFT Collection #120.13 Margery Morton collection

Edna Rayner and Margery Tunn went aloft August 27, 1916.

Of the four airplanes commenced by the Hamilton Aeroplane company, only one is known to have been completed, this being a single seat, two-bay biplane powered by a Maximotor. It was first tested in May 1916 but found to be unsatisfactory and converted into a two seater in which form it was operated by the B.C. Aviation School Ltd. until finally destroyed. Further efforts to build aircraft commercially in Vancouver, however, followed within a year.

After assisting the Aero Club of B.C. by constructing a pontoon float for the old (ex-Billy Stark) Curtiss pusher during 1915, James and Henry Hoffar decided to build an aircraft of their own at their Vancouver boatworks. Their first machine, the Hoffar H-1 was patterned after the Avro 500, from a picture which they had seen in a magazine. The H-1 was original in design and was fitted with a single

CMFT Collection #120.33 Margery Morton collection

Charlie Raynor escaped relatively unscathed from the crash of the Hamilton biplane.

pontoon float constructed on the basis of the brothers' boat building experience.

The Hoffars followed up the successful H-1 with a flying boat, the Hoffar H-2. During its construction, the British Columbia Forestry Department became interested in using the machine to undertake forestry patrols, the first time such a venture was proposed in Canada. Arrangements were made to lease the machine from the Hoffars upon completion after an hour's test flying. This would have placed the B.C. Forestry Department in the forefront of the development of aviation for civil use, but for an unfortunate development.

While thousands yesterday watched the flight of the Provincial Government seaplane over Vancouver, the aircraft which had been riding gracefully along on an even keel a thousand feet above the West End of the city, suddenly turned almost a somersault and like a wounded bird dropped impotently towards the earth.

The machine was driven by Lieut. V. A. Bishop, Royal Air Force, who has been back but a few days from the western front. It fell into the roof of the residence of Dr. J. C. Farish, corner of Bute and Alberni Streets, and in the fall the young aviator was but slightly injured. . . .

CMFT Collection #246.1 Barbara Hicks collection

Lieutenant V. A. Bishop crashed the Hoffar H2 Flying Boat into a house in Vancouver, September, 1918.

Lieutenant Bishop says that the accident resulted from engine trouble. He was trying out the machine for the forestry department of the Provincial Government. When the engine started to miss and the machine began to lose speed, Bishop says he undertook to volplane into the waters of English Bay. When it seemed that he would not be able to make the Bay, the aviator tried to divert the seaplane to

Coal Harbour. He started to fall just about halfway between the two bodies of water with the engine dead and the seaplane completely out of control.

The Provincial Government will be responsible for the damage sustained by the seaplane, which will likely be in the neighborhood of $8,000. The forestry department had leased the machine from the Hoffar Brothers, the builders, for one year, and the government undertook to be responsible for all repairs. The Minister of Lands made this statement last evening in Victoria.

Captain MacKenzie, who made the official test for the government, who circled the city for about an hour at varying heights, said that the machine was quite satisfactory in every respect for the work for which it was built . . . and was a credit to the builders.
(Daily Province, Vancouver, September 5, 1918)

In 1919, the Hoffars completed a second flying boat, the H-3, based on their H-2 design. It had an equally short life.

Striking a log while making a steep descent into the water off pier D, the seaplane built by James and Henry Hoffar at their factory, suffered considerable damage. James Hoffar, the pilot, was slightly injured. . . .

Work on the plane was begun about a month after the previous plane had crashed through the roof of a west end house and was completely wrecked.

The last touch was given the plane late yesterday afternoon and in the evening a trial flight was arranged. It was run out of Coal Harbour into Burrard Inlet and, when it was off pier D and well into the middle of the harbour, a take off was made. James Hoffar, who had experience of piloting the other machines, was at the controls. Before ascending to any height, he decided to try out the controls and, when about 50 feet up, he pointed the nose down and took to the water again, successfully. Taking off again, he ascended to the same height and attempted a steeper de-

scent, flattening out before he plowed into the water. As the boat touched the water, it struck a log which was almost entirely submerged and immediately crumpled up. Water soon filled the boat and the plane had almost sunk when a launch which had been following the plane out of the harbour came up and lent timely assistance.
(Daily Province, Vancouver, May 2, 1919)

The Hoffars ceased their aircraft building efforts following the H-3; although, they did obtain the sales rights for war surplus Curtiss JN4 "Jennies" for British Columbia, setting up United Aircraft of B.C. Ltd. in conjunction with the United Aircraft Engineering Company, a syndicate which had practically cornered the whole supply of JN4Ds released by the Canadian government. The Hoffar designed float, used on the H-1 was fitted to some of these Jennies to convert them into seaplanes. When the supply of war surplus Jennies was exhausted in mid-1919, the Hoffars gave up the aircraft business entirely and concentrated on boatbuilding. It was not until 1929, when Henry Hoffar opened Boeing Aircraft of Canada Ltd. in partnership with the Boeing Aircraft Company of Seattle, that Vancouver again had an aircraft construction company operating within its boundaries.

CMFT Collection #120.7 Margery Morton collection

Hastings Park Racetrack, Vancouver, B.C. 1916. Motorcycles racing against the Hamilton biplane.

CMFT Collection #120.28 Margery Morton collection

The B.C. Aviation School's Hamilton biplane, Hastings Park Racetrack, Vancouver, B.C., 1916.

CMFT Collection #120.24 Margery Morton collection

"Gerry" Hodgson, B.C. Aero School, 1916. Later recommended for the D.S.O. for sinking a German submarine. Hodgson lost a leg in a WWI crash. He finally became a well-known Vancouver lawyer.

3

JOYRIDING IN JENNIES

The first efforts at commercializing aviation

At the start of World War I, Canada possessed a mere handful of trained airmen. At the conclusion of the conflict, with the return of the troops from Europe, the country now had hundreds. The sensible ones, like former Aero Club of B.C. trainee, Charlie (Cy) Perkins, were happy to return to their civilian occupations and forget all about flying.

> *"I had a job offer down in South America,"* relates Perkins. *"Some oil people wanted me to fly a plane but I told them it was not for me. I didn't want any more. Three accidents in a row is bad enough."*

A small proportion of the returning airmen, however, had been infected with a love of flying and established the Aerial League of Canada, branches of which were established in both Vancouver and Victoria, with an immediate rivalry being established between the two groups.

On May 13, 1919 a Curtiss Jenny flown by Captains Alfred Eckely and Ernest Hall of the Vancouver branch made the first aerial crossing of the Georgia Strait between Vancouver and Victoria, returning the same day. The Victoria branch quickly responded and flew a Jenny to Vancouver the following day, claiming a faster time (subsequently found to be in error).

On May 18, 1919 Lieutenant Robert Rideout accompanied by Lieutenant W. H. (Harry) Brown flew the Vic-

CMFT Collection #308.28 Boeing Company collection

First international mail flight – Vancouver to Seattle, W. E. Boeing of Seattle leaving Vancouver March 3, 1919.

toria machine to Seattle carrying an invitation from the mayor of Victoria for the mayor of Seattle to attend the May 24 celebrations. On the nineteenth, they returned carrying a number of letters. Although unofficial, this was the first air mail to travel across Puget Sound though it was not the first air mail to travel in British Columbia. Previously, on March 3, 1919, American Eddie Hubbard flew from Vancouver to Seattle with his employer Bill Boeing in a Boeing C-700 seaplane carrying a sack of mail. This was the first air mail to leave Canada for the U.S.A. in an aeroplane and the first air mail flight in B.C.

Hubbard's visit to Vancouver had been made at the invitation of the Vancouver War Exhibition Committee.

"They were showing war trophies in the old Horse Show Building on Georgia Street and that gave me the idea to get

an aeroplane up here to add to the attraction," remarked E. S. Knowlton to Vancouver City Archivist, Major J. B. Matthews in 1939. *"W. E. Boeing, of Seattle, came up, and thus it came about that the first air mail to leave Canada for the United States left Coal Harbour, Vancouver on March 3, 1919.*

"It was a 'stunt' of mine. R. G. (Bob) Macpherson, former M.P., was postmaster. When I asked him if it would be possible for me to send mail to Seattle by airplane, he replied, 'Yes, I'll give you a new mail sack; then he can keep it afterwards.'"

"The Royal Vancouver Yacht Club gave Mr. Boeing permission to anchor his plane at their float. The mayor of Vancouver wrote letters to the mayor of Seattle, and things like that, and we took the new clean white mail sack down. And in the presence of W. A. Turquand, (for) many years

CMFT Collection #308.25 Boeing Company collection

March 3, 1919. Boeing's Eddie Hubbard and W. E. Boeing.

manager, Hotel Vancouver, Chief Constable William McRae, J. T. Little, (a Director of the Vancouver Exhibition,) and Stuart Thompson photographer, I handed Mr. Boeing the mail sack, the first air mail out of Canada, the 3rd of March, 1919."

Although this first air mail flight between Canada and the U.S.A. was organized somewhat casually, Eddie Hubbard soon developed a regular service operating between Seattle and Victoria (see chapter 5).

CMFT Collection #283.2 Ingwold Wikene collection

Replica of Boeing B & W takes off 50 years later.

During the summer of 1919, flying was being vigorously promoted by members of the Aerial League of Canada. At least five aircraft were based at Minoru Park in Vancouver and one aircraft at the Willows Aerodrome in Victoria; although during the summer, various mishaps reduced the numbers available.

Much of the flying later became known as "barnstorming." The Aerial League organized several displays at Minoru Park with the planes performing various stunts to please paying customers. By Dominion Day 1919, when the largest of the displays was organized, the stunts included wing walking and other hazardous acts.

One of the largest crowds that ever made its way out to Minoru Park attended the aviators' carnival there yesterday afternoon and evening. Flying exhibitions which could not easily be surpassed in cleverness were staged, but the show was somewhat marred by lack of management. . . . A guiding hand for the whole affair was sadly needed and many periods occurred when the spectators were treated to nothing but dust and a scorching hot sun. Practically no announcements were made and people were left to guess what was happening.

The "stunt" flying was carried out by three machines piloted by Lieuts. G. K. Trim, "Miny" MacDonald and Jack Clemence. They stayed up for well over forty minutes, going through most of the stunts known to war flyers. Clemence and MacDonald climbed high up for their stunts and kept high, looking like mere specks in the sky to the spectators on the ground. Trim flew at about 2,000 feet in a silver-painted machine and did his stunts in bits at a time. . . . Everybody could follow every move of the machine. . . .

Fieldhouse's climb around the wing and down to the undercarriage of his plane thrilled the large crowd as it has done others on other occasions and the race between an automobile driven by Harry Hooper and an airplane piloted by Lieut. Trim was intensely exciting. It would be hard to imagine a more exciting race. The automobile, a Stutz Special, owned by Mr. J. R. Duncan of the Vulcan Iron Works of this city put up a good exhibition and held the lead against the airplane most of the time.

The house which had been erected on the grounds and was supposed to be "blown up" by bombs from airplanes flying overhead, caused some amusement by electing to "blow up" of its own free will. Nobody seems to know just what set off the powder stored in it.

The total attendance was variously estimated at from nine to twelve thousand.

(Vancouver Daily Province, July 2, 1919)

On Dominion Day, other centers were also being treated to the spectacle of aviation. At Armstrong, one Jenny of the Aerial League of Canada piloted by Captain Ernest Hoy performed at the Dominion Day Sports while Penticton was visited by a commercially operated aircraft.

The arrival of Lieut. Ernest Hall and a mechanic in the "Vatoo" plane from Vancouver, Monday evening, marked the farthest inland point yet reached by air route in British Columbia. The Curtiss machine of the Vancouver Aerial Transportation Co. made the trip from the Coast in three hours and forty-five minutes sailing gracefully over the surrounding mountains into the Okanagan Valley at 9:30 Monday evening.

The fliers made a half hour stop in Chilliwack and then "hopped off" for Princeton. There the first difficulty of the trip was met, for the plane would not ascend to a height of more than nine thousand feet, which made it impossible to fly above the mountains of Coquihalla Pass. Lieut. Hall accordingly followed the railroad track and found it "bumpy" riding in the valleys and canyons of the Kettle Valley road. . . .

A landing was made at Princeton which proved rather dramatic. . . . Finding no open field in which to land, Hall descended into the open street and promptly carried away several telegraph wires.

After having a refill of gasoline the aviators "took off," running the plane right up the main street. They had a

narrow escape when rising to avoid a clump of trees at the end of the thoroughfare.
(Daily Province, Vancouver, July 2, 1919.)

While most of B.C.'s flying activities in 1919 were of a barnstorming nature, one challenge attracted the interest of the local airmen, a challenge which led to an informal race and ultimately the reduction of the active flying fleet by two aircraft – the aerial crossing of the Rockies.

While the Vancouver branch of the Aerial League of Canada formulated plans for the flight, three newspapers, the Vancouver *Daily World,* the Lethbridge *Herald* and the Calgary *Herald,* put up a total of $950 in prize money on condition that the flight be made by a Canadian or British pilot flying a Canadian or British machine and the flight be made in less than eighteen hours. Also, the pilot had to be a member of the Aerial League.

This latter stipulation thwarted the efforts of the Vancouver Aerial Transportation Company's Ernest Hall, who set off for Calgary in July in hopes of winning the prize. He halted in the Okanagan when he learnt that he did not qualify and awaited developments.

Two Vancouver airmen, Capt. Ernest C. Hoy, D.F.C., of the Aerial League of Canada, and Lieut. Ernest O. Hall, of the Vancouver Aerial Transportation Company, are in a race today for aerial honors—that of making the first flight across the Rocky Mountains to Calgary. . . .

Hall left Vancouver about two weeks ago, with the intention of flying to Calgary with as few stops as possible. When it was learned that the prize for which Hoy is flying will not be awarded him whether he reaches Calgary first or not, he was forced to make one of two decisions—give up the flight and return to Vancouver or go on with his plans and make his flight pay by carrying passengers at the towns through which he passed. He chose the latter plan and has been flying in Merritt, Kamloops and Vernon for some time.

When he learned that Hoy was setting out for Calgary, he took his machine to Penticton yesterday and there awaited developments. . . . He waited to give Hoy a fair sporting chance and then set out for Calgary.
(Daily Province, Vancouver, August 7, 1919)

Aviator Hall's Coast-to-Calgary flight came to a sudden and disastrous stop (in Nelson) about 2 o'clock (on August 7th). Finding his engine running short of gasoline he was compelled to make a landing in a hayfield near the mill of the Canyon City Lumber Company, his first stop since leaving Midway. More than an hour was taken getting on the cargo of gasoline and oil, quite a gathering of spectators lending a helping hand at the work. Immediately the power was turned on to resume, engine trouble developed. The plane did not rise more than half a dozen feet . . . it started to descend, plunging into an automobile which was standing 100 yards from the starting point. The plane went nose-on into the motor car and described a somersault wrecking it almost completely. Fortunately the aviator escaped with only a few bruises . . .
(Daily Province, Vancouver, August 8, 1919)

Hoy, who had departed Minoru Park at 4:13 A.M. and refuelled at Vernon, Grand Forks, Cranbrook and Lethbridge, was more successful, arriving over Calgary late the same evening.

Guided by the third of a series of rockets sent up by the Calgary Aero Club, a number of flares and the three brilliant electric lights turned upward and arranged in the form of the letter "L," Captain Hoy circled above the Bowness Park grounds and made a perfect landing at 8:55 p.m. amid the cheers of a great crowd of Calgary people. He had made the flight from Vancouver to Calgary in 16 hours 42 minutes, one hour and 18 minutes under scheduled time . . . it demonstrates that the crossing of the Rockies can be made without difficulty.

Captain Hoy brought with him forty-five letters from Vancouver and various points along the line. . . .
(Daily Province, Vancouver, August 8, 1919)

Hoy's return flight by a more northerly route four days later was less successful.

Captain Ernest Hoy smashed his machine . . . on the second stage of his flight from Calgary to Vancouver. . . . Hoy arrived in Golden shortly after 12:30 (noon on August 11th) and remained slightly more than two hours. Rising at 2:46 p.m., the machine was seen almost immediately to bank and crash over to the left, crumpling its wing . . . he was seen to extricate himself from the wrecked machine and stand up, apparently unhurt.
(Daily Province, Vancouver, August 12, 1919)

This accident in Golden was no reflection on Hoy's skill as an aviator but had been caused by the novelty of the occasion. Two young boys had raced the aircraft down the field during take off and swerved into the path of the machine. Rather than run them down, Hoy had elected to crash the machine by attempting a turn at perilously low altitude.

This accident was not the only one suffered by the Aerial League that summer as the Vancouver newspapers reported mishaps on several other occasions. These were responsible for the demise of the league as a flying organization by the end of 1919, with purely commercial operations dominating the aviation scene in B.C. in 1920.

At the start of 1920, the Pacific Aviation Company had two Curtiss JN4s operating at Minoru Park, but, on May 24, it suffered a major catastrophe.

Before the eyes of about 2,000 spectators, including his wife and father-in-law, E. H. Beasley, manager of the Union Steamship Company, met death when a plane owned by the Pacific Aviation Company, and piloted by Major A. Baker, plunged from a height of over 4,000 feet at Minoru Park

yesterday about 4:12 and was totally wrecked in a field about a quarter of a mile from the hangars. Major Baker, the pilot, was terribly lacerated about the face, but otherwise escaped serious injury.
(Vancouver Sun, May 25, 1920)

Within a year of this accident, the Pacific Aviation Company had disposed of its remaining Jenny and ceased operations. An associated company, Aircraft Manufacturing Company of which the ill-fated E. H. Beasley had been president, lost its only aircraft, a newly acquired Boeing seaplane in a further fatal accident less than three months later, on August 18, 1920.

Before the eyes of at least five thousand persons, Capt. Hibbert B. Brenton, fell to death in the waters of English Bay when the Boeing flying boat, in which he was making a test flight for a commercial aviator's license, turned over in the air at a height of 1,000 feet, throwing him from the cockpit.

About 6:30 he took the machine from its hangar at the mouth of False Creek and circled around the English Bay section of the city, making a landing at almost the same point where the machine later fell.

He took off again and about 7 p.m. was at a height of about 1,000 feet when he appeared to prepare for a similar landing to the one previously made. But the seaplane suddenly started a steep descent and then apparently turned over in a half loop, the under side of the machine being skyward. Eyewitnesses state that they saw the aviator fall from the cockpit of the craft as it completed the half loop. . . . The machine had just been repaired under his supervision by Hoffar Brothers and had been fully tested and accepted by the Aircraft Manufacturing Company.
(Vancouver Sun, August 19, 1920)

The Aircraft Manufacturing Company obtained a further aircraft, a Curtiss JN4 fitted with a Hoffar pontoon and wingtip floats, which was registered in 1921 but had faded into obscurity by 1924.

On Vancouver Island, the Victoria Branch of the Aerial League of Canada lasted longer than its mainland counterpart, retaining one of its aircraft, "Pathfinder II," a Curtiss JN 4, until May 1920, when the plane became the foundation for Vancouver Island's first commercial flying service.

> *W. H. Brown, Secretary of the Aerial League, . . . and N. A. Goddard, of Courtenay, have purchased the Pathfinder II from the local branch of the Aerial League and will commence commercial flying operations under the name of the Vancouver Island Aerial Service.*
>
> *The new company has secured rights to landing grounds at Comox, Courtenay and Victoria, and will operate the Curtiss aeroplane both as a seaplane and an aeroplane. . . .*
>
> *The company will commence commercial flying immediately and will handle all classes of passenger carrying and special survey work. . . . The Vancouver Island Aerial Service will commence flying operations immediately, using the*

CMFT Collection #476.1 Alberni Valley Times collection

In June of 1920 this JN-4 "Jenny" flown by W. H. Brown and N. A. Goddard became the first aircraft to land in the Alberni Valley.

Curtiss as a land machine, and later, when the floats have been constructed, as a seaplane.
(Victoria Daily Times, May 11, 1920)

Brown and Goddard's pioneering effort lasted only until November 20, 1920.

Lieut. Brown was on his way to Prince Rupert when his plane developed engine trouble, which resulted in disaster, causing the loss of the plane and almost taking the life of the aviator. . . . When in the air an hour and thirty minutes, something went wrong compelling him to descend. Darkness overtook him before he could complete the repairs and, buffeted about at the mercy of the wind and waves, the plane was dashed against the rocky shore of Nalau Island. . . . Morning found Brown alone on a desolate spot in the ocean, drenched to the skin with only a few sea biscuits in his haversack.

Wednesday morning found things had not improved, and realizing that to stay any longer on the island would mean starvation, Brown decided to straddle a log and paddle it out into the channel in hopes of being picked up by some passing craft. After being afloat on the log all day Wednesday, all the while paddling in an effort to get into the lane of sea travel. . . . Brown espied a small craft . . . which proved to be the cannery tender Hidden Inlet. . . . Brown was hauled aboard in an exhausted condition, his legs being numb and feet swollen from being submerged for hours in the cold northern waters.
(Nanaimo Free Press, September 25, 1920)

Following this narrow escape from death, Brown joined the Canadian Air Board serving as a pilot at Jericho Beach Air Station. His partner, Goddard, found new backers, bought a newly repaired Jenny from the Aerial League of Canada's Victoria Branch (presumably Pathfinder I) and commenced a second attempt at commercial flying on Vancouver Island.

> *The Vancouver Island Aerial Transport Company . . . will ply from this city and along the west and east coast of the Island as far north as Comox, and will find its main work in the carrying of passengers and freight to inland waters of the Island . . . where remoteness and difficulty of access make the aircraft desirable for rapid and convenient transportation. Seattle and Vancouver have had commercial aircraft transportation on a limited footing for some months now, but the establishment of the new Aerial Transport Company will be the first to be operated on this Island since last Fall.*
>
> *While operating as partner in the Vancouver Island Aerial Service Ltd., Mr. Goddard discovered that there was a practical application for the use of aircraft in the northern end of the island and more especially to connect coast with inland waters. Prospectors, timber cruisers, surveyors and many other types of field workers were interested in the former venture and the Aerial Service Ltd. was in a fair way to becoming firmly established and adding to its craft when misfortune befell it.*
>
> (Victoria Daily Times, June 14, 1921)

Goddard's second attempt at operating a commercial flying service on Vancouver Island survived only slightly longer than his first, being crashed out of existence on March 19, 1922 following an engine failure while the Curtiss Jenny was being operated on wheels at Victoria. The pilot, K. F. Saunders and his wife were injured.

Goddard soon became involved with yet a third Vancouver Island venture, Commercial Aviation School, which was established to teach flying to Chinese students, replacing an earlier school in Saskatoon.

In 1919, a group of North American Chinese had purchased some surplus Curtiss JN4 Jennies, hired some World War I veterans, and established a flying school at Saskatoon. The Keng Wah Aviation School was ostensibly training Chinese students to meet the needs of civil aviation in China, but, in actuality, was training these volunteers to provide the nucleus of an Air Force for the Nationalist elements in Chinese politics. The Chinese school made its first appearance in British Columbia when an aircraft was brought to Vancouver for the 1921 Chinese Nationalist Convention.

> *A Curtiss JN4 training plane has been taking up passengers from the aerodrome at Brighouse, Lulu Island. The flying was in connection with the Chinese Nationalist Convention and the machine was piloted by officers from the Keng Wah Chinese Aviation School at Saskatoon. . . .*
>
> *When delegates from the various parts of Canada and the United States were attending the Chinese Nationalist Convention in Vancouver, Lieutenant Charles Ray MacNeill of Fiske, Saskatchewan, Chief Pilot and Training Officer for the Keng Wah Aviation School, Saskatoon, is taking up passengers from the aerodrome at Brighouse, Lulu Island. Each day that the weather permits, aviator MacNeill carries an average of five persons. . . . Keng Wah's cadet school is financed by the Saskatoon members and the students who are assessed a tuition fee of $200.00. It is said that the other branches of the Nationalist League have been asked to help finance the school which is the only one in Canada. Some of the students have already gone to China to engage in commercial flying.*
>
> (Vancouver Sun, May 15, 1921)

These demonstration flights foreshadowed the movement of Chinese flight training from the harsh prairie winter to the milder conditions of the B.C. coast, where in May, 1922 the Commercial Aviation School commenced operations with a Curtiss JN4D Jenny on Hoffar pontoon floats. Norman Goddard was hired as air engineer, while his former partner from Vancouver Island Aerial Services, Harry Brown, was hired as instructor.

Believed to be the first flying instruction ever given in this city (Victoria) flying was commenced this morning at the Inskip Island hangar of the Chinese Commercial Aviation School in Esquimalt Harbor when eight pupils of the school were given lectures, and one began his dual instruction in the air.

W. H. Brown M.C. of this city is acting as instructor for the school. The machine used is a Curtiss JN4 type aeroplane with Hoffar pontoons, taking-off and landing on the water. N. A. Goddard, also of this city is acting as air engineer.

W. H. Brown is well known in local flying circles being one of the founders of the former Aerial League and being identified later with commercial flying on his own account. For the past two years Mr. Brown has been acting as a pilot navigator for the B.C. Air Station at Jericho Beach, and was in charge of a substation at Kamloops last Summer.

The Chinese Commercial Aviation School was inaugurated here recently by a group of wealthy young Chinese, all of whom are naturalized British subjects. The founders of the school plan to make it a permanency, and will give a complete course of commercial aeronautics.
(Victoria Daily Times, May 27, 1922)

The main object of the school it is said, is to turn out pilots for commercial aviation in China, a great field being open in that direction as soon as conditions in that land have settled once more.

Purchased from the Vancouver agents of Ericson Aircraft Ltd., Toronto, a Curtiss 80 horse-powered aeroplane is being used, equipped in this instance with a Hoffar pontoon and operated as a seaplane. The machine is fitted for dual control. The instructor flying in the rear seat with his pupil in the forward cockpit.

William S. Butterfield, an author, has undertaken to evolve for the instructor a code of flying terms in Chinese. . . .

The course used for flying is from the harbor at Esquimalt to Albert and William Heads, thence to Brotchie Lodge off the Dallas Road, and return to Esquimalt. The flight is made at an altitude of 1,200 feet, instruction taking place only in still air, that is, in the early morning and just before dusk.

(Victoria Daily Times, June 12, 1922)

The Commercial Aviation School operated only until February 24, 1923 when Hip Kwong stalled in a turn and sideslipped into Esquimalt Harbour damaging the school's solitary aircraft beyond repair. As this was the only commercial flying operation still active in B.C. at the time, the province's commercial flying came to a temporary halt.

CMFT Collection #316.2 Jeanne Ambrose collection

Boeing C204 Thunderbird under construction at the Coal Harbour (Vancouver) Boeing Canada plant. The Thunderbird was similar in construction to the B1 flying boats used for fishery patrols.

4

FISHERY PATROLS

The cornerstone of west coast commercial aviation

One of the foundations of commercial aviation along the west coast was laid by the civil servants who saw in the aeroplane a tool for forest fire detection and for the effective policing of the fishing regulations. From the initial establishment of a Canadian Air Board base at Jericho Beach in 1920, through the establishment of Pacific Airways in 1925 and into the west coast operations of Canadian Airways from the late 1920s and throughout the 1930s, fire and fishery patrols formed the cornerstone of B.C. coastal flying.

Immediately after World War I, Canadian flying activity was hampered by a state of chaos. While cheap war surplus aircraft (mostly Curtiss JN4 Jennies) were readily available, the clubs, small companies, and individuals who purchased them were all competing for a very limited amount of business. By 1920, many of these aircraft were no longer in service, having been damaged, destroyed or idled by lack of finances. Into this chaos came the Canadian Air Board, established by the Canadian government to assume control over aviation. Its mandate included the development of civil flying operations and military training.

In 1920, the Civil Operations Branch, foreseeing a need for a seaplane base suitable for year round operations, selected Vancouver's Jericho Beach as the site for an air

CMFT Collection #98.3 Ken Swartz collection

Felixstowe F-3 Jericho Beach Station.

station. Four single-engine Curtiss HS-2L flying boats and a twin-engine Felixstowe F-3 were shipped to Vancouver by rail and trucked out to Jericho Beach for assembly. Initially, canvas hangars were used to provide sheltered facilities for maintenance; then, in 1922, permanent hangars were erected.

As a means of developing civil aviation, the Air Board provided aerial services to the various government departments, both federal and provincial. Forest fire patrols, aerial surveys, aerial photography and fishery patrols formed the bulk of this work with the occasional rumrunner patrol for added excitement.

> *"Earl McLeod and myself were on the first flying boat that ever went up the coast,"* says Harold Davenport, who served at Jericho Beach from 1923 to 1925. *"I'm telling you that it really made a tremendous difference that one H*

CMFT Collection #140.5 CPA collection via Gordon Croucher

Curtiss HS-2L. Major Don R. MacLaren at controls.

boat (Curtiss HS-2L) patrolling around the mouth of the Skeena. We'd go right down south, way down south to Namu, Bella Bella and the Queen Charlottes. It tightened the thing (fishing) up enormously.

"For instance, at the mouth of the Skeena, looking down on a fishing day when it wasn't raining, you could tell the length of the nets. They were allowed 400 yards but some of them were at least twice that. We would throttle back, glide down, land and taxi up to them. The fisheries people would tell them to pull the net in and recount the corks. 'Okay, let the net out again.'

"In the bottom of the boat is the handling belly where they kept the other nets. 'What's in here?' 'Oh, nothing.' 'Well, take the boards up and let's take a look.'

"We'd find another 1,000 yards of net. We'd take all the details, the certificate and the licence, and get back and take

it to the fisheries man so that he could turn it in. In other words, these guys could not get away with that (using over-length nets) any more and it tightened (fishing) right up. It was rare after about two weeks to see a long net. It worked beautifully, one airplane, very little expense."

These fishery patrols and other government work continued to be flown by the Air Board machines until 1925 when Don MacLaren, Canada's World War I third-ranking ace, persuaded the Canadian government that the Air Board monopoly was hindering the development of civil aviation.

"MacLaren started Pacific Airways with an H boat and I became the flight engineer," says Harold Davenport, who resigned from the Royal Canadian Air Force to work for MacLaren. *"'Why not develop civil aviation? We have a chance to do it. We have an aeroplane and we know how to handle a plane and get around the country,' MacLaren argued."*

"I knew," continued Davenport, *"every fjord between the north end of Vancouver Island and Alaska, had been on most lakes adjacent to them, walked hundreds of miles up streams looking for fish for the fisheries people.*

"So we started off in the same business that Jericho Beach had handled—fishery patrol and we started at Jericho beach. We got an aircraft crate that had held a Fokker DR7 and used that as our working headquarters. We were at Jericho Beach for the whole season, and the next season.

"The first year, on the first flight, the engine packed up. A rod let go and virtually destroyed the engine and we didn't have a spare. We went to Butedale and got a wire off to Vancouver. They got a replacement engine in the States and shipped it to us at Swanson Bay, where we were in operation. There was nothing there except the place to stay, a wharf and a derrick.

"Ten days later the boat came in and unloaded the engine on the dock. It was in a brand new crate.

"'Gees,' I thought, 'we'll get going now.' I took our derrick, lifted up the lid, and set it (the engine) down. Brand new cylinders, brand new paint, it hadn't been touched since before the war ended. I took hold of the end of the crankshaft where the propeller goes and lifted just to check and "click, click, click." I got play of about a sixteenth of an inch. I took the cylinder off and there were no pistons in there. I dismantled the top end and the pistons were lying in the crank-case.

"You know, I had to take it all apart, scrape in the set of bearings and then put the crank-case together. The rings had to be fitted and everything that went with that. The valves and cylinders were all intact so it was just a matter of putting on the cams, making a timing disc, which I did out of steel, and then timing the valves and ignition and then firing it up.

"I think we were getting paid $180 a month. I worked ten to fifteen hours a day, but when you are young you do it."

By 1928, Pacific Airways Ltd. had a virtual stranglehold on the fisheries patrol contract for the west coast but was struggling along with the bare minimum of equipment, a single HS-2L flying boat. James Richardson's Western Canada Airways was expanding westward from its Winnipeg base and had the finances needed to upgrade Pacific Airways fleet; so MacLaren sold out to the Richardson interests and was appointed general manager of Western Canada Airways, west coast operations.

"Pacific Airways was purchased by Western Canada Airways," says Gordon Ballentine, who had just commenced working for the company at the time. *"James Richardson's Western Canada Airways was expanding, and I'm sure that MacLaren needed money. Any small enterprise like that does. The staff down there had grown*

from its original MacLaren and Davenport to include Art McCurdy, who was an airframe engineer, a stores officer by the name of Jock White, and two or three others. MacLaren started a ground school for all us new hires.

"It was Western Canada Airways from about May that year (1928). Instead of one big HS-2L, they were buying modern equipment. The first one was the Boeing B1D, a cabin biplane with crank-up windows and all sorts of goodies on it with a Wright Whirlwind engine. It proved to be sadly underpowered and was succeeded by the Boeing B1E with the Pratt and Whitney (Wasp) in it.

"The big contract was the federal fisheries patrol contract which was greatly expanded to about five aircraft, at one time, in Swanson Bay. The first Boeing B1E was sent up to Swanson Bay with a pilot by the name of Ted Luke and an Air Engineer called Bill Partridge in late June 1928. On July 13th, they crashed the aircraft between Butedale and Swanson Bay, killing the air engineer and totally destroying the aircraft."

Western Canada Airways problems in 1928 were not limited to the crash of the Boeing, G-CASX, which crashed into the water when Luke reached for a cloth to clean the windshield while flying low in fog. Just over a month later, on August, 15, the company lost a second aircraft when the Vickers Vedette, G-CASW, sent to Swanson Bay as a replacement aircraft, crashed (again in fog) on Porcher Island, near Prince Rupert. The crew, consisting of Neville Cumming, Alf Walker and Gordon Ballentine, survived the crash and continued to fly for many years thereafter (see chapter 7).

While new crews were learning the trade the hard way, the old hands carried on. Harold Davenport remembers 1928 as the year when he made his most memorable catch.

"The funniest thing I saw there: We were coming down along the inlet in fog. We had landed and were taxiing along

CMFT Collection #132.5 Gordon S. Williams collection

A Vickers Vedette, G-CASW, Jericho Beach, B.C.

there, crawling along making about six knots. Dead ahead I saw this seine boat. I clobbered off the ignition and coasted to the side of the boat. The skipper turned to me with, 'You son of a bitch! How the hell did you so and so's know that I was here?' He had his purse seine right out, running it in the inlet. We told him, 'Cripes, we can see in the fog.' And do you know what? He believed it!"

In 1930, Western Canada Airways, was amalgamated with other Richardson aviation companies to form Canadian Airways which covered virtually the whole country for the next ten years. Fishery patrols remained an important part of the company's business on the west coast, albeit with some changes in equipment and in tactics as the fishermen found ways of outwitting the aerial policemen.

"We were basically out to watch for infractions of the Fisheries Act, which included fishing at times outside of those designated for fishing and for the unspeakable crime of tying seine nets to the shore," says Rex Chandler, who

flew with Canadian Airways during the '30s. *"Instead of having a dingy and the seine boat go around in a circle joining the net, they would tie the net to the shore then bring the boat in so that they could catch more fish.*

"We used to fly at low altitude up Johnston Strait then hop over a projection of land and catch them from behind. They didn't hear us, you see. It was rather funny. You could see the black smoke of the diesel starting up as they pulled their nets from shore. Actually that was all right, because it was a preventative situation, something like a policeman patrolling the highway for speed. The fact he's there prevents the offence. We had a lot of good relationships with the fishermen. They didn't seem to hold it against us."

Despite these good relations, the fishermen still attempted to evade the regulations and the fishery patrols became more ingenuous in their efforts to catch the offenders.

"We had the Boeing Totem and Bellanca Pacemaker, CF-BFC, based at Alert Bay in July, August and half of September," says Larry Dakin, whose first good job was flying fishery patrols for Canadian Airways in 1939, *"Then we were based in Nanaimo until about the end of October.*

CMFT Collection #334.16 Ewan Boyd collection

Boeing Totem.

"What they tried to do was use the seine net as a fixed net, have the boat out in the middle of the straits and, of course, with the current, the fish would be coming down the strait. We'd come down the strait in the Totem or Bellanca, doing about ninety miles per hour, and all you would see was a guy in a rowboat, about ten feet from shore, rowing like hell!

"The only way we could catch them was to drop two fishery wardens in the bush on a Tuesday and pick them up on a Friday. They just put the guy's boats names on their list.

"We had Tate, the fishery supervisor, with us and if we'd see a boat with the name on the list, we'd go down and Tate would send them into Alert Bay. On Saturday morning we got the magistrate from Nanaimo. I've got a picture of the old Totem tied up in Alert Bay with all these fish boats lined up one after another."

With the merger of Canadian Airways with nine other companies to form Canadian Pacific Air Lines in 1942, the importance of fishery patrols as a cornerstone of west coast commercial aviation diminished considerably. In addition, the wartime expansion of aviation activity led to a new start in the postwar period, one in which the economic lifeline of the 1930s was of much lesser importance. The fishery patrol had, however, played a very important part in introducing the use of aircraft to many communities on the B.C. coastline and its contribution to the health of the industry should not be forgotten.

CMFT Collection #182.1 Jim Spilsbury collection

Bellanca Sr. Skyrocket CF-DOH suffered an engine failure while on fishery patrol at Growler Cove, Cracroft Island, B.C. and was totally destroyed.

5

THE TRIANGLE ROUTE

The start of passenger services in British Columbia

While Vancouver Island Aerial Service Ltd., Vancouver Island Aerial Transport Ltd. and the Commercial Aviation School may be considered to be the first B.C. commercial aviation enterprises, by far the most significant flying service with British Columbia operations in the early 1920s was Eddie Hubbard's Seattle-Victoria Air Mail Line.

In 1920, Eddie Hubbard resigned his position as chief pilot for the Boeing Company of Seattle and commenced a series of trials flying mail between Seattle and Victoria. The objective was to provide a faster mail service connection between Seattle and the Far East, by meeting the trans-Pacific steamships at their first port of call in North America. By October 15, 1920, he had secured a contract under a foreign mail appropriation to operate the service at $200 per round trip.

Within a year, Hubbard had established an enviable reputation for reliability.

> *The aerial postman was bound by contract to make a maximum of ten trips a month, and was bound, too, to meet every call on time. He was obliged to carry up to 600 pounds of mail and could not choose his weather nor occasion. It was in the first contract of eight and a half months that Eddie Hubbard won the tribute of all, for he made trip after trip in weather that delayed trans-Pacific liners at their*

docks, and landed his mails behind the Outer Wharf when the Empress liners ran for Esquimalt to put ashore their passengers and mails, refusing to dock at the Outer Wharf at all. He flew over the 78 air miles in fog that crippled shipping up and down the Straits, and made trips at the close of the day, leaving on his return for Seattle by moonlight.

It was on this showing that Hubbard was awarded the second contract without any trouble, being successful also over many competitors. . . .
(Victoria Daily Times, September 3, 1921)

For over five years Hubbard's Seattle-Victoria Air Mail Line operated its famous "red boats" (Boeing B1 flying boats) on a regular service between its base on Lake Union (east of Seattle) and Victoria. Between 25,000 and 50,000 pounds of mail was flown annually, in all kinds of weather, not always without incident.

"As a small boy I often used to go down and watch the old open cockpit Boeing flying boats come into the Victoria harbour," says George Williamson, who flew Grumman Goose amphibians from the late 1940s until the 1980s. *"My grandmother lived close by, and often, on a Saturday, I'd watch the Eddie Hubbard boats load up. They never seemed to go much above fifty feet when they were flying over the water.*

"On one occasion, the pilot had taken off and was flying past the old St. George Hospital when the engine appeared to stop. It was later reported that he had not stowed a rope properly and it had snaked back and hung up in the pusher propeller, bringing it to a halt. He ended up crashing into the side of a house on Rupert and Haywood, removing part of the bay window. The pilot was reported to have stepped out of the airplane into the dining room where the people were having breakfast, excused himself and asked them if he could use the phone."

By 1927, Eddie Hubbard had established such a high reputation for his service that, in association with Bill Boeing, he was able to bid successfully for the transcontinental air route from Chicago to San Francisco. This was to lead to the formation of United Air Lines in 1928. The Seattle-Victoria air mail service, however, passed into other hands. It remained a flying boat service until June 30, 1937 when it was discontinued following the opening of a scheduled service from Seattle to Vancouver by United Air Lines.

While the time savings possible by flying overseas mail from Victoria to Seattle led to the early development of commercial aviation links between these two cities, the introduction of passenger services between Vancouver Island and the mainland had to await the end of the decade. Today, the route between Vancouver and Victoria is the most saturated in Canada. In the '20s and '30s it was not so well served even though its commercial potential was recognized by everyone interested in flying passengers. The first company to attempt to profit on this route was B.C. Airways, formed in Victoria on January 1, 1928, by two brothers, Ernest and Cecil Eve.

B.C. Airways commenced business, with two Alexander Eaglerocks and a smaller Driggs Dart, training pilots and barnstorming for passengers. They erected a small hangar on a square field flanked by Richmond, Newton, Shelbourne, and Lansdowne roads, which became Victoria's first airport, Lansdowne Field. Running diagonally across the field was Bowker Creek, an ever-present hazard for the pilots.

B.C. Airways' first aircraft, an Alexander Eaglerock arrived in Victoria just a week after the company was formed.

"The Eaglerock was powered by a Curtiss OX-5 motor, ninety-horse, and was a three place job, two passengers

An Alexander Eaglerock similar to this one was B.C. Airways' first aircraft.

CMFT Collection #322.5
Robert W. Spires collection

front and a pilot in the rear," relates Ted Cressy, an experienced aircraft engineer who worked for the company. *"It was a very handy kind of aircraft, with a Clark high lift wing and a fairly slow landing speed.*

"In 1928, we salvaged an engine from the dockyards. We had OX-5s, ninety horsepower. This was an OX-10, about 105 horsepower. It had been dunked in the sea, but it was in pretty good shape and I had it overhauled. It made a difference to our Eaglerocks. We could really carry two passengers at a time."

The Eve Brothers entry into scheduled service commenced later in 1928 when they acquired a Ford Trimotor.

"This ambitious endeavour was the result of farsightedness on the part of Ernest and Cecil Eve, both of whom were aviation enthusiasts, but whose practical knowledge of aviation was nil," reflected A. H. (Hal) Wilson, many years later.

"On the inaugural flight, the Vancouver civic dignitary in Vancouver rushed forward to greet the civic dignitary of Victoria, which resulted in Mayor Taylor receiving a crack over the head from one of the propellers. This, it is felt, is of historical note, in as much as Mayor Taylor survived the ordeal.

Ernest Eve at right of Aeronca C3 during refuelling in Victoria, 1932.

CMFT Collection #259.30
Joan Jordan collection.

"Prior to the purchase of this Ford Trimotor the company hired Mr. H. Walker from Seattle, who delivered the Ford Trimotor to Victoria and commenced the tri-service. During the first week's operation he took me as his co-pilot and after a week's operation I flew the Vancouver-Victoria, or Canadian Division, while Walker flew the Victoria-Seattle Division.

"As this service got underway, through lack of experience, various problems presented themselves, the first of which was the selling of tickets in excess of the number of seats available in the aircraft. The aircraft's normal capacity was fourteen passengers and two pilots, while on occasion seventeen passengers would be carried. This was taken up by the pilots with the business manager, Mr. Cecil Eve, whose knowledge, as stated above, of aviation matters was not excessive. At first his ruling was that if the aircraft was not full of gasoline, then extra human freight should be carried to make up the difference.

"I had an unfortunate experience, on one occasion. When taking off from Vancouver I found the elevator trim exceedingly difficult to move. The aircraft had been

trimmed too tail heavy and in an endeavour to crank the trim I was prevented from doing so due to this additional human freight strap hanging on the trim rod which traversed down the length of the fuselage about four inches from the top of the cab. This trim control undoubtedly offered a very secure grip to passengers for whom no seats were provided, but nevertheless, it presented a situation which needed a remedy. It was only after a united front which was put up by Mr. Walker (the other pilot of the Ford) and myself that Mr. Eve conceded to our request and ruled that when all seats were occupied the aircraft would be regarded as full.

"Another problem to be overcome, of course, was the minimum weather conditions under which the aircraft operated. There was no radio—air to ground, ground to air—meteorological reports or what have you, and since neither Mr. Walker or myself knew how to use the bank and turn indicator, it was suggested that weather minimums be set at 1,000 foot ceiling and three miles visibility. Once again Mr. Eve overruled. As far as he was concerned, fifty feet off the water was OK. As a result of this decision, a few weeks later on September 12, 1928, the aircraft on its way to Seattle flew into the water under conditions of bad visibility, killing all seven persons aboard.

"During the short life of this aircraft, G-CATX, 1,287 paid passengers were carried between the three cities, Vancouver and Victoria supplying an estimated seventy-five

B.C. Airways' Ford Trimotor G-CATX, carried passengers and mail between Vancouver, Seattle, and Victoria in 1928.

CMFT Collection #667.5
Charles W. Wilson collection

percent of the traffic. Rates were $11 each way or $20 return. In addition, mail was carried, the company having its own five cent airmail stamp consisting of a multi-engine aircraft in flight. Insofar as the operation of the Eaglerocks were concerned, chartered flights were made between Victoria and Vancouver at the rate of $60.

"It was only a matter of time before the company had to fold its operations. It sold its two Eaglerocks, which were still intact, to the Aero Club of B.C. in Vancouver, and the Driggs Dart to the Sprott-Shaw School of Aviation."

Following the demise of B.C. Airways, an American company – Alaska-Washington Airways – which was developing a route structure in the Pacific Northwest, decided to develop the triangle route (Vancouver-Victoria-Seattle) to feed passengers into its U.S. services.

CMFT Collection #667.3 Charles W. Wilson collection

Alaska-Washington Airways' inaugural flight, Vancouver to Victoria, 1929. A. H. Wilson on far right.

Hal Wilson on the float of Fairchild 71 CF-AJP, Alaska-Washington Airways' first aircraft, at Victoria prior to inaugural flight to Vancouver October 15, 1929.

CMFT Collection #667.10
Charles W. Wilson collection

"In the fall of 1929 an American company formed a subsidiary in Canada known as the Alaska-Washington Airways of British Columbia," continued Hal Wilson. *"Since I always had an inclination to become engaged in scheduled operations, I temporarily left the Flying Club to commence the Victoria-Vancouver scheduled service between False Creek—where the Burrard Bridge is now located in Vancouver—and the inner harbour in Victoria. This operation commenced October 15, 1929 and a Fairchild 71, CF-AJP, was the aircraft used.*

"Mr. Gordon MacKenzie, who had been brought in from the U.S.A., was promised this job, but due to him not being able to obtain his Canadian licence until he had written the necessary examinations, I was put to work temporarily. Six weeks later, however, Mr. MacKenzie obtained his licence and took over from me, placing me in the reserve position of flying one day a week. In January 1930, however, he had the misfortune to crash in the fog in English Bay, which resulted in the aircraft having to be placed in the newly organized Boeing Aircraft Factory, situated near Georgia Street at Stanley Park, for major repairs. In the meantime, the company was without a Canadian aircraft and accord-

ingly laid me off. This action caused me considerable annoyance since it was the second time that I had been crashed out of a job."

Ted Cressy, who was employed by the company as an engineer, was called up from Seattle to recover the damaged aircraft and still recalls the cause of the accident.

"MacKenzie was on his last run for that day coming back to Seattle, and it was a foggy day. In the 71, the pilot sat in front by himself in the single seat. It was only about two feet six inches from the front windscreen to number one cylinder; so, when you were taking off, you would generally be looking out the left hand side. Well, he was taking off marvelously, but forgot there was a big iron buoy right in the middle of English Bay. This day, his right float hit the boom, swung the aircraft around and broke off the float. The aircraft went down but MacKenzie and the four passengers were picked up by a nearby boom boat.

"MacKenzie lashed a line on the framework that protruded from the bottom of the fuselage, where the tail plane would normally sit, and tied it to the buoy. The machine sank completely but he had a short line on it and the tail was still exposed.

"We hauled the aircraft out by barge with an A-frame. I dropped the wings off with the help of two people and tied them alongside the fuselage. I started working on the engine. Before we got back to Burrard Inlet, I had that machine completely stripped and all the parts covered in solvent or coal oil."

When the Fairchild finally emerged from Boeing Aircraft of Canada following repairs, the company's fortunes were starting to change. Temporary accommodation was found at the newly constructed Air Land Manufacturing float plane hangar on Lulu Island, (now a Keg Restaurant) which featured such modern amenities as an electric winch. The firm resumed service on the triangle run for a while. The parent company, however, went out of business late in 1930, bringing the Alaska-Washington Airways of B.C. operations to a close.

Commercial Airways, a small company which shared a corner of the Air Land hangar with Alaska-Washington Airways, then attempted to operate a Stinson floatplane on the Vancouver-Victoria route, without success. But it was not until Canadian Airways introduced a Sikorsky S38 amphibian to the route in 1932, that a commercially successful service was achieved. This eight-seat aircraft brought a new degree of luxury to the service.

"It was a pretty nice looking aircraft for the time and I was quite proud to be able to work on it," says Bill Jacquot, who joined Canadian Airways as a maintenance engineer when they commenced the service. *"It was an amphibian and, to my mind, doing a very important daily service,*

CMFT collection #282.1 Dick Hammond collection

Fokker Universal, Vancouver Bay, B.C. Dick Hammond in photo.

operating between Vancouver and Victoria. The public response to it was quite good. It made two or three flights a day. It wasn't that expensive for its time, about $20, but only the well off could afford it. They had a ticket office in Coal Harbour, at the foot of Cardero Street. They would load the passengers there and fly to Victoria and discharge them.

"After about two years they decided to put other aircraft on the service —a Fokker Super Universal and a Fairchild 71, both on floats. They sold the Sikorsky."

The Sikorsky was withdrawn from service after a brief two years because its structure was not suited to salt water.

"It was an amphibian but it was not built with the idea of salt water in mind," says Rex Chandler, who also worked as a maintenance engineer for Canadian Airways. *"The aluminum alloys used were not suitable for salt water operation, but, unfortunately, not only did it land and take off in the salt water to go to Victoria and back, but it was maintained at Vancouver Airport. Every morning, it deadheaded from the airport to Coal Harbour, picked up passengers, and flew several times a day between Vancouver and Victoria, then deadheaded back at night. They were landing and taking off in salt water all the time. After two years, they looked into it quite deeply, opening the wings up, and they had to ground it just like that. It never flew again. It was just one gob of corrosion."*

Canadian Airways continued the Vancouver-Victoria run with other aircraft until the beginning of the war, eventually flying de Havilland Dragon Rapide floatplanes on the service. After the war, the availability of a land airport at Sidney enabled various airlines to offer a land based service while several floatplane operators turned the harbour-to-harbour, service into keystones of their operations. It remains a very important route, even today.

Although Canadian Airways ran a successful Vancouver-Victoria operation from 1932, the other leg of the triangle route – Vancouver-Seattle – took a while longer to develop. In 1934, United Air Lines finally started flying Boeing 247s landplanes up from Seattle into Vancouver Airport.

"Bill Templeton, the airport manager, used to talk about getting an airline into the airport," says Joe Bertalino, who became United Air Lines' first Vancouver employee. *"At the time there was no business at the airport and an airline would certainly start things moving. He was able to contact United Air Lines' Seattle superintendent, a Mr. Hall, and they decided to come up. I was introduced to Mr. Hall at the time. They gave me some instructions and said they would hire me. They started operating on July 1st, 1934.*

"I had to look after the passengers and issue the tickets. I would get the passengers off the plane and unload the baggage. Then load the plane up again and help them start the engines. It was a one-man job.

"The reason United Air Lines came in was that they were interested in the long-haul passengers and figured that they could pick up enough business here to feed their Chicago, New York, San Francisco, and Los Angeles route to make it worthwhile. They also hoped to get the airmail contract, but when Trans Canada Air Lines was started in 1938, it was decided that the airmail would be carried between Vancouver and Seattle by the Canadian carrier so United did not get the airmail."

Following this setback, United maintained the service until the start of World War II, when other priorities determined the shape of airline transport services.

Canadian Airways eventually competed with United Air Lines on the Vancouver-to-Seattle, commencing the service with a de Havilland Rapide which was soon replaced with the Lockheed 10A.

"The purpose of Canadian Airways assigning a Rapide to the Vancouver-Seattle route was to lay the groundwork

for ultimately establishing a transcontinental air service across Canada," says Maurice MacGregor, who flew on this route for Canadian Airways. *"It was soon quite obvious that the de Havilland Rapide was not adequate for the job. The company was so serious about becoming the principal operator of a transcontinental air service that they decided to buy two Lockheed 10s, CF-AZY and CF-BAF. This was in 1936."*

CMFT Collection #132.27 Gordon S. Williams collection

Canadian Airways de Havilland Rapide at Vancouver Airport, 1935. Original Vancouver Airport terminal building in background.

Canadian Airways ambition to operate the transcontinental air service was thwarted by the Canadian government, which decreed that a national airline, Trans Canada Air Lines, would be established to serve the route. Both national railways and Canadian Airways were invited to join with the government in forming this company, but the private companies would not accept the government having control through its holdings in Canadian National

Railways. Trans Canada Air Lines was set up with the government owning fifty-one percent and CN forty-nine percent. In 1937, it purchased the two Lockheed 10s from Canadian Airways and took over the Vancouver-Seattle route, which for almost a year was its only passenger carrying operation. When the plans for the takeover were announced, the pilots already flying the route were sure that they would become employees of the new company.

Aerial view of Municipal Airport, Vancouver, B.C. circa 1935.

CMFT Collection #601.9
George Fawkes collection

"We knew that they needed people with experience," relates Maurice MacGregor. *"We had all this training which many bush pilots had not obtained; so we were disappointed that Canadian Airways had failed to get the transcontinental service but not particularly alarmed, just impatiently waiting for the day it would happen.*

"When it happened, around August 27, they just said, 'We'd like you to join Trans Canada Air Lines on September 1st. Fly the first flight. You are part of the equipment. We are buying the two Lockheed 10As, a Stearman mail plane, one truck and the maintenance equipment; so therefore, you and the maintenance people are part of the package.' So we just carried on with our Canadian Airways uniforms and flew T.C.A. aircraft."

With the government backing for a transcontinental air service behind it, Trans Canada Air Lines commenced a year of intensive training operations, flying across the Rockies on instruments and familiarizing its pilots with the sophisticated airline-type flying about to be introduced into Canada. On March 1, 1939, the first official air mail flight from Vancouver to Winnipeg and onward to Montreal was flown by Maurice MacGregor, a pilot who had flown the Vancouver-Seattle route. At that point, air service across British Columbia could be said to have finally matured.

de Havilland DH89A Rapide seaplane operated by Canadian Airways 1942-1946.

CMFT Collection #198.144
Canadian Airways collection

CMFT Collection #98.2 Vancouver Public Library photo

Lockheed 10 of Canadian Airways. Aviation enters a new era.

CMFT Collection #275.100 Gordon Peters collection

A Lockheed 12 Electra CF-CCT at Patricia Bay, B.C. October, 1939. The first aircraft to land at Patricia Bay Airport, Victoria.

CMFT Collection #132.28 Gordon S. Williams collection

A United Air Lines Boeing 247 waits while a T.C.A. Lockheed takes on baggage at Vancouver Airport in the late 1930s.

6

THE COMPANIES OF LANSDOWNE FIELD

The beginnings of small-time aviation

On the west coast of British Columbia, apart from the brief flurry of activity in surplus Curtiss JN4 Jennies during 1919 and 1920, all early '20s flying development had concentrated on waterborne aircraft using the facilities around the Jericho Beach Air Station. As a result of this preoccupation with seaplanes and flying boats, no facilities for the use of landplanes existed upon the lower mainland. In late 1927, all this changed, when the three Dobbin brothers, William, Clare, and Ted, obtained the Western Canada agency for the de Havilland DH 60 Moth series of airplanes. They commenced operations under the name Dominion Airways.

"They had to find a field for their business," says Joe Bertalino, who started earning his Air Engineers ticket while working for Dominion Airways. *"They discovered a good one alongside the Lansdowne Park racetrack and made a deal with the farmer, Mr. Summerfield, and rented the field for their flying activities.*

"I was taken out to the field when I started with the company. They had about four huge crates broken open and pieces of aircraft lying about. There was nothing else except a small shed where we kept our tools and things.

"After a while, the City of Vancouver, which wanted an airport, got interested in the location and Bill Templeton, who had been a flier in the early days, came out and looked

things over. He decided it would be a suitable place for a small airport, went back to City Hall and the city council decided to lease the field from the farmer and put up a hangar."

All this did not take place quickly and without fuss. The lease of the field on Lulu Island was seen only as a temporary expedient, and an immediate answer to the shock which had been delivered late in 1927 when Lindberg had refused to visit Vancouver on his tour of North America following his trans-Atlantic flight, expressing the opinion that Vancouver did not have a suitable airport. Lansdowne Field was not to be the permanent Vancouver airport but was to buy time while a better site was obtained and prepared.

Lansdowne Field on Lulu Island was officially opened in May 1929, following a brief delay. The date had original-

CMFT Collection #10.6 John Whittle collection

The Aero Club's fleet at Lansdowne Field, 1929. Aircraft are two Fleet 2s, and an Alexander Eaglerock. Note the original hangar at right. This hangar is now held for future exhibit by the Museum.

ly been set for the Easter holiday period but had been postponed:

> *. . . due partly to the field not being sufficiently dry for heavy traffic by a number of planes, and partly owing to the delay in securing an airport license . . . the result of a request from the Department of National Defense for the provision of accommodation for customs and immigration officer.*
> (Canadian Aviation, June 1929)

While the Aero Club was prevented from flying off Lansdowne Field until it could be upgraded to meet government specifications, privately owned Dominion Airways were not so restricted and continued using it for their Gipsy Moth training operations, in addition to operating further afield.

"Their main office was in downtown Vancouver in the Vancouver Block," relates Joe Bertalino. *"They had one airplane on floats which was working out of English Bay. This seaplane was used in the spring and summer time flying forestry patrol out of Nelson. Also, they were selling aircraft, the Cirrus Moth and Gipsy Moth. They had folding wings, which at that time was something special; it was the airplane for everybody because you could put it in your garage.*

"In addition to those activities, they were operating the flying school at Lulu Island (Lansdowne Field) and a night school so that people could learn something about aviation. This they ran at an office on Fourth Avenue, just near MacDonald.

"They offered me a job with the company but said that they couldn't pay me very much. I could work on the aircraft and take the night school to learn more about aircraft. So I went to work for them. I used to go out in the daytime and help assemble airplanes and in the evening I would go to the night school.

"There were three Dobbin brothers involved in the business: William Dobbin was the manager downtown, Clare

Dobbin was in charge of all the aircraft and the maintenance, and Ted Dobbin, who was known as Captain Dobbin, he was the instructor and did all the teaching and flying.

"Ted Dobbin had had a twin brother and both he and his twin had been fliers in the war. His twin had been killed but Ted came home and had continued flying in the east before he returned to B.C. He promoted the idea of starting a flying business to his brothers and they decided to contact de Havilland in England and obtain the agency for the Moth aircraft."

In 1930, the Dobbins managed to interest the Yarrow Shipyard in taking a financial interest in the company which was renamed Yarrow Aircraft Corporation. But almost immediately the company met with disaster. A Stinson Reliant, newly purchased to carry larger loads, was left unattended with the engine running and ran amok, damaging three other of the company's aircraft.

"Ted Dobbin, who was flying it at the time, parked it facing the other machines," relates Joe Bertalino. *"He set the brake and got out while he waited for the next load of passengers. He left the engine just ticking over."*

"While he was out, he met a young fellow from the Air Force who asked him if it would be all right to go inside the plane and take a look. Captain Dobbin said, 'Sure, go inside and take a look,' because it was a new machine and naturally of interest.

"While the young fellow was looking at the instrument panel he bent down to look at the pedals and his head or shoulder bumped the throttle, which was in the center of the panel, the first aircraft in Vancouver to have such a position for the throttle. When he heard the roar of the engine as the throttle opened, he grabbed for the lever on the side of the panel, which he took to be the throttle, and pulled it back. It was actually the brake release.

"There were no chocks under the wheels, so when he pulled the lever, which released the brakes, the aircraft started rolling forward toward the parked aircraft. At the time, I was sitting in the center one running the engine up. I heard all the noise and looked around to see what was happening. Paint was flying all over! I chopped the throttle of the aircraft I was in and ducked as far into the cockpit as I could get. The runaway came right up behind me and I could hear all the churning but couldn't see what was happening until it all stopped.

Airport Manager BIll Templeton describes the accident in which Dominion Airways' Stinson Reliant damaged three de Havilland Gipsy Moths.

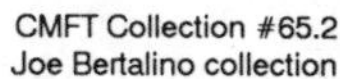

CMFT Collection #65.2
Joe Bertalino collection

"Finally someone got to the Stinson and got the engine stopped and it quieted down. I looked out. There were airplanes piled up all around, and the one that I was in was chewed up right to the back of the seat.

"That accident sure caused a lot of trouble. The insurance companies complained about it, and it was the cause of the company going out of business."

By the time the new Vancouver Airport at Sea Island was opened, Yarrows had withdrawn their support from Dominion Airways, and the company that had given Vancouver its first airport no longer existed.

Victoria-based B.C. Airways Ltd. of the same era had an even shorter existence (see chapter 5), and its surviving aircraft were sold to other users, one of which was Sprott-Shaw Schools of Vancouver, which then set up the Sprott-Shaw School of Aviation.

If the Sprott-Shaw secretarial school expected aviation to be a profitable activity they were quickly disillusioned. In November 1928, the Driggs Dart, G-CAIR, was delivered to them by Hal Wilson, and although all three of its cylinders were operating when Wilson departed from Victoria, only two were operating when he reached Vancouver. The following day, Ted Cressy, the B.C. Aviation engineer, managed to get all three cylinders functioning again but when Ted Luke, the school's instructor, took the aircraft up, he inadvertently spun it just after take off and crashed into a nearby dyke. Luke survived the accident but the aircraft did not. This may have been fortunate for the potential students for Hal Wilson felt that:

> *"This aircraft would never have been any use for training, since although it had dual controls, it weighed only 380 pounds and was exceedingly sensitive and somewhat tricky to fly."*

The school next obtained a Waco 10 with a Curtiss OX-5 engine in February 1929, which was supplemented, in July of 1930, by a Barling NB-3G, CF-AMG. This latter aircraft was registered, not to the school, but to its proprietor R. J. Sprott, possibly because he was having second thoughts about his entrance into the aviation business. The Sprott-Shaw School of Aviation ceased operations at the end of 1930 and thus did not make the move to the new Sea Island Airport which opened in 1931.

Yet another short-lived operation of the Lansdowne Field era was Commercial Airways which commenced operations in the summer of 1930 with a Golden Eagle Chief, CF-AKB, rapidly adding a Stinson Junior, CF-ANE, and a Fleet Model 2 seaplane, CF-ANF. George Silke was employed as chief pilot and the main activities

Sprott-Shaw Aviation School's Waco 10 with a Curtiss OX-5. Aviators unknown.

CMFT Collection #242.9
K.E. Jordan collection

were charter flying. For a brief period in 1930, it attempted to operate a Vancouver-Victoria service which it maintained for only a few months. The Golden Eagle and Stinson were sold at the beginning of 1931, and the Fleet seaplane was turned over to the Aero Club for operation. It was eventually sold, in 1932, for the low sum of $1,500.

None of the commercial operations which commenced business at Lansdowne Field during its short period of operation survived long enough to move to the new Vancouver Airport upon its opening in May 1931. Only the government subsidized Aero Club of British Columbia was able to make the transition. Aviation was a poor business proposition back in 1930.

CMFT Collection #65.18 Joe Bertalino collection

Dominion Airways' crew in front of Vancouver's first hangar at Lansdowne, Lulu Island 1930-31. From left to right: Finney Magar, Barney Jones-Evans, Bill Dean (squatting), unknown, Joe Bertalino.

7

THE HAZARDS OF EARLY OPERATIONS

Crashes, searches and rescues

Up to the early 1930s, few facilities existed in British Columbia to support aviation. The airmen of that era were pioneers in the true sense. They flew in unreliable aircraft into uncertain weather, and when they got into difficulties they were largely on their own resources for survival.

The attempted flight by W. H. (Harry) Brown of Vancouver Island Aerial Service from Alert Bay to Prince Rupert in a Curtiss JN4 Jenny floatplane on September 20, 1920 typifies the risks of those early days. As related in chapter 3, Brown was forced to land in the open water due to engine troubles, drifted onto Nalau Island where he remained for a day, then paddled a log out to the shipping

Liberty engine of the type used in the Curtiss HS-2L.

CMFT Collection #179.21
Marjorie Nicol collection

channels to avoid facing starvation. He was picked up almost a day later suffering from exhaustion.

Unreliable engines continued to plague airmen for the next few years as stocks of wartime aircraft continued to be the mainstay of flying operations. Unlike today, when a single pilot can fly an aircraft up and down the coast in safety, in the early '20s an air engineer was a necessity in the aircraft flying fishery patrols. If necessary, these rugged flying boats could alight on the water for the engineer to make running repairs on the engine.

> *"The Liberty engine was not reliable. It was built, in 1916, in the United States of America by Ford and by Packard,"* relates Harold Davenport, who started his aviation career working on these engines. *"It burned twenty-five gallons an hour but it was not reliable in a good many ways. The cylinders were at forty-five degrees. One of the connecting rod bearings had a forked end which fitted over the throw of the crankshaft, and the other was a steel connecting rod with a bronze bearing that fitted over the back of the other bearing. Having a bronze articulated rod working on the bronze back of a brass-backed bearing is not very efficient.*
>
> *"The load on the bearings was high, and when it failed it usually ripped . . . a side out of the crank case and probably cut into the wooden engine mounts and set fire to the oil. It was very spectacular to see a bunch of burning oil leaving behind the airplane, but that happened a good many times relative to the number of hours we flew."*

Davenport experienced one such failure while on patrol in a Curtiss HS-2L in appalling weather but by good fortune was rescued.

> Says Davenport, *"We had taken off and it was a terrible day. . . . It was a Sunday. Since then I've very seldom worked on Sundays. There was a south-east gale blowing and the visibility was very poor. We headed out into Milbanke Sound flying along about six or seven hundred feet*

and . . . another connecting rod failed. The oil had spilled out very quickly as the crankcase was smashed badly. This set fire to the oil again. Hull (the pilot) slipped the airplane to keep the flames off the tailplane.

"We made a forced landing in quite heavy seas. It was rough. With the shore line about five or six miles away, there was scud blowing that day. You could see the waves riding over the beach from the distance . . . whitecaps.

"Looking around toward the sea, I could see the upper structure of a very large boat. This was a bit of luck. It disappeared through the scud and even the sea. I got the Very pistol, waited for a clear part and fired the first red shot. Within seconds the nose of the boat turned and steered directly towards us.

"He came in, swinging the lead from the front. It was the S.S. Alaskan, *a really big boat. They dropped the line down. I got it and they dropped a heavier line down. We made touch and he backed out. He backed out several miles.*

"At the same time, we'd been working on our radio. By luck again, the Givenchy, *a fisheries boat happened to be within a very few miles. They picked up the signals and, in not more than an hour, they came on scene. The big boat pulled away and disappeared under the scud in a few minutes.*

"The Givenchy *got a hold of us. Some men went back with a hawser, the biggest line I've ever seen in my life! It was three and a half inches in diameter. I made it fast to the boom that ran down from the engine mount to the nose that took the thrust from the engine and the* Givenchy, *by this time about 1,000 feet ahead of us, played the line out.*

"They started off too fast and, the first roll, I'm looking down at the sea then, the second roll, the aircraft turned right over. So we wound up, Hull on one side and me on the other, with our heels digging into the wing. And then they had the job of getting us off. That really was a tough show,

getting off from the trailing edge of the wing. They eventually got us off but it was a difficult thing. The boat would be down and we'd be up but one after the other we got off."

Unreliable engines were not the only causes of problems during the 1920s. The lack of adequate weather forecasts and a willingness to fly in poor conditions led to incidents like the loss of a Canadian Airways' Vickers Vedette in 1928.

"The big contract was the federal fisheries patrol contract which MacLaren had taken over from the Royal Canadian Air Force about 1926," says Gordon Ballentine, who joined Pacific Airways early in 1928. *"In 1928, when Pacific Airways sold out to Western Canada Airways, the fisheries patrol contract was greatly expanded to about five aircraft. In late June of 1928, the first Boeing B1E was sent up to Swanson Bay with a pilot by the name of Ted Luke and an air engineer called Bill Partridge. On July 13, they crashed the aircraft between Butedale and Swanson Bay, and killed the air engineer and . . . totally destroyed the aircraft.*

"To replace this lost aircraft, the contract required that they get another one up there; so MacLaren flew me and Alf Walker, an air engineer, up in a Boeing B1E to Swanson Bay . . . and we were followed by Bill Upham in another Boeing B1E.

"We started out for the Charlottes from Swanson Bay in a Vickers Vedette and went up to Prince Rupert for the first night. We left Rupert with a ceiling of about 1,500 feet, gray and drizzly. Gray and drizzly in an open airplane, I might say, is not comfortable. We were flying the channel headed for Hecate Strait when, all of a sudden, from having visibility we were in cloud. I'm presuming that the pilot was just as surprised as I was.

"Suddenly we were in cloud, but we didn't have any instruments . . . not the sort of thing you need to fly in cloud,

Western Canada Airways' Boeing B1E CF-ABB circa 1930.

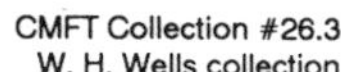

CMFT Collection #26.3
W. H. Wells collection

so immediately the power came off and we started down. I expected the first thing we would see was water, the water we'd seen prior to running into this cloud. Instead of that, about ten or fifteen feet underneath us, were some very tall trees. We were right over the forest and very close to it, and so the power came on with a roar and we started up. In cloud, without instruments, there's no way of knowing what sort of gyrations we were going through, but every few moments we'd see trees and then into the cloud again, eventually, nothing ahead of us but scrub and rock, and "bang," we hit the mountain. If you want real terror, you want to sit helpless as a passenger. The pilot's too busy to be frightened.

"We hit the mountain with a good crunch. I was out and running right away, because we all knew enough about air planes crashing to know that they usually caught fire. I guess I stumbled maybe fifty feet. I fell down because I'd banged one knee a pretty good thump in the crash. I sat there sort of stunned and looking around, looked back at the airplane. The engine was still running , but was now vertical like a helicopter engine with clouds of steam coming off it. It took me a moment or two to realize that this was an air cooled Wright Whirlwind. It just didn't make steam, that was

gasoline. The engine running merrily along at about, I guess about 1,500 rpm. No sign of fires; so I went back, and tried to figure out how to get at the two fellows still in the cockpit. The wings were just a mass of junk and wire, mixed up with the scrub at the level on the mountain at which we had hit.

"It took me a bit of a struggle through this mess of wires and scrub to get to the cockpit. I went in on the left hand side because I wanted to switch off the engine. When I got there, Neville (Cumming) was slumped forward with his face down and so was Alf. Alf's face looked like chopped liver and he looked dead. I was pretty sure he was dead. I thought Neville was dead at first, then just as I was trying to reach in to get at the switch, one of his hands came up, knocked the switch off, and he went back to dreamland.

"There I was, with one dead friend and one more or less alive. I crawled out through the wreckage again, got an axe out, and started back. I was going to do something about chopping Neville out.

"When I got back there, I got my first real shock, not counting the shock of the crash. The dead guy was gone. That really shocked me. You're not normal after an incident like that. I'm sure I wasn't. Neville was sitting there, still in the same position, passed out cold, blood all over the place, instrument panel smashed where their faces had smashed it, and the dead man had disappeared. With the fog swirling around and not knowing where we were, it was quite an eerie feeling.

"I thought I'd better go find my dead friend; so I took the axe and went out again around to the front. Just as I got around to the front of the airplane, there was Alf coming around from the other side. We looked at each other, and we both started to laugh . . . sort of hysterical laughter.

"We didn't know where we were, if we were on the mainland or on an island or whatever, and we were still in cloud. So we decided first we ought to get Neville out. He

was totally unconscious and didn't come to for some hours. Alf and I took turns wandering around the mountain trying to figure out where we were. About five o'clock, the clouds started to break enough; so we suddenly got a glimpse of water away down below.

"We decided there was no point in staying where we were. In those days nobody knew where you were. You didn't have flight plans or anything else, and if you didn't help yourself, nobody else would. They wouldn't have even known we were lost for a couple of weeks, because they expected us to be working in the Charlottes.

"We decided to carry Neville down to the beach. We didn't know if it was a lake or the ocean or what it was. I chopped a couple of poles to make a stretcher, a Boy Scout stretcher. We got my jacket on the poles and then we sat Neville up to get his jacket off to make the rest of the stretcher, when he came to and wanted to know what we were doing. When we informed him that we were going to carry him down the mountain, his response was, 'Like hell you are, I'm going to walk down. . . .' and this guy, with his nose broken, a gash in his head an inch wide and four inches long and with more gashes on his face, walked down the mountain.

"We decided we'd do a little exploring, and we tossed a coin to see which of us would go first, and another coin to see which way to go. It came out that Alf would go, and go to the right. About an hour later, Alf came back, incoherent, his eyes bugged out. It turned out that, about half a mile along the beach, he'd come upon a bay with a launch in it. He yelled and whistled and had thrown rocks at it with no response, but a little farther on was the start of the trail coming down the mountain. He went up this about twenty feet or so, and lo and behold, on a tree there was a telephone, one of these old crank-up telephones. This place was the shore base for some mining exploration up the hill.

Not long after, along comes a rowboat into our bay, and out of it jumped three guys. They took us to the launch and into Rupert. Alf and I promptly wired our respective homes in Vancouver that we were alive and well."

Brown, Davenport and Hull, and Ballentine and his associates, all had rapid rescues. Far less fortunate was E. J. A. (Paddy) Burke and his party whose disappearance in the Liard River country of northern B.C. sparked one of the greatest aerial searches of the time.

Burke, who was chief pilot for the newly formed Air-Land Manufacturing Co., was operating the Junkers F-13 CF-AMX, with Emil Kading as his air engineer. They left Liard Post on October 11, 1930 to fly a prospector, Bob "Three Finger" Martin, into a mining claim near Atlin and vanished. Since charter flights in the area were prone to delay, especially when they were involved in prospecting activities, no great consternation was felt for over a week. However, with winter approaching, attempts were made to locate Burke's party after his wife advised the authorities that the plane and three men were overdue.

At the time no search and rescue organization existed and the initial search efforts were conducted by the missing men's friends. Frank Dorbrandt, a well known arctic pilot, commenced search operations from Atlin, but was forced to abandon them to fulfill a contract flying trappers into the north. The Yukon-Tredwell Exploration Company's Fairchild FC-2W, G-CARM, flown by Everett Wasson joined the hunt while other aircraft flew in from the south. The search achieved tremendous proportions and resulted in the loss of or damage to several other aircraft.

"There was an American outfit, Pacific International Airways, going up to Alaska, with a Fairchild and a Fleetster," says Ted Cressy, who joined the search some time later, *"They came into Vancouver to gas up, heard*

about Paddy Burke and said they would look for them on the way. They landed, at either Terrace or Burns Lake, whichever one had a field, because they were on wheels. The Fairchild busted an undercart on take off and went on its nose. The other aircraft had engine trouble somewhere around Ketchikan."

Initially, the Royal Canadian Air Force took no part in the search. Its flying boats were not suitable for use in the Liard River country where the freeze-up was turning all the lakes and rivers into solid ice. In any case, the Air Force pilots would have been operating in unfamiliar country, since their activities had concentrated upon coastal waters. They came into the search, however, when yet another aircraft went missing on its way to the search area.

"We had established a temporary base at Comox Lake, on Vancouver Island," says Larry Dunlap, who piloted one of the two Air Force machines which joined the search at this point. *"While there, we had instructions to proceed at once to Prince Rupert to participate in the search for a missing pilot, Pat Renahan, who was a very experienced pilot with Alaska-Washington Airways.*

"Renahan was concerned that his friend Paddy Burke, who was missing in northern B.C., had not yet been found. He felt that he knew exactly where Paddy Burke would be.

"One of the reasons that Paddy Burke wasn't found was that he was on an assignment to a mining promoter taking supplies into a secret gold mine, and they were being very secretive about the whole operation. Nobody knew quite where Paddy Burke was flying when he became overdue.

"Renahan had had something to do with this promoter and had a pretty good idea where this gold mine was located. He may even have been in there at some time. He appealed to his principals in Seattle and said that if he could have the weekend off he would fly up there and find Paddy Burke. He took off on a Friday afternoon and reckoned he could

be back on Monday morning. He was a very cock-sure type of fellow.

"He refuelled at some place a hundred miles south of Rupert. He was running out of daylight, so he didn't even stop to strain the fuel. Fuel drums sitting on a dock have a habit of taking on a bit of moisture, if for no other reason than condensation inside the drum. Also, when you've got drums sitting on end with an inch of water sitting within the rim, you can get a little bit of water going in around the bung. We always filtered our fuel into aircraft in those days. The chamois filter always filtered out the water.

"Renahan didn't take time to do that and his engine was heard at one or two points, after he took off, missing rather badly. Then darkness set in. Somebody heard him flying by in the dusk. Then were was nothing else reported. He wasn't heard beyond Rupert, but we presumed that perhaps he got beyond. He was heading for Ketchikan, Alaska, and he was going to refuel again and go on from there. So we were ordered up there.

"We got there in early November and the search lasted until the end of November. We put in a lot of time. I'm sure we put in fifty or more hours apiece covering all the inlets that he possibly might have gotten into. We searched up the Alaskan coast. We searched up to Portland Inlet, way up to Stewart, and we searched over the north end of Queen Charlotte Islands . . . we searched in the islands to the south of Prince Rupert. All the time our aircraft were taking a terrible beating because they were tied up at the Imperial Oil docks. Sometimes the winds would get up to fifty or sixty miles an hour in the middle of the night with the pontoons banging against the docks. You couldn't anchor out in the mooring there because the harbour was so deep. We were exposed to frightfully hazardous flying. I have never experienced such severe air pockets as we encountered at various stages of that search.

"The closest that anybody came to seeing anything was a famous clairvoyant of Prince Rupert who sat all the time that we were out on search, looking at a crystal ball and seeing the location of the crashed aircraft and seeing us get near the location from time to time. She was so highly regarded in the Prince Rupert area that we were invited to make contact with her and let her try to explain to us where we were in relation to the crash.

"Of course we weren't inclined to put any stock in this, but having searched already for three weeks and found nothing we went along with it. It was rather an interesting and amusing session but the poor lady was no good on locations or directions. She was entirely unable to explain to us where she thought this aircraft was located and where we were in relation thereto. So it didn't prove beneficial."

It was to be several months later, long after the search had been called off that any trace was found of the Renahan's missing Lockheed Vega. Pieces of the fuselage were eventually picked up near the Piercy Islands, proving that Renahan and his crew had been forced down into the Sea and had perished, adding three lives to the cost of the search for Paddy Burke and party.

While the RCAF's flying boats concentrated on looking for Renahan, a search committee was formed to coordinate the efforts to find Burke. Don MacLaren of Western Canada Airways was appointed chairman and took control of further movements of aircraft into the search area.

At this point the other Air Land Manufacturing Junkers F-13, CF-ALX, arrived back at base and were immediately dispatched to Atlin. Ted Cressy, who was aboard as air engineer, can still recall the difficulties this crew encountered.

"We came home and found this trouble and they said that we were to gas up and get going. We figured that we'd get up to McDame's Landing, just this side of Juneau and

fly up the McDame and get into the Liard that way. But they had so much trouble with the Burke search, having lost Pat Renahan, that MacLaren, the searchmaster, said, 'No, you have got to go overland.' We didn't like the idea of that at all. Anyway, we went up.

"In the mean time, prior to this, they had removed the licence from Bill Joerss (the pilot of the Junkers). Since we had to take a licenced pilot with us, they hired Van der Byl, who had never flown a Junkers. We packed him around just for the licence.

"We got to Prince George where we bent a float strut on landing. I took it off and into Prince George and straightened it. That took us a day and a half. We then went up to New Landing at Takla Lake and gassed up there. Taking off, we figured we could make Dease Lake, but we couldn't. Half way up the Driftwood River, snow and low clouds came in; so we had to go through the canyon, which wasn't very nice, and land at Thutade in a snow storm.

"We stayed there three days, and then the ice started to come up pretty fast. We kept the machine going as often as we could, thinking that we could take off on floats on the ice and get back to Takla Landing. On the third or fourth day, we built a raft to make a channel in the ice, breaking it as we went along. We got out to the middle and tried to take off. Well, the water spray got onto the floats, the float struts and underneath the wing. We were completely overloaded and couldn't take off from weight of ice. So we came back through this channel we had cut through the ice, cleaned everything off, and decided that we would have to do the same thing the next day, but strip the machine down, Van and I staying there to let Bill get out. If the aircraft didn't get out, people would be worried about where we were as well as where Burke was. So we stripped the machine down, gave Bill just enough fuel to get down to Takla Landing, about twenty-five minutes flying time.

"We broke the ice and got out into the middle of the lake. We figured that Bill could taxi slowly until the middle of the lake came along and then he could get on heavy ice. He would be partly on the step, and he could hit the ice, go along the ice on the bottom of his keel and take off. Well, the theory was O.K. and it worked. He taxied until the spray was just under his wings, instead of hitting his wings, came to the main stream of the ice, in the middle, which was hard enough and heavy enough to hold him. He broke a little of the ice getting up there and then his keel hit the main ice and he got off. We watched him go.

"We figured he would get down there and it would be about nine days for Joe, the number one Indian at MacDonigal's place at Takla, to get in and get us. We didn't want any help or anything, just a guide to take us out. Well, we waited there sixteen days and there was no Bill, so we figured, maybe he had hit the mountain.

"It so happened that, when he got to Takla, Joe was taking his son—who had severely cut his foot with an axe chopping wood—down to Fort St. James.

"We then found that there was an Indian trapping crowd at the bottom of the lake. One came up and we started mushing out with him as guide. We got out in thirty-one days. On December 23, we got to Fort St. James and that was the first time we got into a bed and I was able to telegraph to our friends and my wife that everything was OK.

"In the mean time, while we were up in the bush, Wasson, who was flying a Fairchild out of Carcross—had found the Burke party and found that Burke—who suffered from diabetes and hadn't got the necessary injections—was dead. Emil Kading and Three Finger Martin were still okay and he flew them back to Carcross and that was the end of that."

The Burke party was found only due to the persistence of Ev Wasson, who was convinced that the party was in the

Liard River area. He had continued his flights whenever the weather permitted, long after all other aircraft had been withdrawn. On November 24, flying with Walsh, a prospector familiar with the region, he had sighted the snow-covered Junkers on the frozen Liard. A few days later he was able to land on a frozen lake fifteen miles away, mush in through deep snow to the machine where he found a note saying "Leaving for Wolf Lake, food low."

After making several flights between the stranded machine and Wolf Lake, he sighted two of the missing men, landed on a lake ten miles away and walked in to the camp, to be greeted by the haggard and exhausted Martin and Kading, who told him of Paddy Burke's death from exposure and exhaustion on November 20.

The Burke search was one of the greatest searches for a missing aircraft in B.C. and one of the largest searches in Canada to that time. With most of the search efforts being organized on an ad hoc basis, it was a rather hazardous and haphazard undertaking. This search stimulated the RCAF to accept a more dominant role in search and rescue operations leading to the services we enjoy today.

CMFT Collection #30.3 Brian Burke collection

E. J. A. "Paddy" Burke and Emil Kading circa 1930. They and aircraft CF-AMX figured tragically in the greatest air search ever conducted in the west.

Flight Officer E. J. A. "Paddy" Burke, in Fairchild FC-2W RCAF, 1928.

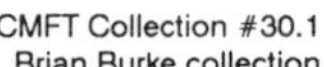

CMFT Collection #30.1
Brian Burke collection

CMFT Collection #41.1 Gordon Moore collection.

A Junkers F-13, CF-AMX, with a 6-cylinder BMW engine owned by Charlie Elliott is shown here on charter at Clowhom Lake, B.C. to Pacific Air Services/Wells Air Harbour, circa 1935.

8

THE AERO CLUB OF B.C.

The 1930s social center of Vancouver Airport

During the 1930s, when the Vancouver Airport was a small place, the social center of the airport was the Aero Club of B.C. Formed in 1928, when the airport was Lansdowne Field on Lulu Island, the Aero Club was the only organization of that era to relocate to the new Sea Island Airport after its opening in 1931. During the Second World War, the Aero Club operated Elementary Flying Training Schools for the British Commonwealth Air Training Plan (BCATP), then re-emerged postwar as Vancouver's most important flying club and finally withered in the late 1960s when the training activity was pushed out of Vancouver to Pitt Meadows Airport.

During the 1920s, a group of ex-World War I flyers – the Air Force Club of B.C. – were actively lobbying the federal government for the support of flying training. They, along with other like-minded pressure groups across the country, were crowned by a measure of success when, on November 10, 1927, J. A. Wilson, Controller of Civil Aviation, announced government support for lightplane training clubs that could qualify under a new Canadian Flying Clubs plan. The proposed plan was patterned after an existing program in the U.K., and five major cities, Montreal, Toronto, Hamilton, Winnipeg, and Vancouver were prime contenders for early eligibility. To qualify for federal support, flying clubs would require approved airfields, qualified flight instructors and mechanics, hangar facilities and adequate bonding to cover the replacement of any government aircraft should they be damaged or destroyed.

The government plan called for the donation of two DH Gipsy Moths to each qualifying flying club, and an additional ten machines to be held in reserve for other interested communities intending to qualify. In addition Ottawa proposed to donate a further gift aircraft for each one subsequently purchased by an approved club to a maximum of two. A $100 subsidy towards the cost of each student's licence tuition rounded out the governmental largesse, all of which imparted a sizable fillip to Canadian aviation and hastened the Canadian division of de Havilland Aircraft Ltd., into a modest manufacturing plant on de Lesseps airfield, Mount Dennis, Ontario in 1928. In 1944 the "city" flying clubs were granted the appellation Royal in consideration of their wartime training contribution.

The Aero Club of British Columbia was rapidly organized but only just managed to obtain the last two of the twenty Gipsy Moth biplanes allotted to the scheme in 1928. Bonds posted by Brigadier General J. W. Stewart and H. O. Bell Irving, covering the value of the machines, removed the last obstacle in the path of the club's flying activities in August 1928, the two aircraft arrived from the RCAF station at High River, Alberta. G-CAKH was unofficially named "Mariposa" and G-CAKW "Manana."

Upon arrival, the two aircraft went into storage since the club's instructor, Percy A. Hainstock, was still at Moose Jaw taking an instructors' refresher course. Upon his return, the condition of the Lulu Island Airport (Lansdowne Field) was criticized by the RCAF and the cancellation of its licence as a temporary airport was threatened unless major upgrading was undertaken. The aircraft remained in storage while the field was prepared and a hangar, "fit for the storage of the government's property," was erected.

In March 1929, after a delay of almost a year, flight training finally started with twenty-seven students enrolled for instruction. On July 22, 1929, "Manana" was destroyed, being spun into the ground on a training flight with Hainstock, the club's instructor and a student, Henry Colin, aboard. Hainstock was killed.

By fortuitous circumstance, a qualified instructor was available locally.

> *It was happy chance that brought A. H. Wilson to Vancouver on business last week just as the matter of the appointment of a new club instructor was under consideration by the directors. This being the case it was possible to negotiate with him personally at once, to secure the approval of Ottawa to his appointment and to resume flying the following day.*
> (Canadian Aviation, September 1929)

In the fall of 1929 Wilson resigned his position to fly for Alaska-Washington Airways but in January 1930, the company's Fairchild 71 crashed in fog at English Bay with Gordon MacKenzie at the controls and, for the second time in under two years, Wilson was crashed out of a job by the action of others. The Aero Club, who were not happy with Wilson's replacement, rehired their former instructor, who remained with them until World War II.

In addition to the two government supplied Gipsy Moths, the club had purchased two Alexander Eaglerocks formerly owned by the defunct B.C. Airways Ltd. In August 1929, one was put in service. The other, G-CAIS, obtained in damaged condition, went into service at the end of February 1930 but collided with the club's remaining Gipsy Moth while landing on March 9, 1930, putting the club in a precarious financial condition. The Eaglerock was damaged beyond repair while the Moth had some $900 damage.

As it had become apparent that the wooden airframe of the Moth was not ideally suited to the damp Vancouver climate, it was decided to replace the club's aircraft with a different type. The Canadian-built Fleet Model 2 was selected. The directors arranged to refinance the club in order to obtain two Fleets, one of which, CF-ANL, was provided by the government as a matching contribution to the one purchased by the club, CF-ANN. These two aircraft, which arrived in August 1930, were to remain the mainstays of the Aero Club's operations throughout the 1930s.

During 1930, the club dabbled briefly with the new craze of gliding. Boeing Aircraft of Canada offered one of its primary gliders to the club in return for Hal Wilson's services piloting a gliding display at the 1930 Pacific Coast Exhibition. This led to the first aero tow in Canada as, on July 31, 1930, the Boeing primary was towed into the air behind a Fleet 2, CF-ANH, leased by the Aero Club from Hump Madden. This flight by Wilson was a test for a proposed tow to the exhibition grounds but the latter was prevented by a telegram from Ottawa,

> *"Under no circumstances is a glider to be towed by an aeroplane."*

Although the test flight showed the idea was feasible, officialdom ruled and the glider was dismantled and moved to the exhibition grounds by truck. Wilson's displays at the exhibition took place as planned, although they were not elaborate.

> *"They would tow me up behind an old Maxwell coupe and we'd get up to 200 feet. I would cut off, turn left over the stand, turn back to the right again and go down. One day I left it a little late; I went a little too far. As I was coming down I had to come over some horses in a corral and I just*

held it off. As I passed over the corral I said 'Whoa, Whoa, Whoa,' because I thought that if one of the horses were to buck, it would knock the bottom out of the glider."

The Aero Club was not enamoured with the idea of gliding, however, and, apart from this display put on at the exhibition, left this form of flying to others.

A. H. "Hal" Wilson in front cockpit and Gordon Bulger in rear cockpit of a Fleet biplane.

CMFT Collection #667.1
Charles W. Wilson collection

With the arrival of its new aircraft in August 1930 and the move to the new Sea Island Airport in 1931, the Aero Club settled into the pattern that would see it through the depths of the depression. They operated with a fleet of two Fleet 2s, Hal Wilson as instructor and Bill Bolton looking after the maintenance. It had prestige which the other operations lacked, Wilson and Bolton being two of the best men in their trade.

"The Aero Club seemed to be the elite," says Larry Dakin, who started in aviation with one of its competitors. *"It had a government subsidy, Hal Wilson, who was a mogul at the airport, and Bill Bolton, who had a lot of credibility as an engineer. They seemed to be in a class by themselves. Noticeably so, I thought. I went back to the airport in the '40s and the Aero Club hadn't the same status it was during*

the '30s era. Everyone recognized Wilson, he was in a class by himself. He had a great background. Everybody wanted Wilson. He was a great instructor."

Rex Chandler, who learned the mechanic's trade with the Aero Club, feels that a lot of the Aero Club's status was due to the high maintenance standards set by the club's mechanic, Bill Bolton.

"Bill Bolton was a natural born mechanic," says Chandler. *"He lost his right arm in a threshing machine accident on the prairies. He could put a set of rings on a piston with the greatest of ease quicker than a lot of people with two hands. He taught me a tremendous amount of knowledge and practical ways of doing things. Because he did them all with one hand it made it that much easier for me to do it with two."*

The factor which had the greatest impact on the fortunes of the Aero Club, however, was the government sponsorship and the prestige which this gave the organization.

"The Aero Club had one advantage over other organizations," continues Rex Chandler. *"It was subsidized by the government. When a person learned to fly with the Aero Club they were given a grant. The rationale behind it was that they (the government) decided that it would be appropriate to have a nucleus of pilots available in the event of a national emergency.*

"That was really why the Aero club existed throughout the depression. Other organizations, not having those subsidies, had additional problems keeping above water.

"The club was also a social organization. They had a club room in the administration building at the airport which consisted of a few chairs, chesterfield and tables, a coffee shop, and a very small office in one corner of this area, where Finney Magar presided, looking after all the log books."

In this regard, the Aero Club had an advantage over the commercial operators who moved in during the mid and late '30s and worked with the bare minimum of facilities.

"The Aero Club people looked down at the other operators," says Gordon Peters, another mechanic who trained under Bill Bolton. *"Not that there was anything wrong with the flying of the others but the Aero Club did things a little different, a little closer to the line. Foggin, for example, didn't see things like that . . . he was in there to make some money, which he did."*

As the clouds of war approached, the Royal Canadian Aero Clubs were prepared for an expanded role. Senior instructors were taught the mysteries of instrument flying, and additional aircraft, equipped with blind flying hoods, were supplied by the government. In 1937, the Aero Club obtained a Fleet 7 for such instrument training. Then, with the outbreak of war, massive changes took place.

"I remember going to the airport on September 3rd when they declared war," says Gordon Peters. *"It wasn't but a few days later when the army came out and set up tents and guys with guns. Then, from that point, things just seemed to mushroom."*

During early 1940 the Aero Club continued to function on a relative peacetime basis—it was the period of the "bore" war—although signs of pending changes were apparent. Arnold Feast arrived in Vancouver during early January 1940 and flew the Aero Club machines until May of that year. He recalls:

"In the spring, as I remember, the Aero Club had their first intake of P.P.O.'s (Provisional Pilot Officers) who, after successful completion of the ab initio program, became direct entries into the RCAF. The modest P.P.O. scheme preceded the massive British Commonwealth Air Training Plan, that was still about a year down the road then.

"I was quite startled by the amount of ultralight home-built plane activity at Sea Island Airport. This was unheard of in Toronto where I learned to fly and in fact, back east, the D. of T. (Department of Transport) seemed to frown heavily on the whole idea and actively discouraged it.

A. M. Feast March, 1940. Fleet CF-ANN in background.

Loaned from Arnold M. Feast collection

"The Aero Club was interesting for several reasons; the economy of their rental rates compared to Toronto levels—approximately one half—and a certain carefree approach to regulations pertaining to the dual controls in their Piper Cub BIP and Fleets ANN and CEM a Fleet 2 and 7 respectively. The club left them installed all the time, which proved to be very helpful.

"It became a flying club within a flying club as it were. I would catch the streetcar from Jericho Beach Air Station and, accompanied by eager aircraftsmen anxious to fly, trundled out to Marpole and walked across the bridge and

CMFT Collection #512.5 Graham Bell collection

This 1938 Piper J3 was one of the Aero Club's trainers.

up the long road to the airport. Then, depending upon my trainee's finances, as mine were negligible, a Cub or Fleet were rented and away we sailed into the blue. Well away from the field I socked the air work to them. My passengers paid the plane's rental charge to me and I passed it along to the club. Each time I arrived at the club there was that tense moment when the machine of the day was seemingly casually inspected by me to ensure that both sticks were in. The club never let me down."

"The Aero Club," recalls Gordon Peters, *"became No. 8 Elementary Flying Training School and, all of a sudden, we needed people, all kinds of people. All of a sudden we seemed to have about a hundred Tiger Moths. It was amazing that they got the people to fly them and to look after them. In no time at all, they had instructors, students and mechanics. Some of the instructors had been Sunday pilots*

with the Aero Club. They liked flying and here was a chance to get in some flying and get paid for it. They seemed to become instructors overnight.

"There just weren't that many people in aviation prior to this happening and so they just went downtown to all the garages. If you were a car mechanic, they'd ask: 'Do you want to become an aircraft mechanic?' And they became aircraft mechanics."

To ease congestion at Vancouver, a new airfield was built at Boundary Bay and No. 8 EFTS was moved to that location as No. 18 EFTS. When the Japanese struck at Pearl Harbour in 1941, the west coast airfields were cleared of training schools and No. 18 EFTS relocated to Caron, Saskatchewan, becoming No. 33 EFTS. In 1943, when the air station at Abbotsford was completed, training resumed in B.C. as No. 24 EFTS, with No. 33 EFTS supplying about half the personnel.

Following the war, the equipment used by these schools was made available to Canada's Aero Clubs which reopened for business. The Aero Club of B.C. quickly returned to resume operations at Vancouver Airport in 1945.

"The Aero Club of B.C. were quite active at the airport as soon as the war was over," says Al Michaud, who reopened Gilbert's Flying Service about the same time. *"Of course, they were just in the flying, training, and rental business. We were selling airplanes, servicing and doing charter business, all the things they couldn't do. On the other hand, they had certain benefits—they had free hangars. We had to rent or buy hangars and if we were fortunate enough, we paid some income tax. . . .*

"As time went on there was more competition and they became more of a club than a commercial operation, although they continued flying training until after they moved to Pitt Meadows Airport, when it opened."

Government policy moved training operations from Vancouver Airport in 1963. Some operators, such as West Coast Air Services, gave up flight training and concentrated on the more profitable charter business. The Aero Club did not have this option. Business dropped due to the move to the distant and restricted (single runway) facilities of the new airport. The Aero Club suffered. In 1969, it sold its remaining aircraft, ceased its training activities and became strictly a social club.

CMFT Collection #102.19 Art Seller collection

Chief Instructor, Len Milne; General Manager, Ben Valerie; and Terry Finney, "the Walking Encyclopedia" who instructed, taught ground school, and did whatever had to be done at the Aero Club.

CMFT Collection #102.8 Art Seller collection

Aero Club of B.C. fleet including Tiger Moths, Cornell, Fleet Canuck, Luscombe, and Piper PA12.

CMFT Collection #102.16 Art Seller collection

The Aero Club's Tiger Moth in a P.N.E. parade in Vancouver, circa 1946.

9

FROM A MOB TO LEGITIMATE BUSINESSES

Vancouver's commercial flying schools of the 1930s

"None of the flying schools or operations at the airport were really financially very solvent," says Bryan Mahon, who spent much of the 1930s around Vancouver Airport. *"The Aero Club of B.C. was, of course, the best one because it got a government subsidy. If the Aero Club put up enough money to buy one aeroplane, the government would give them a matching aeroplane. That meant that the cost of acquiring aircraft was cut in half and, in addition to that, it was respectable. As an officially sanctioned club, it was a social attraction for people with lots of money, who could indulge themselves in flying, and who would join the club for social and prestige reasons.*

"When we (Columbia Aviation) operated our flying school we hardly owned anything. We tied in with Len Foggin on a kind of a commission basis, just hoisted our banner above his Bird, so to speak. There weren't a lot of flying schools in Vancouver. There were really only the Aero Club and the commercial competitors, and the commercial competitors were sort of a mob.

"The people around the airport in those days didn't run flying schools like an established corporation that you might find today. They had an aeroplane and they barnstormed. They'd find a student, or a potential student, looking over the fence and give them a sales pitch and get him to start taking lessons and charge him so much an hour. So there

probably wasn't any office or anything; the fellow just drove up in his car and kept his books in his car and cranked up his plane and went. There were a lot of people in that category. One of the most remarkable was Clifford Peene.

"Clifford Peene was a plumber from New Zealand," continues Mahon. *"The Victoria Aero Club had two OX-5 Eaglerocks and these aeroplanes were taken over by the Aero Club of B.C. in Vancouver. An OX-5 was not a very attractive engine and the Club got more advanced aeroplanes, Fleets, so Cliff Peene bought this Eaglerock for a song. He took it home to his house in New Westminster and rebuilt it.*

"These were depression years, and he didn't make any money; so he had to scrimp and save on materials. Finally, he brought it back to the airfield. He got the big parts in a truck, but I remember him bringing an aileron, which is a pretty awkward thing, from New Westminster on his Harley Davidson motorcycle. Finally, he got the aeroplane together and got it licenced.

"He didn't have a pilot's licence so he hired instructors and his office was a saddle bag in his motorcycle. He used to taxi it over to the gas pump and back. One day, instead of taxiing back from the gas pump, he taxied down to the end of the runway. I remember remarking, 'Look at Cliff going out to the runway. Has anybody given him any instructions?'

"Everybody looked at everybody else. 'No, No. . . .' We all started looking with interest to see what was going to happen next.

"So Cliff lined up and started down for take off. Naturally the aeroplane swung with torque. He chopped the power and went back and tried again. I don't know how many tries he made, at least a second and maybe a third, but he got off. He just disappeared into the blue, he seemed to be going off to New Westminster. We didn't really figure it out till

later, but what he had done was taken off for New Westminster to fly around his house so his wife could see him.

"When he came back he made his approach for landing, but he didn't flare it right; so it bounded like mad. After two or three horrendous bounces he put the power on and went back up. As he went by us, he was waving out of the cockpit. Then he went around the tower and back in for another landing approach. He must have made four of five approaches to the field ending in wild bounces and putting on the power before, finally, he made a wild bounce and didn't put on the power. Naturally it came down, and so then he taxied it and got out all smiles and said, 'Well, I think I'll be good with a little practice.' He had just soloed that machine with no dual instruction at all.

"He went on to get his commercial licence in the minimum time it takes to get a commercial licence and then he set about preparing for a barnstorming trip. At this point he took the engine out and put in an OXX-6 which has dual ignition, an OX-5 has only single ignition. The OXX-6 had 100 horse power where the OX-5 had ninety.

"The Civil Aviation Department then had a rule that you had to have a minimum 600 feet per minute rate of climb and Cliff wanted to show he could get 600 feet a minute with two passengers in the front cockpit so that he could double his revenue. Well, he never seemed to go above about 200 feet because he was so broke that he didn't want to spend the money on gas. We never saw him climb so we didn't think the aeroplane could climb. But he put in the OXX-6 saying that would improve the climb enough to get the licence while everybody around scoffed.

"When he went out and did the test, he shoved the throttle forward and the thing gave a great belch of black smoke and went up 600 feet a minute. So he went barnstorming and had quite a successful trip. I heard later that he became a chief in the Ontario Provincial Air Service."

If Clifford Peene was the most remarkable of the Vancouver Airport "mob," he was closely followed by Len Foggin, one of the earliest and most durable of these characters. From a free-lancer, flying passengers in a three-seat, Bird biplane, he built his flying business into a formal flying school, Foggin Flying Service.

Len Foggin is reputed to have been a "remittance man" from England, wealthy enough to be able to afford the then expensive pastime of flying. In 1933, he purchased a (Kinner) Bird BK biplane which could seat two passengers in the front seat, offering distinct economic advantages in the era of "cent-a-pound," joyflights.

Initially Foggin, who had a regular job as a B.C. Electric Company gas works steam engineer, operated alone using the services of the Aero Club's Bill Bolton for maintenance but, in 1934, he acquired the services of Larry Dakin as a maintenance helper at bargain prices.

> *"When I started working at the airport,"* says Dakin, *"my father came down to make sure everything was satisfactory. He paid my board and gave me less than $10 a month for expenses. I was working strictly to gain experience. I never received any money from Foggin until I got my engineer's licence in 1936. After that he paid me $50 per month.*
>
> *"I used to scrounge the odd bit of flying time off Foggin. I paid him about $3 per hour for it. Normally it would have cost $9 just for the flying and $12 for dual; so I was just paying for the gas. Bill Bolton used to take sympathy on me. He felt Foggin was cheap; so every now and then he used to do some work on the plane after which he'd say, 'This requires a test flight to 10,000 feet,' and wink at me. Bill would then take me along on the 'test flight' which was just great.*
>
> *"When I started there, Foggin had just the one airplane and during the week Jack Wright used to do some instructing. Our main source of income was actually on the*

CMFT Collection #353.20 Neil Cameron collection

Foggin's Kinner powered Bird BK CF-AUB at Vancouver Airport.

weekends, taking up passengers on Saturday and Sunday afternoons. Len didn't get into instructing himself until a few years later. Then the business got so busy that he had to quit his job at the gas works and go into flying full time."

The reason for this surge in fortunes was twofold. As the cloud of war loomed on the horizon, flying training in general became more popular, and, early in 1938, Neil Cameron came to work for Len Foggin on a commission basis. Cameron became a virtual legend "working the fence" at Vancouver Airport and provided Foggin with a real competitive edge. Cameron, a nonflier, entered the aviation business quite by chance.

"I was out of work," says Cameron, *"but I had a motorcycle and always had my eye open for something. I used to go out to the airport and hang around there for a while. When Len Dakin was working on the planes I used to chip in and help him.*

"One day, when I was helping him, Dakin said to me, 'See that guy down at the gate, the one with the leather jacket? He's been here before and he looks like he's got ideas about flying.' I said that I'd go down and tackle him.

"I got talking to him and asked him if he had thought about flying. He said that he had been giving it some thought so I said, 'Come on in and I'll show you our planes.' Soon I had him sitting in the cockpit and was explaining the controls. I sold him on the idea of flying and he went right through and got a commercial licence. He was number one on my list. I was to talk hundreds into flying in those years.

"When Larry quit, Foggin asked me to take over his job. I told him that I didn't have mechanic's papers but he said that it was okay because he had got his mechanic's licence and could sign off the work for me. So I took over the responsibility of looking after the planes in the morning and in the afternoon I'd work the fence."

Cameron soon had working the fence down to an art, handling the daily crop of spectators the way a carnival barker handles his crowd. If the spectators were going to come and watch the planes flying, then Cameron was going to try his hardest to have them fly and enrich himself to the tune of ten percent of what they spent. He invested considerable time and money in perfecting his sales pitch.

"I also had a lot of brochures printed up that gave information about flying," says Cameron. *"When persons came out to the airport they always had lots of questions that they wanted answered so I capitalized on that by preparing these pamphlets. I had a space on them on which I could stamp the arrival and departure times of the airliners because people always wanted those. This information was just the worm on the hook because, when they got all this information about learning to fly, well, that was the hook.*

"I'd come up to the party and hand them one of the brochures I had printed up saying, 'Here's some informa-

tion about the airport that might interest you. If you're thinking about taking a ride, we have our planes here and experienced pilots to fly them.

"We'll give you a nice ride over Vancouver for $3. It's a nice experience and we'll give you a souvenir card autographed by the pilot.'

"At that point they'd start to breathe hard on the idea. If they took the bait, I'd sell them a ticket which I had all numbered and tell them to wait around until I called the number.

"I had a big advantage in that I was not a pilot. Most of the other fellows working the fence were pilots and, as soon as they got a passenger, they would leave to fly. I could sell a ticket and have the passenger go for a ride and be selling another ride while he was flying."

In addition to making smart use of handouts, Cameron used camouflage to ensure that he had a better opportunity of luring the customers his way.

"I went to Bill Templeton, the airport manager, and asked his permission to put up a little shack near the gate, because it was a little hard on the hoof to be standing around out in the sun all day. The opposition got a little jealous when they saw my booth. It was about the size of a double telephone booth and had enough room for a chair and shelf for use as a table.

"I also got myself a uniform and cap. I looked quite official sitting there right by the gate and people would come up to me and ask if it would be all right to come into the airport to have a look. I would reply, 'It is as far as I'm concerned, I don't own the place.'

"My cap had 'Neil' on it and in all my advertising I had the advice 'Ask for Neil' at the bottom; so when they came to the gate or if I was out along the fence they would see at once that they were talking to the right man. That was the way I wanted to have them trained."

As Foggin's business started to boom, he enlarged his fleet of aircraft; adding a Fleet 2 in 1936 and a Gipsy Moth shortly after. Cameron, however, viewed the open cockpit with its requirement for protective clothing as antiquated and a hindrance to his sales pitch.

"One day, I saw an advertisement for a Luscombe which was a high-winged, cabin monoplane," says Cameron. *"It was light, nice and neat, and had eye appeal. I thought, 'Oh boy, if I can sell Foggin on the idea of using these we can make a fortune.' Well, it wasn't long after that a fellow came to the airport who had the Canadian agency for them. I almost grabbed him. I said, 'I've been trying to talk Foggin into buying one of those for a long while. Don't go away until I get you and Foggin together.' The fellow was leaving in an hour and I had a hard job locating Foggin, but I knew most of his haunts and by phoning around I eventually found him. He got to the airport with twenty minutes to spare. I got the two of them together and got working on the thing. Foggin saw that my idea was logical and signed up to buy one before the fellow left.*

"That Luscombe arrived in May of 1939 and business really boomed. We got the second one in 1940, by which time we were going hand over fist. By the time we had got all the planes in and the cash fixed up it would be around 11 o'clock at night.

"The war was going and we had a lot of fellows coming in to get instruction so that they could get jobs as flying instructors in the British Commonwealth Air Training Plan and stay out of the trenches. We also had some Air Force fellows coming over to take extra instruction so that they could get ahead faster.

"Sometimes Foggin would have somebody contact him directly or someone else would bring them in and introduce them to Foggin. I wouldn't get anything from those ones, but over the three years I was working with Foggin I started

CMFT Collection #373.3 Neil Cameron collection

Neil Cameron, at Vancouver Airport, circa 1941.

541 people flying. I had to keep track of them all because I was working on a commission basis."

Cameron's bonanza ended on May 13, 1941. While Foggin was out flying aerobatics in the Fleet biplane with Jack Haws, former student who had joined the RCAF as a pilot, the Fleet 2 crashed at Boundary Bay in an inverted spin. Foggin and Haws were both killed.

Although Cameron hoped to be able to carry on with the business, the authorities ruled otherwise.

"That accident put me out of work. I could have carried on but the government had a rule that no new outfits would be allowed to start up at the airport. As I had been working for a ten percent commission I was unable to continue; although I tried awfully hard. It would have been different if I been signed up as a partner, which in effect I was; a ten percent partner, but there was nothing in writing; so I ar-

ranged for the sale of remaining aircraft and closed the business."

Len Foggin at Vancouver Airport.

CMFT Collection #373.1
Neil Cameron collection

Foggin's main competitor among the "mob" of joyride pilots of the early '30s was Frank Gilbert. Like Foggin, he did not rely on his flying for his livelihood, being a projectionist for a city theatre. Also, like Foggin, he remained in business right into the early war years and Gilbert's Flying Service grew to be a sizable operation.

Gilbert entered the flying business by chance. It was the actions of his wife, Alma Gaudreau, that led to him taking up flying and eventually led them into the operation of a flying school.

Alma Gaudreau was no ordinary woman. Not every landlady would buy an aircraft from a lodger to enable him to return home, but Gaudreau did exactly that. As a girl in Quebec she had read about the exploits of the Wright brothers and decided that one day she would fly. The opportunity to turn the wish into action occurred in 1931.

"In October of 1931, I bought a small two seat Aeronca C3 from William Ressinger, who had flown it out from

Toronto for the Aero Corporation of Canada as part of the Trans Canada Air Pageant," says Gaudreau. *"He was anxious to return to the east but needed to sell the plane first. As the depression had started, there was some difficulty selling it; so I was able to buy it from him for a good price.*

"As neither my husband, Frank Gilbert, nor I could fly, we leased it out to Harold Davenport and Gordon Ballentine, who were running a business at the airport at the time. They rented it for about two years, using it for passenger rides and as a training plane. During those two years, my husband and I learned to fly it and got our pilots' licences.

"When we saw how much money our little plane was making for those two fellows, we decided to enter the flying business for ourselves. Once my husband had his commercial pilot's licence, we took the plane back and commenced Gilbert's Flying Service.

"Gilbert was working as a projectionist in a movie theatre, so we had a steady source of income other than that from our airplane, but it was easy to make money with a plane, even in the depression. People used to come out to the airport by the hundreds just to see a little plane fly around. We would sell them rides for $2 each.

Frank Gilbert stands in front of Aeronca C3 CF-AQK. This aircraft flew across Canada in 1931 and became the nucleus of Gilbert's flying adventures.

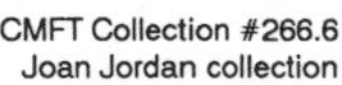

CMFT Collection #266.6
Joan Jordan collection

"There were others who tried to do the same as us, but apart from Len Foggin, none of them stayed at it for long. Our advantage was that Gilbert learned aircraft maintenance and got his engineer's ticket. This meant that we did not have to pay for an engineer to sign the aircraft out each day and our costs were just the rent on the hangar and the gas for the plane.

"At first, we mostly flew passengers, but if someone wanted to learn to fly, we would hire instructors to teach them. We rented the plane for $10 per hour, and collected $4 per hour for the instructor.

"After about three years, Gilbert got his rating and did the instructing, but working as a projectionist at night and instructing by day was very tiring; so mostly we hired instructors.

"Although I had learned to fly—I got my private pilot's licence in 1934 and my commercial pilot's licence later—I did not instruct. I sometimes flew passengers, and taught the ground school. Because I flew, our flying school was able to attract many women students. So many that Hal Wilson of the Aero Club of B.C. pushed Rolie Moore into flying aerobatics as a counter measure.

"In 1936, we sold the little Aeronca C3, and replaced it with the BAT (Aeronca LC, CF-BAT). We went to Cincin-

Gilbert's Flying Service fleet with 65-h.p. Aeronca TAC CF-BTU, 90-h.p. Warner powered Aeronca LC CF-BAT, and Aeronca CA65 Chief CF-BTR.

CMFT Collection #565.1
Al & Lloyd Michaud collection

CMFT Collection #353.11 Neil Cameron collection

Neil Cameron with Foggin Flying Services' Luscombe CF-BNB, at Kamloops, 1942.

nati to pick it up and flew it back. Over the next five years I made three trips to Cincinnati to pick up airplanes. We also bought one of Len Foggin's planes after he was killed; so we had a total of five planes by 1942.

"As the war approached, more people wanted to learn to fly. At the time the Air Force would not accept people for flight training unless they had graduated from high school or had a private pilot licence. We, therefore, got a lot of boys who had not graduated from high school coming to us to get their licences so that they could join the Air Force. To help us handle the extra business, we took on partners. At first, Ian Bell worked with us, but he joined Trans Canada Air Lines; so then Lloyd Michaud became a partner.

"By 1942, it had become too dangerous to keep operating around Vancouver because of all the military airplanes; so Lloyd went to work for Canadian Pacific Air Lines in Edmonton. Gilbert moved the flying school to Kamloops

and kept it going there until Lloyd's brother, Al, bought out our share of the business. When they restarted after the war ended, they renamed it Vancouver's U-Fly and built it up into a much bigger business. Later, they called it West Coast Air Services and became millionaires when they sold it."

Although the Gilberts got out of the flying business during World War II, Alma continued to fly until she was over 60 years of age, often borrowing a plane from her friends, the Michaud brothers. She had not learned to fly until well into her '30s but says:

"When I got tired of the world down below, I would take the little plane and go to Chilliwack, or somewhere else, and come back feeling better."

CMFT Collection #353.18 Neil Cameron collection

Charter and flight school aircraft at Vancouver Airport, B.C., circa 1947. Runway 8/26 and taxiways were under construction.

10

AIR LAND MANUFACTURING AND WELLS AIR HARBOUR

Vancouver's alternative airport

From the late 1920s until the commencement of World War II, a seaplane base on the middle arm of the Fraser near Marpole was an important center of aviation activity. Generally known as Wells Air Harbour, after its early '30s operator, Hunter Wells, it was actually established in the late 1920s by the Air Land Manufacturing Company, who erected a hangar and commenced operations with three Junkers monoplanes in 1929.

"Two factions were negotiating with Mr. W. Anderson of the Hayes-Anderson Truck Manufacturing Company, who was in the process of forming the Air Land Manufacturing Company," stated Hal Wilson, who was chief instructor for the Aero Club of B.C. *"One faction was headed by Mr. Paddy Burke, Messrs. Bill Joerss and Leonard Miller, who had some get-rich-quick scheme in mind, operating in the northern part of the province and the Yukon on some very secret gold mining mission. I, on the other hand, was trying to persuade Mr. Anderson to operate a Canadian coastal service taking in Vancouver, Victoria, Nanaimo, Powell River, etc. The final outcome was that Burke and his party won out. Since I had no desire to become involved in the operation, which I regarded as being a risky one, I returned to the Aero Club."*

"Air Land bought one used and one new Junkers F-13 and a little two-passenger floatplane Junkers," says Bill

Jacquot, who went to work for the company after leaving Canadian Airways. *"The pilots for the F-13s were Paddy Burke and Bill Joerss, and they had a flight engineer, Emil Kading, who went with Burke to work for a company based at Carcross. They were forced down in the wilderness up around Liard Post and Burke lost his life."*

The Burke accident, and its repercussions (see chapter 7), left Air Land Manufacturing in a precarious position, and the company went out of business.

The Air Land hangar was used briefly by Alaska-Washington Airways of B.C. and by Commercial Airways—both shortlived operations (see chapter 5)—then came into the possession of Wells Air Transport, operated by Hunter Wells.

"Hunter Wells had been operating a small service with a Fairchild 71 and a Boeing Flying Boat out of Vancouver Airport," says Cy Charters, who was just getting interested in aviation at the time. *"The seaplane hangar was a bit crowded because Canadian Airways used it too. The Air Land building was not being used so he moved over there about 1933."*

"This location became known as the Wells Air Harbour," related Hal Wilson, expanding on the use of this facility, *"and the company operated many aircraft which had been purchased from companies going out of business or purchased in crashed condition and repaired locally.*

"The old Fairchild 71, which had been purchased from the Alaska-Washington Airways, and surplus Boeing B1E boats from the Boeing factory, in addition to one of the Dominion Airways crashed Moths, CF-ADY, were all made serviceable.

"One phase of this operation was a twice-weekly service from Vancouver into the Bridge River country. The aircraft could be assured of at least two passengers northbound prior to the weekend and the same passengers returned the

Two Boeing B1Es similar to this one of Canadian Airways were operated by Hunter Wells out of the Air Land building in Richmond, B.C.

CMFT Collection #491.18
Earl Gerow collection

following Monday or Tuesday. Although these people were unknown to the pilots on this run, it turned out that they were ladies of easy virtue being transported by a syndicate into the mining area.

"The charter phase of this operation did not prove too successful, since one of the boats was crashed on the west coast in an endeavour by Gordon MacKenzie to taxi the aircraft onto Long Beach in a heavy swell. The Fairchild 71 was also crashed by the same party on Seton Lake, killing several passengers.

"The second flying boat was crashed at Alta Lake by Mr. McClusky, which took the lives of everyone including UBC's Dean of Engineering, Dean Brock, and his wife.

"The flying school operation was a success. They had for their instructor Jack Wright. It was not until Wright had left their employ that the company went out of business."

Sharing the Air Land hangar with Wells Air Transport was the repair business of Tommy Jones, which was to outlast Wells Air Transport by several years. Jones was one of the few Vancouver area people to operate a profitable aviation business during the "dirty '30s."

"Tommy Jones was a Welshman, who came out from England in the late 1920s," relates Cy Charters. *"He worked as a foreman for the Leyland garage on Richards Street, then he picked up the pieces of the Dominion Airways fold-up (see chapter 6). He got a couple of Moths out*

Lock Madill collection

Lock Madill's Cirrus powered Moth C-GAUM at Wells Air Harbour, 1936.

of it. Then he picked up a Fairchild 21 and was running the three aircraft as a flying school at Vancouver Airport.

"When he moved to Wells Air Harbour, he didn't want to bother with the flying school; so he sold the two Moths to Columbia Aviation. Within a month, a student up on his first solo had a connecting rod fail and was lucky to make it down to a forced landing. Columbia decided the deal was no good; so Jones had to take the airplanes back.

"At Wells Air Harbour, the Jones operation was mostly overhaul, although he also had a Stinson Jr. and a Fokker Super Universal which he operated as a charter service. If somebody wanted to go somewhere, they could phone up and get an airplane, but his main business was with the Air Force. He was about the only one in Vancouver that got any Air Force contracts up until the war. The only other shop,

CMFT Collection #65.13 Joe Bertalino collection

This de Havilland Cirrus Moth was one of two owned by Dominion Airways. Both were damaged by a runaway Stinson. It is probably one of the two mentioned as being picked up by Tommy Jones and repaired in his shop in the Air Land building in Richmond, B.C.

Harold Davenport and Gordon Ballentine's Aircraft Service of B.C., had closed down.

"Jones' problem, one reason that he went out of business, was that he didn't want to pay any money. You were supposed to pay a minimum wage for Air Force contracts and he didn't want to pay that. All the fellows went on strike and Jones just left the place shut down."

With the closure of Tommy Jones' maintenance operation, the Air Land building was put to other uses and Wells Air Harbour fell into disuse, passed up for the superior facilities which were developed around Vancouver during the war years. In more recent years, the old Wells Air Harbour building has been converted into a Keg Boathouse restaurant.

Noorduyn Norseman at Wells Air Harbour, 1938.

CMFT Collection #49.58
Maxse M. Tayler collection

11

THE INDEPENDENT OPERATORS

Barnstorming their way into careers

Immediately after World War I, the availability of cheap war surplus Curtiss JN4 "Jennies" tempted many a young aviator to make a living providing joyrides to the public, an activity that later became referred to as "barnstorming." The early Jenny operations in British Columbia barely lasted into the early 1920s, following which commercial aviation stagnated locally until Don MacLaren's Pacific Airways was set up in 1925.

While Pacific Airways' main source of income was the government contract for fishery patrol, this work was supplemented by carrying out barnstorming-type operations when business was slack. Being operators of waterborne aircraft from their base at Jericho Beach, the barnstorming was carried out from popular beaches in the neighboring area.

"We sometimes came into English Bay and people would pay $5 for a short ride around Vancouver," says Bill Jacquot, who worked for this company following service with the Canadian Air Force. *"The aircraft would be taken up the beach to offload passengers, then a fresh load of two or three would be taken aboard. All we would do was turn the aircraft around and ask the pilot if their were any complaints or problems, which we would have to rectify.*

"On a nice sunny afternoon, flocks of people would surround the aircraft and, once they saw other people get-

ting aboard, they would come forward of their own accord and say, 'Can I go for a ride, too?' "

Towards the end of the 1920s, land airports were developed at Vancouver and Victoria. These became the home bases for several companies and individuals operating wheeled aircraft. Business at these airfields was quite competitive and rather sparse; so the pioneers were often forced to venture out to the less well prepared surfaces of a farmer's field in order to have their aircraft earn their keep.

When B.C. Airways commenced operations at Victoria's Lansdowne Field in January 1928, the small aircraft, used for charters and training, were also put to use on barnstorming trips – not always uneventfully.

"*One of the most successful barnstorming days,*" stated Hal Wilson, who instructed for the company, "*was carried out in a hay field near Courtenay halfway between what is now the Comox Airport and the Village of Courtenay, when on July 1st, 1928, 103 passengers were carried, bringing in a total revenue of $425.*

"*From a flying point of view, this consisted of six hours flying—a tiring ordeal, when it is taken into account that the field measured, from corner, to corner 1,200 feet. During this period two things happened. The propeller was broken by a rock and repaired by a local carpenter, whose wife and family had to be given a free ride in compensation thereof. The tail skid broke, and this had to be repaired by the local blacksmith who likewise was given a free hop, in addition to the owner of the land and his nine children, who were all circled around the field.*

"*An unpleasant incident occurred when, on one of these flights, it was discovered, when several hundred feet in the air, that one passenger was drunk. Only by rocking the aircraft violently could the man be confined, by centrifugal and other forces, to the cockpit.*"

When Vancouver also opened an airport and small flying schools opened for business there, they too found that the number of training flights was low and sought to supplement the income of these machines by getting local pilots to take the aircraft away on barnstorming expeditions. Sometimes these achieved greater success than anticipated.

"Sprott-Shaw School of Aviation was started up at Lulu Island Airport (the original Vancouver Airport, now the site of Lansdowne Shopping Center in Richmond)," says Maurice MacGregor, who went on to set up Pakistan International Airways for the Pakistan government in the 1950s. *"Sprott-Shaw was a bookkeeping training school, and when they entered the aviation school business, knew nothing about airplanes.*

"On July 1, 1930, I took their three passenger Waco to Courtenay. We'd made a deal with the local Chamber of Commerce to be part of their Dominion Day celebration. I had a crew man with me who was a member of the Aero Club, Noel Humphries. He helped collect the money and also helped to steer the aircraft to take off position. The field was so small that I had to get the tail up heading towards a fence and use maximum revs. He would dig his heels into the ground and we would swing the aircraft around with the tail up and he would let go. Every take off was like that.

"We carried passengers, loggers, and all the local people all day long. We gave them ten minute rides, not from an airport but from a field close to the town. We had a good day, came back and gave them $400. Sprott-Shaw was astounded that an aeroplane, a little old aeroplane, could make that much money in a day.

"I flew for Sprott-Shaw on several occasions, and then a former colleague of mine, who started with B.C. Airways but didn't complete his course—Humphrey Madden, obtained a small inheritance and decided to buy a Fleet. He

didn't have a pilot's licence; so he got me to fly it and we did the rounds barnstorming. He collected the money and I did the flying. We travelled around throughout this general area, Ladner, Sidney, before there was an airport, and we barnstormed out of Breather's Field (that's close to the town) a grain field.

"We'd put on a show to attract people to come to the field. We'd do aerobatics, fly upside down, do bunts and loops and rolls and generally cause people to come to see what was transpiring, and then we'd look for the $5 for a ten minute ride.

"Occasionally we would carry some people who were, at that time, bolder than the younger people, people of seventy. In those days, people of that age were quite venturesome really, when they agreed to get in a little old aeroplane and go flying. They had confidence, I guess, in the pilot or something.

"Madden would organize the sales and collect the money, and generally look after everything on the ground, while I did the flying. The only reason he did this is because he didn't have a licence and he could not fly passengers until he obtained enough time. I did all the passenger flying until he obtained his licence, and then he was on his own."

When "Hump" Madden, as he was known, finally obtained his licence, he moved his Fleet biplane to Victoria, and attempted to earn his living by giving flying instruction and providing joyflights, but his career in the Victoria area was cut short.

"The good fathers of Victoria," says Hump Madden, *"decided I was making too much noise flying over the hospital. The little field we used there, Lansdowne, was right in line with the general hospital; so I really couldn't blame them too much; the airplane was noisy and I was making circuits and bumps with passengers. So I moved over to Vancouver.*

"Vancouver was very crowded. There was only one little hangar there and about four or five outfits competing for the little bit of business. It wasn't a very profitable place to stay. So I decided to go to Kamloops. I hadn't been there before. An air engineer agreed to go with me."

Joe Bertalino and a DH Cirrus Moth during the time that he worked for Dominion Airways Ltd.

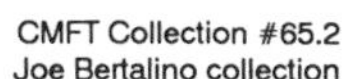
CMFT Collection #65.2
Joe Bertalino collection

Joe Bertalino was the air engineer who helped Madden get established in his speculative venture, and he maintains a vivid recollection of this period of his life.

"I was out of a job for awhile, but at that time people were planning all sorts of things." says Bertalino, *"Everybody was trying to make money in any way. I met Humphrey Madden, who was purchasing an airplane. He asked me if I'd be interested in going on a trip with him. I said, 'Sure, I wouldn't mind going barnstorming.'*

"So we took off and left for the interior. His idea was that we would go to Kamloops. It seemed to be a very nice place where there was a chance to start a school. That's how I got started going barnstorming.

"The idea was that we'd get as many students as we could and then, on weekends, we'd fly around to the little towns like Merritt, Penticton, or over to Salmon Arm, and do

barnstorming. Any day that we were free, when we had no students, we would leave and spend the day someplace else.

"One weekend I remember we went to Merritt. We flew over the town. We were flying down the street and we saw all the kids and people rushing down the street. They followed us down; we turned around and came back. We were looking for a place to land as close as we could to the town. The noise of the airplane and all the commotion was quite exciting to watch. We landed in a field not too far and then started taking passengers."

Bertalino parted company from Madden in 1931 after Madden broke his arm in a motorcycle accident in Trail, where the pair were then operating. By the time his arm was healthy, Madden had left B.C. accompanying the Trans Canada Air Pageant back east and remained in the Maritimes for several years. Bertalino remained in Vancouver, spending his time at Vancouver Airport, which was not very busy at the time. There the pilots and mechanics had to resort to many of the barnstormers' tricks to eke out a living.

"During the hard times," continues Bertalino, *"the main thing was to try and make a living at the airport; so we used to do a lot of the 'cent a pound days.'*

"We had a scale and, if you would come along, we'd put you on the scale. If you weighed a 170 pounds, it would cost you a $1.70 for a trip around the airport. It depended on your weight. It was a good way of doing it as it was cheap and we'd get people to fly.

"Flights were between five and ten minutes. In some cases we had two people together; so we got $3. The most we could get was $3.50 a flight.

"We had the Fleet and the Gipsy Moth; we had an airplane called a Bird, and an Eaglerock, quite a mixture.

"Everybody who had an airplane would put it in the pool just to make money. I used to work with the boys on the

'cent a *pound day' and we used to split up anything we made."*

Gordon Peters, who was also trying to earn his living at Vancouver Airport as an aircraft mechanic in the 1930s, remembers how the airport "regulars" made absolutely sure that no dollar, in the form of flying business, escaped them.

"Everyone was trying to make a dollar during the depression days. When I think back it is kind of humorous. Tommy Laurie was a pilot. He had a commercial licence and he was working on this runway. In those days United Air Lines were coming in; so they had him as a flag man at the end of the old runway to stop the trucks from crossing the line of the runway. We made a deal. I would work the fence and try and con people into going for an airplane ride.

"We had the Bird, two people in the front and one in the back. If I could get a couple of people to go for a ride, I'd put them in the front, start the airplane up, and taxi it to where Tom, the pilot, was with his flag. I'd get out and then he would fly them around the circuit. After doing whatever he was going to do, he'd come back and then I'd get back in the airplane and taxi it back to the hanger. I got fifty cents out of that. The pilot got a dollar or two and the operator of the plane, Foggin Flying Service, got a few bucks for the use of the airplane. So we all made a dollar."

In the 1930s, however, flying was a precarious way of making a living. Sometimes the fliers almost starved. One of those who experienced such hard times was Larry Dakin, who ventured into the Okanagan with Tom Laurie on an unsuccessful barnstorming expedition. His experience did, however, lead him into finding greener pastures.

"In 1936, Tom Laurie and I left for the interior: Vernon, Oliver," says Dakin. *"But we were only gone for about a week. Tom was flying the airplane, I was the mechanic. We*

just about starved to death. We had sleeping bags and slept in the airplane overnight. I remember in Oliver a guy came out in the morning. We tried to charge him $5 for a ride but he said that he only had $2. We threw him in the airplane, got the $2 and dashed off to get something to eat. We hadn't eaten in about three days. We hung around there all day and we didn't get anything. As a matter of fact, I don't think we made a dime up there.

"It wasn't until '37 that I got the idea of logging camps. They were the only place to go. Loggers were the only guys that had any money, really, lots of money. That summer Foggin left the Fleet on floats. It was one of the nicest summers I ever had. I knew a girl at Buccaneer Bay and I would go over to Youbou logging camp on Lake Cowichan on Saturday and Sunday. I would be working all day at Youbou and Camp 10 on Lake Cowichan.

CMFT Collection #353.9 Neil Cameron collection

Fleet 2 seaplane CF-ANF in Nanaimo Harbour circa 1938.

"Another weekend I went up to Great Central Lake, just around Courtenay. I had them lined up. It was great, absolutely fabulous. Of course, taking off of water is still a hell of a nice way of flying. The loggers just loved that. Going down the lake there were different things they wanted to see. They'd say, 'Fly me over here. Fly me over there.'

"I would come back with $120 to $130 every weekend. But I'd fly Saturday and Sunday and then, on Monday, I would either go to Buccaneer Bay or come back to Departure Bay. I'd probably fly back into Vancouver on Tuesday or Wednesday. It was just a hell of a nice way to spend the summer."

With the advent of World War II the whole character of flying changed. Public awareness of aviation was heightened, leading to another boom time for barnstormers in the immediate postwar years. The general public, flooded with the wartime reports of Air Force activities, welcomed the opportunity to experience flight, which came with the lifting of the wartime restrictions and the return to civilian life of thousands of airmen.

Aviation, however, was more highly regulated in the postwar era, and the new breed of barnstormer was a professional pilot, employed by a struggling company, which sought any opportunity to extend its existence. The Okanagan Valley, in particular, offered a lucrative trade in joyflights and was oversupplied with entrepreneurs attempting to make a living from aviation.

"Dave Smith didn't know much about flying," recalls Dan McIvor, who joined Smith's operation as chief pilot. *"He was a fruit farmer who loved airplanes. We used to go out on weekends, go down to Oliver, for instance, and barnstorm, just fly passengers.*

"We went over to Keremeos one time and dug an airport out of the sagebrush, and operated there for three or four weekends. Boy, the people would just swarm out to fly. We

were doing all right. The Super Cruiser, with two great big men in the back and me in the front, would stagger off, go over the hill, and pick up speed. We'd get five ten-minute flights in an hour and charge $5 a flight."

Vernon's L & M Air Services also took full advantage of the joyflight trade trying to bring in the money necessary to avoid insolvency.

"We did a lot of barnstorming on weekends," says Dick Laidman who struggled (unsuccessfully) to make L & M a paying proposition. *"We would go out where there would be a picnic or a fair and hop passengers. Flying on floats, at the Regattas, was always popular. In the wintertime it would work well too, because we would have skis on. It was the type of thing people liked. But you would have to constantly be trying to figure out a way to make an extra dollar out of this. The postwar boom had burst."*

These activities, in most cases, only served to delay the inevitable, and, as the 1950s rolled around, the small operators were squeezed out of the business. Flying had matured, and, for the general public, the novelty had worn off. As the bigger and more stable companies consolidated their operations at the major centers, barnstorming activities vanished.

CMFT Collection #338.26 Joe Lalonde collection

Cessna 140 of L & M Air Services Ltd., Vernon, B.C. in 1946.

CMFT Collection #376.8 Joe Lalonde collection

Vernon City Airport during L & M's time. The aircraft is an Avro Anson.

Loaned from R. H. Laidman collection

Dick Laidman and Stinson Gullwing "Mother Goose," 1990.

12

FROM GROUND SCHOOLS TO OPERATING AIRPLANES

The story of ambitious empire builders

While to most people the term "aviation" conjures up a vision of flight and flying machines, others see it as a realm of opportunity needing trained people who in turn need training. The acquiring of training services is a lot less costly than buying flying equipment and several organizations have attempted to enter the aviation industry in British Columbia by this cheaper route.

In 1928, Sprott-Shaw Schools of Vancouver, who already offered training in office procedures, attempted to expand their field into aviation by setting up the Sprott-Shaw School of Aviation and offering an aviation ground school course. This soon expanded into a full-fledged flying school (see chapter 6), but the time was not right for this venture which closed in 1930.

In 1929, Harold Davenport and Gordon Ballentine, with Art McCurdy, all laid off by Western Canada Airways, attempted to build up a business of their own by opening Aero Schools of Vancouver.

> *"We rented a building on Fourth Avenue and started a school of ground instruction,"* says Davenport. *"We taught aircraft structure, aircraft theory, engine theory and structure, and tied it all pretty well in with the glider school we started soon afterwards.*
>
> *"Gordon and I were the principal instructors. Art McCurdy and I started the construction of the glider, then*

Gordon joined us. Money was scarce and Art was not able to stay with us long.

"When we finished the glider, we started flying it out at the Lulu Island Airport, charging 50 cents a flight. We certainly didn't make a mint of money at it, but we trained quite a few people.

CMFT Collection #300.18 Eldon Seymour collection

Primary gliders such as this one built by Eldon Seymour and Jimmy Duddle were an inexpensive way to learn to fly.

"The primary glider was a single-seater with a simple frame fuselage, but Gordon and I occasionally took passengers up for flights. The passenger had to stand on the frame clinging to the vertical post. Fortunately, the Department of Transport never heard about it. We made good and sure Carter Guest (the local aviation inspector) was nowhere about when we did it.

"We only operated the Aero School for a short time, until we moved out to the new Vancouver Airport and got a little flying school going. We stopped the gliding about that time also.

"We moved to the airport as Aircraft Service of B.C. and dropped the Aero School because there was very little business in that line. There were very few aeroplanes about, and for years, everyone thought you were nuts when you even got in an aeroplane. We did set up the flying school, however. The idea was that Gordon would run that and I would handle the maintenance business.

"We didn't have enough money to buy our aeroplanes so we rented them from various aircraft owners. We started off using an Aeronca C3 CF-AQK, owned by Frank Gilbert, then Lew Findlay bought another, CF-ATL, in 1932, and we used that as well. We also used a Gipsy Moth.

"By the end of 1934, things were changing in the aviation scene. Jobs were coming up in the flying end of things and Gordon was more interested in that line. I was more interested in the technical side of things, and some opportunities

CMFT Collection #259.47 Joan Jordan collection

Aeronca C3 CF-AQK, Vancouver Airport, B.C.

arose in that area; so we let the company dissolve itself. It sort of became non-operational."

When Davenport and Ballentine had vacated and closed Aero Schools of Vancouver, they had left a vacuum for other individuals to enter, and it was not long before another group of entrepreneurs attempted to make their fortune teaching aviation topics to would-be mechanics and airmen.

Robert Pike, a Vancouver teenager, who had observed the operation of various aviation ground schools while living in California during the late 1920s, decided to stake his future on the demand for the training of air engineers, and, with a borrowed $25, started a ground school club for a group of King Edward High School students.

Every Saturday morning, at eight o'clock, Pike taught the theory of flight and related topics to these schoolboys, charging them 50 cents a lesson. In order to offer them more than just theory, he approached Bryan Mahon and Ewan Boyd, who had taken over the assets of the Glider Club of Vancouver and were flying a glider at Vancouver Airport.

Pike suggested that Mahon and Boyd, teenagers like himself, teach his class gliding. He offered them 25 cents per student each Saturday. Mahon and Boyd were thus induced into an association with Bob Pike that eventually led to the formation of the Columbia School of Aeronautics.

About 1933, while still in High School, Pike expanded his operation by opening Vancouver Aero Tech, a night school offering courses in aviation topics. Desmond Murphy, a pilot in World War I, was hired as instructor. He was later replaced by Bill Lawson, a 1920s flier. The business later expanded to include day classes; although, for the first year, there were only two daytime students. Late in 1933, Mahon and Boyd threw in their lot with the young entrepreneur, and Vancouver Aero Tech was renamed Columbia Aviation Ltd.

"When the three of us got together," recalls Bryan Mahon, *"we incorporated the company as the Columbia Aviation Company. At that time, I think that the only things that the Aero School had were just thrown into it. Ewan taught the power plant subjects and I taught the air frame subjects.*

"We had a night course, a night school. You couldn't buy a suitable text book for a prepackaged course; so we had to write our own. That meant researching the subjects and all sorts of publications. There were lots of books on aeronautics and so forth, but nobody wrote a text book suitable for a school. Nowadays, you can go to purveyors of aviation books and pick up the text books you need, but we didn't have that."

As the market for such courses was limited in Vancouver, the company commenced marketing correspondence courses in aviation under the name Columbia School of Aeronautics. Once again, the pressure of preparing the courses fell on Mahon and Boyd.

"We started to sell correspondence courses," relates Mahon. *"Ewan and I had to write those courses. At the first stage of it, I was still going to university. The strain on me was high as it was difficult to do my university work and keep up with this.*

"We had a lot of trouble getting the government to approve us. They thought we were irresponsible and fraudulent and incompetent and all the rest. On the other hand, though, you can see that a government official would perhaps look on us with some suspicion. We were ambitious and hopeful and I think that we did a much better job than people were prepared to credit to us."

The next stage in the development of the company was a logical move closer to the center of aviation activity, the

Vancouver Airport. The school had started in a rented room on Main Street using borrowed chairs, relocated to a corner of the Air Land Manufacturing hangar down at Wells Air Harbour, then leased premises on the corner of Sixth and Granville. However, as Ewan Boyd has stated, "You can't run a flying school on Sixth and Granville, and we wanted airplanes."

In September 1934, Columbia Aviation Ltd. leased space at Vancouver Airport and moved there. In addition to four offices attached to the landplane hangar, the company found it necessary to lease two offices in the administration building. For about a year, Columbia Aviation Ltd. was one of the largest operations at the airport.

> *"By that time we were becoming more established and we were just ambitious and expansion-minded,"* comments Bryan Mahon. *"We looked for any opportunity that came along. We aspired to have a repair station and a flying school and a ground school and everything that is now called a fixed base operation.*
>
> *"As we didn't have any money, everything we got was a dollar down and the rest when they caught up with us. We got two de Havilland 60M Moths from Tommy Jones, one of the commercial operators, and I remember we paid $200 down and $400 a month payments. Then we discovered they were in pretty bad shape. The longerons were rusted through and so forth. There was a lot of hard feelings about all that.*
>
> *"Also, we used the method that's common now. I guess, in present parlance, you'd call it the lease-back method. Somebody buys the aeroplane and hands it over to the operator and the operator pays so much an hour. We had a Bird that belonged to Leonard Foggin that we operated in that manner. Desmond Murphy and Jack Wright were the pilots. We, the three kids who started this, Boyd, Pike, and*

I were not really qualified. Boyd had an engineer's licence, but nobody else had anything; so we were really entrepreneurs. We had to hire people with licences and that's one reason we went broke. They got all the money.

"We didn't pay them much. They were on a semi-starvation basis. They got paid by the hour for flying instruction and so on. But that kind of a business will not stand employees that get all the money. If we, the promoters, had been fully licenced and had hired nobody, we still wouldn't have made enough money to make a good living, but to try to organize it and then have to hire somebody is having too many tiers in management."

The one person who managed to earn better than semi-starvation wages while working for Columbia Aviation was Stan Sharp, who went to work for the school in 1934 as salesman.

"When I walked into Bob Pike's office on Sixth Avenue, I knew nothing about aviation. I was just checking the school out for an acquaintance. I saw some letters sitting on his desk and one was an enquiry from a lad on the prairies who wanted to take a course. I asked Pike what he had done about it and was flabbergasted when he told me he didn't have time to write a reply to it. That letter was over a month old and still unanswered.

"I could see that the school was a pretty good setup but lacked students. I asked them if they had any salesmen working for them and what they were paying. Pike answered that they had a salesman selling the courses for $10 commission, but he was not producing many students. My response was that they couldn't expect a salesman to do much for $10 and that the commission should be at least $25. Pike said that they couldn't afford to pay that much because they were only charging $98 for the course.

"'That's your first mistake,' I said, 'this course should be priced at $198, not $98. That way you can pay a decent

commission and the customer is going to think that he is getting something worthwhile. Right now it looks too cheap to be any good.'

After a few more suggestions about how they could improve things, I made the suggestion that they really needed a sales manager and that I was the man for the job."

Applying the sales techniques that he had learned while selling correspondence courses for the Automotive Institute of America, Sharp, who was only twenty-four, promoted the Columbia School of Aeronautics throughout rural B.C. and across the Alberta prairies.

"One of the first things I did," says Sharp, *"was to make a deal with Eric de Pencier, who had an aeroplane. He flew me all through the province to promote the course. I ran advertisements in all the various papers, and I would take the mayor and local councilmen for rides in the aeroplane. This helped me get a lot of business."*

Sharp, in fact, is reputed to have been the only person to have made money out of Columbia School of Aeronautics and he admits to having made a "pretty good living out of it." As the salesman, Sharp retained the $25 down payment for any course he sold, while Columbia's share was the twelve follow up payments of $20.

"I don't doubt that on many days he would take in over $200," says Cy Charters, a former student and an employee of the school in 1936. *"It was fantastic. He made more out of it than Columbia did."*

Columbia School of Aeronautics did not remain in business very long, however, for the partner's ambitions were always straining the purse strings.

"After a short while, they started making money and were able to move out to Vancouver Airport," explains Sharp. *"They bought an old Moth and were spending money faster than I could make it for them. Pike was getting to be the big time operator and spending money like it was going out of*

style. It was pretty obvious to me that they were going to go broke."

Towards the end of 1935, the company attempted to further expand its area of activities by becoming a charter aircraft operator. Three Boeing 40H4 mailplanes, which had been built by Boeing Aircraft of Canada in 1930 and had been sitting idle since the cancellation of Canadian Airways prairie airmail contracts in 1931, had been optioned by New Zealand Airways. Due to licencing difficulties, it appeared that these options would not be taken up; so Columbia Aviation made New Zealand Airways an offer for the options. On the final day of the options, New Zealand Airways accepted the Columbia offer and the final payment of $3,000 per aircraft was rushed down to the Boeing plant on Georgia Street.

"Boeing were madder than hell," relates Ewan Boyd, *"because they were going to sell them the next day for $12,000. There was an Alaskan fellow who was prepared to pay Boeing that much for them. When he found out that we had bought them out from under his nose, he offered us the $12,000 for each of them, but we had other plans."*

Hiring Sheldon Luck as their pilot, the partners readied one 40H4, and, leaving Mahon in Vancouver to look after the school, Pike and Boyd departed for Alberta with intentions of operating an air service to the Lake Athabaska gold fields. Setting up such an operation was not as easy as they had hoped, since MacKenzie Air Service and Canadian Airways had tied up all the fuel supplies. The aircraft was then chartered to Grant McConachie, who used it to haul fish from a northern Alberta lake, which suggested an alternative use for the 40H4. Columbia Aviation entered the fish hauling business.

"They took one of the Boeings up there," says Stan Sharp, *"but they didn't know anything about lagging fuel and oil lines for fifty degrees below zero. Sheldon Luck had*

CMFT Collection #316.3 Jeanne Ambrose collection

Boeing 40H4.

fuel starvation on take off and the plane crashed. Sheldon was okay and walked out.

"They got a second aeroplane up there with the lines properly lagged, figuring that this time it would be all right, but the fishermen went on strike. So they couldn't get any fish.

"The fishermen didn't go on strike forever, but by the time they came off strike; the fish were on strike, so there were still no fish. The whole deal wound up costing them a fortune; although, it had looked like a real money-maker on paper."

Meanwhile, problems had arisen back in Vancouver. A dispute had arisen with Carter Guest, the Regional Air Inspector. Columbia considered him a "man you couldn't reason with" and had antagonized him considerably by attempting to have him fired. In early 1936, the relationship had soured to the point where a rumour circulated that the Department of Transport would not recognize any training given by the Columbia School of Aeronautics and that "anyone who expected Columbia's training to count toward their air engineer's ticket had another thing coming." Of course, all the students were soon demanding their money back, and new enrollments sunk to zero. Bryan Mahon, the sole partner in Vancouver, was left trying to run a business which had a cash flow of zero. By March 1936, the company had folded.

Columbia Aviation had expanded too far, too fast. If it had restricted its activities to the training of aircraft mechanics for a while longer, and not added the flying school and other operations, it may have survived to cash in on the bonanza that came with the war years. Instead, the school's ace salesman, Stan Sharp—who formed a school of his own, Brisbane Aviation, shortly after Columbia's collapse—went on to build a highly successful business out of training mechanics.

Of the three principals, however, Bryan Mahon obtained employment with Boeing Aircraft of Canada as an engineer; Ewan Boyd became an air traffic controller, while Robert Pike, the driving force behind the operation, moved to California.

Columbia's salesman, Stan Sharp, however, found that the company's demise had left him with a problem and an opportunity. The opportunity was of taking over where Columbia left off. The problem was that nobody had contacted him when the company went bust and he had been accepting money for courses which were no longer being taught.

> *"I was opening up Alberta for Columbia,"* says Sharp. *"I was walking down the street in Calgary one day and a fellow I knew said to me, 'What are you doing these days?' I said, 'I'm still doing the same thing, I'm working for Columbia Aviation.' 'How can you be?' he said. 'They're broke. I just came from Vancouver and they're all closed up.' On the*

strength of that, I thought, 'Well I'd better see what this is all about.' So I sent them a wire, just made up a little story and said, 'Can you handle lots of business?' or something like that in the wire.

They wired back and said, *'Yes, we're just in the state of reorganization, and we can do all the business we can get; so bring it all in, as much as you can get for us.'*

"By luck, I kept both wires—the wire I sent and the wire I received. But I got in my car and came back to Vancouver.

"When I got back to Vancouver, I went out to the Airport, and the whole place was closed down. When I came home (I was staying temporarily with my wife's family) my wife's father said, 'There have been some RCMP officers waiting to see you all day. Must be something pretty serious. Something to do with Columbia School.' So I said, 'That's fine. I'll look after it.'

"The following morning, I went down to the RCMP office, and when I told them who I was, they ushered me in in a great big hurry to the private office of a high ranking RCMP officer who said that charges were being laid against me for accepting money from students for Columbia School when the school was bankrupt. By good luck I had these two wires. When I showed them these wires, they said, 'We're sorry Stan, but there's no trouble with you at all.' Whatever did happen, I don't know, but I then started my own company, Brisbane Aviation.

"I knew all the names and addresses of the Columbia students, because most of them enrolled through me. I wrote to them all and told them that I was starting Brisbane Aviation and that, if they wanted to finish the course they had started with Columbia, I would give them full credit for any money already paid to Columbia.

"Some students had paid in full, so a number of students were given the course for free. But it was right and fair. Also, it was an advantage to me—just starting the company—be-

cause I started up with quite a number of students, and, from there on, away she went.

"I commenced with an operation out of High River, Alberta for the first six or seven months. It was good country for getting students and good country for barnstorming. I took in a friend of mine—a pretty good friend—who had an old Waco with a Curtiss OX4, privately licenced. We did a lot of flying in Alberta, barnstorming and the likes of that, and enrolling students and so forth. We used to have a lot of fun.

"We would go to a farmer and ask him if it would be OK to use his stubble field. Usually they agreed. We'd take the kids up for a free ride, then we'd borrow a car off somebody, probably the farmer, and go down to the Greek Cafe in town. It would probably be a couple of miles away. We'd put the sign over the Cafe, 'Barnstorming at Smith's Farm—a cent a pound.'

"The Greek was always pretty good because he'd usually sell tickets for us. Of course, his business was pretty slack in those days, and, if our customers came to the cafe and waited for a ride out to the airport in the car, while they were there they'd buy coffee. So it helped him.

"However, we had a very bad situation while we were flying out of North Battleford, Saskatchewan. My pilot went up with a fellow, up for a ride, and cracked up the aeroplane. Both got killed on the airport there. I felt like quitting the whole operation then, but I decided to stay with it anyhow. I went back to Vancouver and rented an office in the administration building and half of a seaplane hangar at the Vancouver airport and built up from there.

"I needed my own building. I designed one the way I wanted it and tried to get some money to build it. Well, you couldn't buy land on the Vancouver side of the airport; you could only lease it. Things were kind of bad. I was not very old at the time, and I wanted to borrow $50,000 to build the

building on leased property in the middle of the depression. I went down to the Royal Bank and told them what I wanted to do. They just laughed and said, 'Anybody that's going into aviation has rocks in their head. There's a depression on and you're too young. In any case, we never loan any money on a building on leased property. If you owned the property we might look at it. But you can't buy it'.

"I played around with that for a while, and then I talked to the city, and they agreed to build the building. Within six months from the time the building was built, they doubled the size of it and six months after that they doubled the size again and we had a pretty fair operation.

"When the war started things changed because there was no such thing as paying students anymore. Those people who might have paid to become students were in the Army. However, we trained a lot of people for the EFTS and for pretty well every aircraft company in Canada. Then it got that everybody was being inducted into the services; so I started getting into production of aircraft parts and instruments and that sort of thing. I got a contract from Stanley Burke of Boeing Aircraft and one from Bill Vivian from Vivian Diesel, making diesel parts for submarines and two or three others.

"We put in an instrument shop, a fabric shop, a metal shop and a propeller shop. We had, at one time, about 300 people on staff, and you couldn't miss because it was cost plus ten percent. You just couldn't miss on making money. But we had a good staff, which was important."

A key member of this good staff was Hugh Thomas, who joined Brisbane Aviation just before the war. He remembers the changes that occurred as the school adapted to the times.

"Before the war," says Thomas, *"people were looking for places to send their kids to school a lot more than they are now. We boarded them and arranged everything.*

CMFT Collection #91.111 Maxse M. Taylor collection

Tiger Moths of No. 8 EFTS at Sea Island, Vancouver, 1940-41.

"When the war broke out, there was an awful rush to train people as Lead Hands for all the factories in Canada. Brisbane Aviation was the only big school in Canada at the time. So we trained an awful lot for Boeing and the other companies. Then, when we'd saturated the market, we went into subcontract work for Boeing Aircraft of Canada on the production of Catalina flying boats.

"All the instruments, every instrument in those Catalinas, came through Brisbane. We would make the instrument panels and they were all jigged so that when they went into the aircraft they were all ready to go. They were the last thing actually to be assembled. We were equipped for doing all the instrument work, including Sperry and Norden bombsights.

"The manufacturers were rushing the instruments out so fast that the metals weren't stabilized so that hysteresis set

in. The gimbal links on all the gyro instruments needed at least three months to age. They were moving all over the place. By the time the instruments were shipped to Boeing they were unserviceable. The castings kept shifting and would throw the instruments out of calibration. So we set up the shop to assemble and recalibrate all the instruments including the auto pilots and the Norden bomb sights."

Stan Sharp considers that another key factor in Brisbane's success during these years was their willingness to tackle almost anything, even if the job was an unfamiliar one.

"We had a program at Brisbane," says Sharp, *"where if anybody came in and asked to do something, we just said 'Yes' before we even knew what it was. It didn't matter whether it was fixing a tractor or making cowlings for Trans Canada Airlines.*

"We ended up with, I guess, the best aircraft instrument shop in the country. We had Sperry and the whole bit, as well as an engine shop, a propeller shop, a metal shop and even a wood working shop because there were still aircraft with wooden ribs and spars and that sort of thing. We had a pretty complete operation."

With the approaching end of the war, however, the demand for aircraft diminished. Boeing Aircraft of Canada closed down its production line of Catalinas and Cansos, and companies such as Brisbane Aviation were forced to find other work to sustain their business.

"Stan Sharp could see the writing on the wall, as far as the subcontract work was concerned," says Lock Madill, who had worked as an instructor for Brisbane Aviation before the war. *"However, he realized that there was going to be a demand for aircraft engineers. In the Air Force you specialized. You were either an engine mechanic or an airframe mechanic. To be a licenced aircraft engineer in civilian life you have to have both. So we started the school*

Brisbane Aviation's shops did instrument and systems repairs and overhauls for airplanes like these Boeing built Catalinas during WWII.

CMFT Collection #132.12
Gordon S. Williams collection

up to give the boys what they didn't get in the Air Force. In other words, the engine mechanics took an airframe course, and the airframe boys took a mechanic's engine course. This is where I came in because I had already been with Brisbane prior to the war training engineers.

"We turned out quite a few licenced engineers. They spent six months in the school. Then they could go and write for their engineer's licence. Of course the business became pretty saturated with them and petered out.

"Brisbane also opened a flying school. They had two pilots there, ex-Air Force pilots, doing a little bit of commercial flying with students, people who couldn't or weren't able to take lessons during the war and wanted to learn to fly. Along with the ground school it worked out pretty good."

By the early 1950s, however, aviation was entering a doldrums period. Regulations were becoming tougher and government intervention was inhibiting the free-enterprise spirit upon which Stan Sharp had built his business.

"I put in for an extension of a charter licence," says Sharp, *"and they turned me down. So I figured, 'What the hell. If you've got to hire the people and put up with all the*

things that go with that, take the risks of business and then put up with the Air Board as well—then to hell with it all. I can make money in easier ways. So I closed the business down."

When Brisbane Aviation closed its doors in late 1952, it was the end of an era. The last of the small, prewar aviation companies started in Vancouver in the 1930s had gone. The small ventures remaining at Vancouver Airport were all postwar companies involved in a new dog eat dog struggle for survival.

CMFT Collection #338.8 Joe Lalonde collection

Cessna Crane CF-BXW was one of Brisbane's fleet of charter/school aircraft.

13

SUPPORTING THE MINING INDUSTRY

The development of aviation in central British Columbia

While major population centers were the centers of barnstorming activity and held the greatest potential for passenger traffic, it was in the more remote areas of the Canadian hinterland that the aeroplane became an indispensable form of transport.

In the 1920s, Imperial Oil ordered two Junkers F-13 monoplanes which were operated in northern Alberta in 1921 and 1922. One of these machines, G-CADP, "Vic," was sold to the Railway Employee's Investment and Industrial Association of Hazelton, B.C. and was used to carry hunting and prospecting parties into remote lakes. As the operational costs were excessive, the aircraft was pulled onto the banks of the Skeena River the next year, and lay derelict for six years.

In 1928, the Junkers was purchased by R. F. Corless of Prince George and used to fly supplies to a goldmine in the area. This illegal use of an unlicensed aircraft was noticed by Western Canada Airways, which was just starting to expand their network into central B.C., and a letter of protest was sent to the Controller of Civil Aviation.

> *"We are operating at the present time at 6 Mile Lake, twelve miles from Prince George,"* wrote Leigh Brintnell in June 1929, *"and, while there, noted that the old Junkers F-13, which the Imperial Oil used to have, has been reconditioned and is now flying again. Do not wish to make this*

an official complaint but would like to submit these suggestions to you so that you can take care of them if you deem it advisable.

"The machine has no official licence, and I believe its former licence was G-CADP. The pilot flying it is an old time German war pilot and has no licence either. We have kept our engineers from examining this machine officially as we did not wish to be implicated in any way in the event of a crash. Unofficially, we feel that this machine is very unsafe to fly, as half an aileron pulled away in the air the day before I arrived."

The aircraft was subsequently seized by the RCMP, inspected and, indeed, found to be unairworthy. It was left beached on the shore of Stuart Lake where it was picked apart by local vandals. It was a sad and ignominious ending for a plane that had flown a notable albeit brief career and which was the first Canadian registered aircraft to fly, in 1922, throughout northern and central B.C.

A year earlier, the rugged, all-metal German machine, powered by a 185-horsepower engine, made a number of trail blazing exploratory flights in company with its sister ship G-CADQ "Rene", into northern Alberta and the Northwest Territories. Imperial Oil's primary interest in the air operations was aimed at swift supply and liaison with their oil interests in the Mackenzie River valley. On March 24, 1921 both machines departed their Peace River Crossing base en route to Fort Norman Wells. The ski-equipped machines struggled in the deep, dry snow. On March 28, while landing at Fort Simpson, disaster struck Rene. On touchdown the skis hit a frozen snow drift, and the propeller and one ski were shattered. The Vic landed safely but then developed engine trouble. The crews doggedly transferred the Vic's propeller and a ski to the Rene, checked her for airworthiness and prepared to depart for Fort Norman Wells, their final destination. On take off the deep snow again trapped them, the machine struck a frozen drift that smashed the propeller and a ski. The whole operation was stranded, the crews seemingly fated to enjoy the spartan comforts of a Hudsons Bay post until spring break up.

The crews declined to accept their fate lying down and doggedly set to work. They enlisted the aid of Walter Johnson, the post's skilled carpenter cum cabinetmaker, and he, with the assistance of air mechanic Bill Hill, commenced handcrafting two propellers from oaken sleigh boards. They based their measurements on numerous tin templates they had made, then laminated the layers of wood together with a glue made from the hide and hoofs of a moose, then clamped tightly. There was insufficient oak to complete the second propeller; so the resourceful duo used alternate laminates of birch and oak. Meanwhile the rest of the crew toiled in the subzero temperatures repairing the skis, the wing of Rene, and top-overhauled Vic's motor.

On April 15, Vic took triumphantly to the air; her home-made prop performing flawlessly. On April 20, it was Rene's turn and she soared away on a brief air test. Back on the frozen river, a delighted pilot Gorman reported no vibration and normal revs. They prepared to leave on the 24th, Rene to depart first. Nearing take off speed, the skis broke through the snow crust and the tail section suffered serious damage. The machine was hauled to high ground to await later repairs. Rene's mechanic was detailed to stay at Fort Simpson until parts could be shipped north. With pilot Stan Fullerton at the controls, Vic lifted off carrying Gorman, Hill and Imperial Oil employee Waddell and made a direct six-hour flight to the base at Peace River Crossing. Later, repaired and float equipped, Rene joined Vic in further hazardous flights, both surmounting further misadventures until Rene struck a submerged log on August 21 and capsized. Both aircraft have long vanished from the scene, but their famed home-made propellers live on at the National Aeronautical Museum in Ottawa.

The work that had led Western Canada Airways into the Prince George area in 1929 was a photographic survey of the surrounding region. The base, which they established at the time, was not supervised from the Vancouver station, which handled the Pacific coast section, but from Edmonton.

The 1930 amalgamation of Western Canada Airways with several other air transport companies owned by James A. Richardson created Canadian Airways, whose goal was to build a transcontinental system of air transport.

In the 1930s, Canadian Airways established a base in the Burns Lake area, serving the considerable mining activity which was taking place in that area.

> *"It was in 1930 when Walter Gilbert and Frank Taylor flew into Burns Lake in a Boeing flying boat to pick up an injured mining engineer."* says Earl Gerow, who apprenticed with Canadian Airways as an aircraft mechanic. *"The next year, Stan McMillan and Fred Little came in with the Canadian Airways Junkers long-range aircraft, which was designed for photographic work. I was picked up as an apprentice mechanic to help out during the summer. Then, in 1932, Billy Wells and Bill Hoffner came to Burns Lake with a Fokker Super Universal. I was again taken on. My main job at the time was weighing out loads, refuelling the airplane, and assisting with the maintenance.*
>
> *"A mining group came into Burns Lake and caused quite a furor over a big gold mine. We were flying to Takla Landing and refuelling, then going in through McConnell Lake. These people had heard the legend about the 1896 and '98 gold rush in the area and that people had gone in there and made fortunes. Unfortunately, after two years*

they went broke. They didn't seem to know how to mine gold, or were, maybe, mining the public on stock.

CMFT Collection #202.6 CP Air collection, via Wayne Cromie

Junkers W-34 CF-ABK – workhorse of the 40s, 50s, and 60s.

"The biggest part of our work in 1932 and '33 was taking mining supplies into two mining ventures in the area. It was a case of loading, fuelling, and taking off, go into Takla Landing, refuel, take off and take the stuff on into the mining area. The reason for stopping at Takla Landing is we could carry a heavier payload by stopping at Takla Landing. They stocked the fuel in there by scow in the summer.

"When the weather was bad between Takla Landing and the mine site, we often made four and five trips a day between Burns Lake and Takla Landing, and stockpiled there. Eventually, when the weather cleared we would move the stockpile into the minesite.

"We were using the Fokker Super Universal that summer. Later on, in the fall before the ice set in, we had such a backlog that Stan McMillan was transferred in with the Junkers 34, which would carry a 1,500 pound load on floats, rather than the 800 pounds on floats of the Super Universal. If the weather was good we could go straight through in the 34 without landing at Takla Landing.

"Beside this flying, we flew charter flights for prospectors, and fur buyers. In the spring, after the ice went out, they used to fly around and pick up all the fur from the outposts, Germansen Lake, Takla Lake, and Bear Lake, wherever there was a post with factors buying fur.

"At Takla Lake there were two trading posts, an independent post and the Hudson Bay. We gathered up the Hudson Bay fur and took it to Prince George for them, because they didn't sell it to the local fur buyers. They brought it down to Vancouver to their own sale. We covered the interior up as far as Telegraph Creek, and Stan McMillan was based at Carcross where he served the Yukon and the northern part of British Columbia, and we were kept reasonably busy."

During 1934 the Canadian Airways network underwent substantial reorganization, as it was losing money and appeared unlikely to obtain the hoped for trans-Canada airmail contract. As an economy measure, it withdrew from the Prince George area, which was serviced from Burns Lake. This brought other operators into the district to service the mining ventures in the region.

"United Air Transport were called in to take over from Canadian Airways, who were disbanding the base," relates Earl Gerow. *"McConachie and Gil McLaren came in with two Fokker Universals and one mechanic. I started right in with them. We maintained the two airplanes until the spring break-up when McConachie went back to Edmonton with his two airplanes to do the service work and put them on*

CMFT Collection #413.9 Earl Gerow collection

Earl Gerow with Junkers W-34, January, 1933 at Burns Lake, B.C.

floats for the summer. During the spring and summer, he went direct to Takla Landing and they scowed all the mining goods into Takla Landing. They could take bigger loads, cheaper and faster than flying all the way with the Fokker Universals, which were capable of an 800-pound load. It was obviously cheaper for the mining people to do it this way.

"It was a much smaller-scale operation than Canadian Airways. McConachie only had the two small airplanes, but it was the start of bigger things for him because he was up against pretty tight competition in Edmonton with Canadian Airways and the Mackenzie River Air Service.

"The second winter, before I went to Pacific Airways, McConachie brought in one Fokker Super Universal and the Ford Trimotor, G-CARC. That was only in there for February and March. They were flying stuff into Two

CMFT Collection #26.1 Billy Wells collection

Canadian Airways Junkers F-13 CF-AMX, de Havilland Gipsy Moth CF-AAM, and Fokker Super Universal G-CASQ at McKye Lake, B.C.

Brother's Lake; mining equipment. They brought in a dismantled bulldozer and flew it in, in bits and pieces.

"Late in June that same year, Pacific Airways, owned by Charlie Elliott, came into Burns Lake with a Junkers F-13, CF-AMX, the old airplane that Paddy Burke had got lost in up in the Liard country. Dan McLure and Charlie Elliott bought it and formed Pacific Airways. Financing was done by Dan McLure of McLure's Taxicab.

"I worked with Charlie Elliott for two years on the Junkers and a third year on a Custom Waco, CF-BDT, up to 1936. His home base was Vancouver, but he made his operating base at Burns Lake. Charlie operated out of there to many places; up to Stewart and, on occasions with the Junkers, he did fly people from Prince Rupert, from Smithers to Prince Rupert and people from Prince Rupert

Junkers F-13. The remarkable all-metal aircraft which first flew in 1919.

CMFT Collection #30.6
Brian Burke collection

to Smithers when the Skeena flooded and took a section of the CN Railway out.

"The Junkers went well for two years and could have gone on, but, unfortunately, the upper crankcase had a crack about six inches long in an area that couldn't be welded because of the heat stress. About that time, a fellow with a little black moustache was planning on conquering the world. He converted Junkers Industrial Manufacturing to building bombers and fighters. So the airplane had to be scrapped.

"It was licensed for four passengers and a flight engineer. But in those days I'm afraid we didn't live up to the law very well because we carried as many as six people. They just sat on the floor or on the load. Today, you've got to have seat belts for every passenger, which we should have had then."

Fred. W. Hotson in his definitive book on the trans-Atlantic flight of the Bremen in 1928 (The Bremen, Can-Av Books) also recalled the turbulent history of CF-AMX.

"It was serial number 663 from the Junkers factory in Dessau and was put in service with the Dereluft Airline plying between Germany and Russia, 1923-24. Damaged in a forced landing in Russia, it was thoroughly rebuilt at Dessau and then shipped to the U.S.A. in time for the Dayton Air Meet of 1924. It participated in the 1925 Ford

Air Tour, flown by Fred Melchoir, a former Swedish Air Force and European Airways pilot, then flying for Junkers in America. On January 1, 1926 the aircraft force-landed after dark with serious undercarriage and wing spar damage. Repaired with parts shipped from Germany, it was then registered with the Metal Aircraft Express Corp., a sales and demonstration affiliate of the Junkers Corp. of America, bearing U.S. registration NC-87.

"Following the crash of the Bremen on Greenly Island, NC-87 was flown into eastern Canada by Melchoir in company with Herta Junkers, daughter of the founder. Here they were involved in the slightly madcap rescue operations precipitated by competing newspaper chains.

"Consolidated Mining and Smelting Company also based a Fokker Universal in Burns Lake for about four years, doing exploration work. They were putting mining engineers in various places. Germansen Lake was quite a vast mining operation in there. They were involved in that. So they flew all over that area, covering the whole of British Columbia and the Yukon, but they based at Burns Lake. It was central, then, for B.C. and the Yukon."

This use of aircraft by Consolidated Mining and Smelting (Cominco) had been pioneered by W. M. Archibald, a vice-president of the company, who was manager of the smelter at Trail. In the late twenties, he organized the Cominco Flying Service, hiring a group of World War I pilots to train some Cominco mining engineers to fly at the company flying school set up at Creston, B.C. The Cominco Flying Service was soon an important contributor to the company's mining exploration efforts. It remained active until 1964, when Cominco got out of the aircraft business and went to the use of chartered equipment. Aircraft flying under the Cominco banner were soon ferrying men and equipment throughout the Canadian wilderness.

"Archibald had started the Cominco aviation group in the late twenties with a flying school in Creston," says George Neeley Moore, a retired Cominco pilot/engineer. *"During the depression the aircraft were used for exploration and, also at times, for advertising Cominco's Elephant brand fertilizer across the Prairies. There were two groups of aircraft, the freighting aircraft, since in those early days regular air service was not adequate nor sufficiently developed to serve Cominco's needs, and the small aircraft. In the early 1930s, the company's prospectors were still travelling by canoe, but were being moved by aircraft, not necessarily from lake to lake, but certainly they weren't doing any five mile portages. By this time, they would be moved by aircraft for any appreciable distance, but they were still prospecting by canoe."*

Pat Callison and Fairchild FC-2W2 Northern Airways.

CMFT Collection #327.1
E. P. Callison collection

While the B.C. interior operations were developing around the Burns Lake-Prince George area, aviation activity in the northernmost area of the province was being serviced from Carcross in the southern Yukon. Here too, aviation developed on the back of mining, with George Simmons' Northern Airways dominating the Carcross-Atlin trade.

"George Simmons inherited a mink farm from his father," relates Cy Charters, who worked for Northern Airways in the late 30s, *"but he made an error, moving it to the U.S.A., to Colorado Springs. He went into fur farming down there, but he ended up broke. He returned to Carcross and started again. Then the bottom fell out of the fur business in '29; so he looked around for something else to do. There was an old chap running the winter mail by dog team and horses to Atlin. When the contract came up for renewal, George under-bid him, got the contract and hired people to work for him.*

"In 1932, the Tredwell Yukon Mining Company were disposing of their aircraft which they couldn't afford to run. The pilot of the Fairchild FC-2W, Everett Wasson, came down to Carcross and proposed to George that they buy the airplane between them and use it to haul the mail. He talked George into the idea and they started as partners.

"George's contract for hauling the second-class mail from Carcross to Atlin was for ten trips a year, but he was undecided as to how he would haul it. He could haul it any way he wanted. It just happened that it was more practical to haul it by air. This led George into operating Northern Airways.

"For the first few months they couldn't get passengers because people didn't trust airplanes. Nobody would risk their neck in an airplane. In the days when they ran the dog teams, you paid $15 for the privilege of putting your suitcase on the dog-sleigh and ran behind for the sixty miles, a two-day trip.

When they got the opportunity to fly over in about thirty minutes for $15, they wouldn't take it because it wasn't safe. It wasn't until the provincial mining inspector from B.C. came out to Atlin, found that there was an airplane available and bought a ticket, that George started getting passengers. Then he started to do all right.

Loaned from E.P. (Pat) Callison collection

Fairchild FC-2W2, CF-BXF, at Carcross in 1944 with sister ships, Fairchild 71s CF-BXH and CF-BXI. Northern Airways used these aircraft to support construction of the Alaska Highway and the Canol Pipeline.

"The White Pass Company, which practically ran the Yukon, didn't take kindly to George flying some of their business around; so they decided to get some airplanes. They made an offer to Ev Wasson and he left George, going to them as chief pilot. When I moved up there they had a much bigger operation than Northern Airways. We had a rate war the year I went in and it just about bled George white. George had three airplanes and $10,000 in the bank. About four months later he was practically broke. At this point the White Pass said, 'Let's divide the territory, you take everything south of Whitehorse, we'll take everything north of Whitehorse.' From that day George started to make money because he had their backing."

"When the war broke out, the American army came in and wanted aircraft to do all the surveys," says Gordon

Mechanic Bill Hill with the propeller he made which enabled Junkers F-13 "Vic" to fly out after her factory propeller was shattered. See beginning of this chapter.

Loaned from Imperial Oil Archives #493

Cameron, who later formed Yukon Flying Service. *"Northern Airways got in with the American army, flying on that top end of the Alaska Highway survey. Simmons was busy. He made a lot of money doing that U.S. Army flying.*

"At the end of the war George Milne and I started up the Yukon Flying Service. We had little airplanes like Fleet Canucks, Piper Super Cruisers and the Seabee. George Simmons still had the Travel Air 6000, two Fairchild 71s

and two Ansons. He flew passengers between Carcross and Atlin, but by this time Atlin was dying off. The gold business was pretty well dead. He just wasn't getting the flying.

"Carcross was just a little village, and people would come in and out of Whitehorse, which was a customs airport. They weren't going to Carcross. Also, if there were only one, two, or three they didn't want to take an Anson or a Fairchild 71, they wanted a little plane. They came to us and would charter the little Stinson or the Seabee. George wasn't doing any business. So he came to us and said, 'Buy me out.' So we bought him out."

CMFT Collection # C90,19.23

February, 1990, 50 years later, Fred Gardham, (see chapter 15) is still overhauling warbirds. This Handley Page Hampten bomber was ditched in the ocean off Pat Bay (Victoria) in 1942, where it lay until raised in 1986. Fred has been working on its restoration, one section at a time, since that time. The Canadian Museum of Flight & Transportation seeks volunteers or cash donations to help complete this last remaining example.

14

CIVILIANS OVERHAUL WARBIRDS

An infant industry supports the war effort

The start of World War II brought great changes to aviation in B.C. The conversion of the Aero Club of B.C. into an elementary flying, training school was one aspect. As the west coast was considered a major front during WWII, aircraft swelled new operational and training air bases ready for the impending Japanese invasion, which, of course, never came. The rapid buildup of the RCAF brought a need for new aircraft and maintenance facilities.

One of the major beneficiaries of the demand for aircraft was Boeing Aircraft of Canada, whose factory on Georgia Street had struggled through the 1930s doing any type of work that was available. Established in 1929 by Bill Boeing of Seattle and James Hoffar of Vancouver, the company took over the Hoffar-Breeching Shipyard and commenced building Boeing flying boats for the Canadian market under licence from the parent Boeing company.

Aircraft production had barely commenced when the depression hit and destroyed the market. Boeing Aircraft of Canada completed the few aircraft it had under construction, then temporarily abandoned this side of the business. Abandoned at this time, was its "Totem" single-engine, metal-hulled monoplane flying boat project, only the prototype of which was completed. It was a machine in advance of its time, but like so many Canadian aircraft, failed commercially because of poor timing.

"It was about 1933 when they built the Totem," says James Campbell who worked for Boeing Aircraft of Canada throughout the 1930s. *"The Totem was a local design by the chief engineer and it turned out very good, exceeding expectation. It climbed to a lot higher altitude than they had figured. In fact, it was still climbing well beyond their height estimations, but everybody (on the test crew) was so cold that they decided not to go any higher. They only made the one, however, because there was no market for that kind of stuff in the hungry '30s. They weren't buying anything, fish boats, tug boats or flying boats. The payroll money was coming up from the Seattle plant because we certainly weren't making enough. The Totem was the last aircraft they built before they quit with the aircraft work. After that the shipyard really took over the aircraft plant."*

Boeing concentrated on shipyard work until 1937, when it gained a contract to build seventeen Shark torpedo

CMFT Collection #316.1 Jeanne Ambrose collection

Boeing Totem at the Boeing plant, Vancouver (Coal Harbour), B.C.

bombers for the RCAF under license from Blackburn. As an aircraft, the Shark was not a success, but it was a significant aircraft for Boeing since it did revitalize the aircraft plant and paved the way for future wartime efforts.

> *"When the rearming started in Canada the aircraft plant was re-opened,"* recalls Bryan Mahon, who joined Boeing to work on the Shark contract and whose career with the Canadian company and its American parent spanned over 45 years.
>
> *"When I started there, in 1937, there were seventeen employees. At the end of the war there were 10,000. I doubt that more than 100 of them had ever had anything to do with aircraft before they were employed by Boeing.*
>
> *"When we were building the Shark, we built the whole aeroplane except for the specialized forgings. They came from England. Most of the other parts were locally made as it was an ordinary metal airplane of conventional construction, riveted sheets, welded tubes and so forth.*
>
> *"It was actually a very poor aeroplane. It had everything, a rear gunner, a navigator-bombardier. It had a prone bombing sight so you could get down and drop bombs and a Lewis gun in the back of an open cockpit. It could carry depth charges hung from the wings and it could carry a torpedo slung from the center. It had seaplane floats or wheels and was beefed up for carrier operation. It had just about everything you could imagine, but it had only 800-horsepower. It couldn't even get out of its own way.*
>
> *"When we were building it, we couldn't imagine why anyone would buy it because there were some much better aeroplanes available. At the time, Northrop was building a low winged, . . . modern, fully-cantilevered monoplane floatplane. In my opinion, the Blackburn Shark was the worst aeroplane that the Canadian Defence Department could have wasted its money upon, without any exceptions."*

RCAF Blackburn Sharks of No. 6(TB) Squadron, escorting King George VI and Queen Elizabeth into Vancouver harbour, May, 1939.

CMFT Collection #236.1
Fred Gardham collection

Fred Gardham was one of the last employees on the Blackburn Shark contract when it ended.

"In 1940 when the contract at Boeing expired we had about two options;" Fred says, *"we could quit and look for work elsewhere, or, they were just starting the Terminal Avenue plant and they offered me a job there at 50 cents an hour laying flooring to tide me over. I decided I would rather go back east; so I jumped on a train and followed all the other people that were at Boeing, at Jericho Beach, that went to Fort William (now Thunder Bay), Ontario, where they were building Hurricanes."*

Canadian Car and Foundry were building Hawker Hurricanes for the Royal Air Force and many of the men trained at Boeing joined the production line producing the sophisticated fighter.

"I came out from Fort William in about March, 1941," recalls Gardham. *"National Registration was in effect and I was attached to the Lake Superior Unit. The understanding was that if I left the airplane business I would have to go into the army. I managed to get a discharge from Canada Car to go back to Boeing and then on the way back I made my first flight across Canada from Winnipeg on one*

of the old Lockheed 14s that TCA was flying between Toronto and Vancouver. It took us from 4:30 A.M. until midday to get to Vancouver because you had to stop about every hour for fuel.

"Before Boeing had its main base set up at Sea Island, we started our first overhaul in a sawdust bin down at Sixth Avenue and Pine around the B.C. Hydro railroad line.

"That's where we were overhauling Blackburn Shark No. 526, which had crash-landed in eastern Canada. They had shipped it out to Vancouver and . . . the first job I did was to put some new skins on the fuselage. . . . We made the new skins at Boeing down on Georgia Street.

"A lot of the original Boeing men that went to Fort William came back to Vancouver and joined me there.

"We completed No. 526 and took it out to Jericho Beach to assemble it there. The Air Force A.I.D. (Aircraft Inspection Detachment) was not happy with the way we rigged the aircraft; so we re-rigged it at the Boeing plant on Sea Island. It was the first airplane ever rigged in the Boeing plant.

"The overhaul building was across the apron from Boeing's main plant where they were building PBYs. We had our own ramp going into the Moray Channel just about where Air B.C. is right now. After we got the Shark out we started overhauling a Lockheed Lodestar that crash-landed at Patricia Bay.

"The Boeing shop was also used to re-engine Trans Canada Air Lines' fleet of Lockheed 14 Super Electras which required more powerful engines to make regular flights across the Rockies to Vancouver."

"After building the Sharks, Boeing got a contract to build the PBY. It had long range for those days and was very reliable." relates Bryan Mahon, *"It was used by the RAF and the Australians, New Zealanders, the U.S. Navy and the Canadian Air Force . . . and some were even used by the U.S. Army Air Force.*

"Consolidated provided the detailed parts for those, except for the outer wings and empennage which Boeing built. Apart from those parts, Boeing just put those aeroplanes together, but the aircraft in the subsequent contracts, which were for flying boats, were totally built by Boeing. All forgings and castings came from Eastern Canada; so the aircraft were totally Canadian."

Boeing plant Sea Island, 1944.

CMFT Collection #152.2 Boeing Company collection

The contracts for the flying boats (Catalinas) and amphibians (Cansos) led to a major expansion of Boeing, which moved most of its operations out to a new factory at Vancouver Airport. It also led to a massive expansion of the workforce. As virtually a new industry, Boeing had to take people with very little training and use them as best it could to carry out the necessary work.

An example of how Boeing found the people it needed is the case of Lock Madill, who had rebuilt a Gipsy Moth floatplane in the late 1930s and flown it for a couple of seasons before the war. With the Air Force and British Commonwealth Air Training Plan acquiring most of the country's experienced pilots, a person like Lock Madill was just what the company needed to help test-fly the aircraft about to pour off the production line, in spite of his, by today's standards, limited flying experience.

"When the war came along," says Madill, *"I went into ground instructing for the Air Force. It wasn't on the Elementary Flying Training but it was with the Department of Education. I was there for about three years then I heard that Boeing wanted some test pilots for PBYs; so I went out there and landed a job.*

"They were stuck for pilots at the time, since there weren't too many of them around, and I had enough of the ground training. I had an interview with Pat Howard and went to work there the next day. There were five pilots and four or five engineers in the flight test department. All the engines and controls had to be checked out and there were various procedures that we had to go through. There were altitude flights, high-speed flights and fully loaded flights with shot bags laid out all over the floor to the maximum all up weight of 44,000 pounds.

"For the amphibians, the primary flights were usually done on wheels. It was a little more convenient. Then, while we were out flying around we would shoot a few water landings.

"Believe it or not, one used to roll off the production line almost every morning. We built fifty-five amphibian Cansos and 300 of the flying boats. One of my jobs was to walk around, climb on the wing and generally check that everything was sort of working. One thing I did discover was that if you stood on the wing tip and jumped up and down, if there was anything loose in the wing you could hear it hammering in there. There was often the odd bucking bar left in the wings but one time there was quite a loud bump. It turned out to be a piece of two-by-four which had been left inside when they skinned the wing. I believe they cut a small hole in the wing then cut the two-by-four into a whole lot of little pieces to get it out."

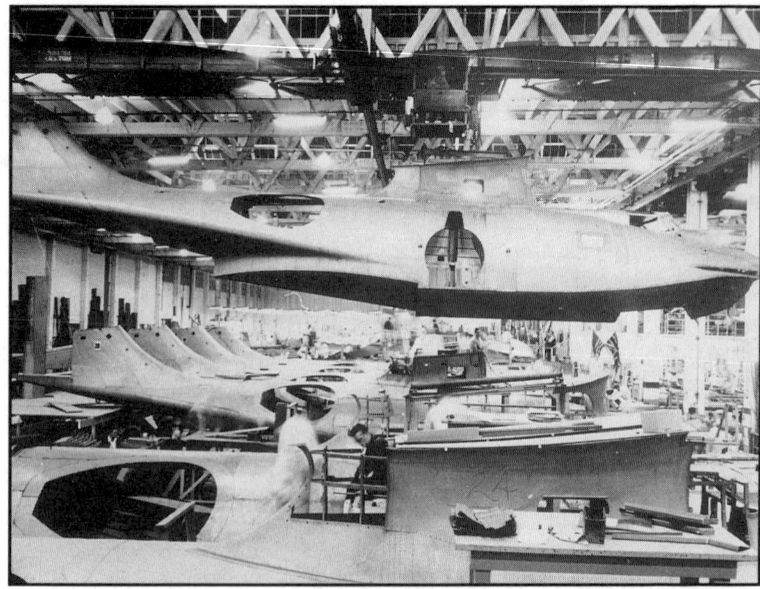

CMFT Collection # 67.3 Vancouver Public Library collection

PBY production line at the Boeing plant on Sea Island, early 1940.

Follow-up orders for lend-lease customers eventually pushed this total to 366 aircraft. In downtown Vancouver, Plant 1 on Coal Harbour was converted to producing sub-components and a new facility was built on Terminal Avenue near the Canadian National Railway station to produce laminated wooden components for such famous aircraft as the Norseman and Mosquito, under construction in eastern Canada.

As the war wound down, the demand for aircraft of the PBY type diminished. The Boeing Aircraft of Canada plant was switched over to building the center fuselage sections for the Boeing B-29s which were carrying the war to the heart of Japan.

"The war in the Atlantic against the submarine was substantially won before the war against Japan," says Bryan Mahon, *"so the market for flying boats went down the tube*

because nobody was going to buy flying boats to sink submarines when submarines were out of the picture. Boeing had nothing more to do in Canada, so they arranged for the plant to build part of the fuselage of the B-29, which was to be the major weapon against Japan. It didn't include the nose or tail but included the fore and aft bomb bays and where the wings attached. It was built in Vancouver and trucked to Renton.

"As soon as Japan capitulated, that was the end of B-29 production, and that work came to a total halt. There was no other work available; so they just shut the plant down and liquidated."

"Boeing had this plant until about the end of 1942 and they wanted the overhaul building as a preflight base for their Cansos and PBYs that were starting to come out of their factories." Fred Gardham comments. *"Boeing relinquished the overhaul shop and turned it over to Canadian Pacific Air Lines. The government then built us another overhaul shop at Queensborough at the east end of Lulu Island. We moved there in the winter of 1942-43."*

At the time, Canadian Pacific Air Lines was an infant organization, newly formed by the merger of ten bushplane and airway companies under the banner of the Canadian Pacific Railway. The overhaul facility was a major undertaking by the company.

On a point of land not far from where the Fraser River splits into the North and South Arms, the Queensborough facility seemed an unlikely location for an aircraft overhaul facility. However, just across the Queensborough bridge was New Westminster, and local politicians had waged a successful campaign to get more war-related work for the local population.

Access for flying boats and seaplanes presented no problem. The aircraft could land on the Fraser River, but landplanes had to be transported from Sea Island airport.

"All our aircraft at Sea Island had to be stripped down and put on barges and towed up the river." reminisces Gardham. *"A hangar was built at Sea Island for our flight crew and that was where Harrison Airways was in the 1970s (occupied by Air B.C. in 1986). After we overhauled them at Queensborough we had to barge them down the river again and take them to Sea Island, put them back together and get ready to flight test them."*

C.P.A.'s Queensborough repair facility, 1944.

CMFT Collection #44.3
Fred Gardham collection

Barging aircraft up and down the river was not without its hazards. On at least one occasion an aircraft emerged from the overhaul shops just long enough to be wrecked when it struck a bridge on the barge trip to Sea Island.

Fred Gardham recalls, *"Canadian Pacific Air Lines at that time was just formulating an airline. They were flying Barkley-Grow floatplanes between Vancouver and Victoria Harbour. They had two Barkley-Grows on floats and they were trying to build the nucleus of an airlines industry. The first contract that C.P.A. got during the war was this overhaul base that was set up at Queensborough."*

Once the Canadian Pacific Air Lines merger had taken place, the Queensborough facility received some of the finest skilled aircraft mechanics that bush flying ever

CMFT Collection #44.2 Fred Gardham collection

Left to Right: Jim Brooks, B. Midian, Fred Gardham, at the Queensborough Repair Facility.

produced. Manager of the facility was Tommy Thompson, a WWI veteran and one of the pilots on the first trans-Canada flight in 1920, flying the final leg which was also the first official airmail flight through the Rockies. G. A. "Tommy" Thompson had also served as general manager of Canadian Airways, the largest single company merged to form C.P.A.

During the Boeing years Lloyd Painter was the chief mechanic, but Albert Hutt, another experienced Canadian Airways veteran, took over following the C.P.A. takeover.

C.P.A. also used to send personnel out from Winnipeg to Queensborough to gain experience. Bob Raven, the aeronautical engineer on staff, found the experience invaluable when he joined Canadian in 1944 as one of the initial engineers working with the Douglas Aircraft Company on the design of the Canadair North Star.

As Raven recalls: "*We must have had about 500 people working there. We had . . . our paint shop, next to that was where we did the dismantling, and then the next bay to that was where we did our sub-assembly and then there was the final assembly. We had a lot of sub-assembly shops up on the second floor where instrumentation and small parts and gear was overhauled. We had an integral organization . . . our own sheet metal works, machine shop and anodizing tempering tanks.*

There were three lead hands. I was looking after all the flying boats like Stranraers and Grummans, and there were other chaps looking after Bolingbrokes, Hudsons, Kittyhawks and the odd Hurricane.

"There were a lot of good people down there. Dick Lake who wound up as vice-president of engineering at Pacific Western, was our chief inspector and Cy Charters who wound up as chief mechanic for C.P.A., was our engine man.

"We had . . . those we picked up from Boeing and who had filtered back from back east. Others had been demobed (de-mobilized) from the Air Force. They had been shot up and got back to Canada and wanted to do something useful. So we had ex-Air Force personnel as inspectors and a lot of women working there too, because by the time 1944 rolled around there wasn't too many single men left.

"One hundred and three aircraft was the total number of aircraft overhauled and repaired in the three year period we were in operation from 1941 to 1944. About half of these were done by Boeing and the other half were done by C.P.A. but basically it was only a change in name, that was all. We were still the same group of people and still doing the same job that we had started.

There were challenges in every one of the shops. We had to adapt and improvise because all during the war we had

CMFT Collection #194.3 Mrs. Beavis collection

Boeing PBY Catalina flying boat undergoing repairs at C.P.A.'s repair facility at Queensborough. Many women were employed in the shops.

difficulty getting spare parts. To give you an illustration, the Ford plant that was out on Kingsway was originally built by Ford to assemble automobiles, but was taken over by the Air Force early in the war, about 1942, and made into an assembly depot for spare parts for Western Air Command. When we went to get spare parts for Hampdens or Bolingbrokes or whatever we were after, we used to go there and make a list out of what we took and submit it to the Air Force because there was nobody in this Ford plant. They never had the personnel to look after the place. It was an interesting way to run a ball game."

The aircraft passing through the overhaul facility encompassed just about every type in operation with the RCAF in British Columbia and Alaska. There were the flying boats and float planes such as the biplane Stranraer and PBY. Cansos built by Boeing and Canadian Vickers for the RCAF, and all sorts of landplanes, from fighters to transports and bombers.

Raven continues, *"We had all the wheeled-aircraft, like the Hampden bombers that were with the 32OTU (Opera-*

tional Training Unit) over at Pat (Patricia) Bay for the torpedo bomber course they were doing for the Royal Air Force. Then there was the Bolingbroke Squadrons that were attached to Pat Bay and were also up at Annette Island in southwest Alaska, just above Rupert. There were Lockheed 10A Electras, the Model 14 Lodestars, the Lockheed 12s that they were using for communications work for the Air Force. C.P.A. managed to squeeze in an old Boeing 247D that they had flying up the Mackenzie out of Hay River and we overhauled that just before we shut down in the summer of 1944.

"We had two or three Douglas DC-3s come in there that belonged to the Air Force. They were relatively new and we'd never seen an aircraft of that size before. We were quite impressed with the DC-3.

"We got quite a lot of Kittyhawks. They were always smashing those up as fast as we could put them out and we had one Bristol Beaufort, but most of our main work was the flying boats, Stranraers and that sort of thing. That seemed to give us the most trouble because they were always punching holes in them and running into trouble somewhere up the coast. We used to get them in pieces on barges and some of them would fly in. Some were time-expired.

"It was always interesting because you never knew what was coming in next and all your shops had to be flexible enough so they could switch from one aircraft to another or from one phase of construction to whatever was required. . . . It was a wonderful experience."

The Queensborough overhaul facility closed in September 1944 and today sits as a forgotten reminder of the war effort that involved hundreds of local men and women. Canadian Pacific, while preparing for the postwar period, was still strapped by the rules that C. D. Howe had set down when he granted Trans Canada Air Lines exclusive rights to east-west travel across Canada.

CMFT Collection #194.5 Mrs. Beavis collection

Bristol Bolingbroke in unusual target tug paint scheme, at the Queensborough repair facility.

C.P.A. could only fly north-south and that prevented many of those at Queensborough from finding jobs with the airline and catching the first wave of the postwar airline boom.

The Overhaul and Support Companies

While Boeing Aircraft of Canada was the only company to actually build aeroplanes in Vancouver during World War II, the contribution of other civilian aviation companies was vital to the war effort.

Years of neglect and restraint had left the RCAF undermanned and ill-equipped to meet the wartime needs. Its rapid wartime expansion led to a demand for repair and overhaul beyond the capacity of its existing maintenance facilities. On the west coast, Vancouver's No. 3 Repair Depot at Jericho Beach was strained to the utmost handling regular airframe inspections and minor maintenance. With skilled personnel being constantly transferred to newly-opened bases, and for service overseas, the Air Force's capability of handling major accident repairs was limited. Only by resorting to the facilities of civilian contractors could the needs for major overhauls be met; so companies which had been struggling to survive were suddenly inundated with opportunities for work.

Although the C.P.A. overhaul shop at Queensborough (and its Boeing predecessor) handled the larger aircraft, other Vancouver companies benefitted from the smaller aircraft which utilized the (then) more traditional steel tube, wood and fabric construction. Before shutting his shop down in a dispute over wages, Tommy Jones at Wells Air Harbour, Lulu Island (see chapter 10) received some war work, but the company which handled most of the small plane overhaul work was Coates Aircraft.

In 1935 Cecil Coates had resigned from Canadian Airways, where he had obtained his experience as an aircraft engineer, erected the first privately owned building on Vancouver Airport and commenced his own aircraft repair and maintenance company, which he called Coates Aircraft.

> *"For the first five years business was quite slow,"* recalls Coates, *"and it was a battle all the way. The trouble was that there had been nobody else at the airport doing overhauls and we didn't know what to charge. There was no precedent to use for comparison.*
>
> *"The government contracts awarded when the war broke out are what changed the situation. That's what made*

CMFT Collection #229.19 C.P. Coates collection

Hawker Hurricane undergoing repairs at Coates Aircraft Ltd., Vancouver Airport, 1939.

things go. The government looked around to see who was available to carry out their work and we got a government contract to overhaul Training Command aircraft and some of the other machines, Norseman and Hurricanes. The work was mostly routine overhauls, but now and then the odd one would come in all smashed up."

With his many years of experience in the repair and maintenance of aircraft of traditional steel tube, wood and fabric construction, Cecil Coates' company retained this specialty, while other companies handled the aircraft of the more modern stressed-skin construction. Coates Aircraft became noted for the large number of Tiger Moths that went through its shop, as well as Lysanders, Hurricanes and even a few Mosquito bombers.

"It was a fairly small operation," recalls John Anderson, who test-flew some of the machines overhauled by Coates Aircraft at the end of the war. *"It wasn't much of a*

Loaned from Ingwold Wikene collection

Yukon Southern Airways' Ford 6-ATS Trimotor CF-BEP at Vancouver after being hit by a RCAF Hurricane, March 2, 1939. This Hurricane, which was the first one to be shipped to Vancouver, had just been assembled, but got away during takeoff.

pretentious looking place, but there was a lot of good work that came out of there, mainly due to a lot of good fellows working there. Some of them were originals in the industry.

"I flew pretty well as required and as the volume going through the shop changed. I had the opportunity to work in the shop as well. Eventually, the military contracts diminished so that pushed me out of the flying end of it, but there just wasn't the demand for that either and eventually the organization packed up."

Although Coates Aircraft was a busy place during the war years, the cessation of hostilities required an adjustment to the cruel winds of a harsh economic climate. While a large company like Boeing Aircraft closed the doors of its Canadian subsidiary and fled home to Seattle with its wartime profits, smaller firms like Coates Aircraft were forced to try to struggle through.

"We figured that there would be a gap when the war finished and things would fold up; so I went into boat building," says Coates. *"That's one of the mistakes I made actually, because if I had waited a while, I would have realized that the Air Force was still supporting us. They had lined up a lot of aircraft for us to overhaul which would have tided us over the gap. We didn't switch completely to boat building, still doing some overhaul work, but our resources were stretched and eventually we ran out of money."*

Coates' conversion of war surplus boats for civilian uses was a dying gasp exercise, however, and was not profitable. His company collapsed into bankruptcy, a sad end for an enterprise that had reconditioned hundreds of aircraft as part of the war effort.

CMFT Collection #194.2 Mrs. Beavis collection

Queensborough facility. Aircraft is a Catalina.

15

EARLY FLYING IN THE OKANAGAN & KAMLOOPS AREA

The first flights in the Okanagan area closely followed upon those in the more major British Columbia centers of Vancouver and Victoria in the early 1910s. Billy Stark, the Vancouver aviation pioneer, brought his Curtiss biplane to the 1912 Armstrong Fair and made a single flight under gusty conditions. As Stark's aircraft could not be entrusted with the dangerous flight over the mountains from the coast to the Okanagan, it was crated for shipment to Armstrong and reassembled at the site of the fair.

On August 13, 1914, Weldon Cooke flew a Curtiss Hydroplane at the Kelowna Regatta. This machine was shipped in, crated, on the steamer *Sicamous* and assembled on the beach. It, too, made only one flight.

With most of the adventurous spirits being fully occupied with World War I from 1914 to the end of 1918, it is not surprising that there was no further flying in the area until 1919, when Captain Ernest Hoy visited Armstrong for the Dominion Day Sports. Lieutenant Ernest Hall flew in Penticton, also on Dominion Day, and Lieutenant Trim brought a Curtiss JN4 Jenny to the Kelowna Regatta to fly passengers from the polo grounds. This latter barnstorming venture proved successful and Trim remained in the area for some time after the Regatta.

Later in 1919, Hall again visited the Okanagan on an attempt to fly to Calgary, but upon learning that he was not eligible to earn the prize money being offered by the World Group of newspapers, barnstormed in the area until Ernest Hoy passed over Penticton on his way to Calgary on August 7, having refuelled at Vernon. Hall then took off in pursuit, but his flight ended in a crash at Nelson. Hoy, however, succeeded and arrived in Calgary sixteen hours and forty-two minutes after departing Vancouver, after a flight involving four refuelling stops. This was the first aerial crossing of the Rockies.

About 1928, Clyde Wann passed through the Okanagan with a three-seat Alexander Eaglerock on a barnstorming tour to the Yukon. If the passengers were light, Wann squeezed three into the front seat to increase his revenue.

> *"After a passenger flight with him I swore I'd never go up again, but I was out the next day for another one,"* recalls Cliff Renfrew of Kelowna, who took his first flight with Wann. *"We did a stall turn. I knew what a stall was, but I didn't realize it was something the pilot had under control. He took off, pulled up and did a stall turn. We had a pretty close look at the airport before he pulled out. I thought that was not too good, but like I say, I was out for another flight the next day."*

Renfrew had his appetite for flying whetted by these joyrides, and when Lowell Dunsmore came to the Okanagan and offered flying training, shortly afterwards, he commenced taking flying lessons.

> *"I got even more interested once Radium Hot Springs Flying Service started operating out of Rutland,"* says Renfrew. *"A group of us started training with Lowell Dunsmore giving the instruction. It was just flying instruction, there was no ground school like they give today. We were simply told that if we had any doubts about the weather then we shouldn't fly.*
>
> *"John Blakeley, the proprietor of Radium Hot Springs Air Service, had a de Havilland Gipsy Moth, CF-AGK, which*

he brought over to the Okanagan for a few months each year from 1928 to 1931 when the weather was fine. He had interests in Radium Hot Springs, so he had Lowell Dunsmore fly it for him. His flying activities were sort of part hobby, part business.

CMFT Collection #298.38 Cliff Renfrew collection

John Blakeley's Radium Hotsprings Air Service Gipsy Moth CF-AGK at Rutland, B.C.

"He commenced operating out of Rutland, but that strip didn't have a licence, so, when the Vernon Airport opened, it was necessary to move there. Dual instruction cost $18 an hour, which was high for the time, but he didn't have very many students, and it wouldn't have paid him to operate at a lower cost. I don't think it paid him anyway, but at least he was operating with his machine kept in nice shape.

"I started my training with him in the fall of 1929, but, with the machine going back to Calgary for the winter, the

training was extended over quite a period, and I didn't finish my training and get my licence until 1931."

It was not just the "summer only" operation of Radium Hot Springs Air Service in the Okanagan region that caused this long interval between the start of training and the achievement of a licence. There was also the matter of making arrangements for a medical examination and getting the Regional Air Inspector up from Vancouver for the flight test.

Corben Jr., Ace, CF-AOM built by Eldon Seymour and Jimmy Duddle at Vernon, B.C., 1935.

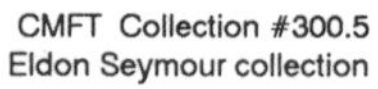

CMFT Collection #300.5
Eldon Seymour collection

"When we took our medicals in Vernon," continues Renfrew, *"they had to bring the doctor from Revelstoke because only certain doctors were approved, and he was the only one in the B.C. interior who was approved."*

For the flight test, the Regional Inspector for Civil Aviation, Carter Guest, came up from Vancouver. Eldon Seymour of Vernon, was another student of Lowell Dunsmore who took his flight test during the 1930s.

"Carter Guest was sitting out on the airport when I flew my licence test," says Seymour, *"but he was sitting in a car. They didn't let the inspectors fly with you on the licence test in those days. From what I was told, he never even looked out of the car while I was up doing my stuff, which consisted of spot landings to a sheet and solo spins. I didn't lose enough speed before I entered the spin and finished up rolling the plane onto its back, the first thing I knew I was headed for the ground with the airspeed winding up at a fantastic rate. I managed to pull it out and climbed up and did it properly, but after I landed they told me that Carter Guest had never even seen it."*

Although Lowell Dunsmore was able to get enough business to make it worthwhile for John Blakeley to base his Gipsy Moth in the Okanagan for a few seasons, he did not choose to keep coming back as the "dirty thirties" damped down the economy.

Later in the 1930s, as the plans for the trans-Canada air route were translated into a series of airports at fifty mile intervals across the country, the first efforts were made at setting up an air service between the Okanagan Valley and the coast.

CMFT Collection #298.22 Cliff Renfrew collection

Lana Kurtzer visits Vernon in the early '30s with the Aeromarine Klemm.

"Shortly after the opening of the Oliver Airport, which was a part of the trans-Canada chain of airports and built as a relief measure without using heavy equipment, just shovels and wheelbarrows," relates Cliff Renfrew. *"A Waco was operated from Vancouver to Oliver to Kelowna. It was quite a short-lived operation, but it was a good attempt."*

Apart from this mid-30s attempt at an air service over the triangle route (Vancouver-Oliver-Rutland-Vancouver), there was no serious effort at developing a regular scheduled flying service to or within the Okanagan until after World War II.

16

LEAN TIMES FOR WWII VETERANS

The postwar development of aviation in the Okanagan

Between 1945 and 1950 the interior of British Columbia, and in particular the area around Kamloops and the Okanagan Valley, was the scene of a struggle for survival by several small aviation companies. Some of the companies found their resources too slender and simply went out of business.

One plunged into a new form of flying and grew to become a giant in the helicopter industry. The others struggled on, some cooperating, some competing. By the early 1950s there was only one company left still operating in its original role, Central B.C. Airways, which subsequently moved to Vancouver and became Pacific Western Airlines.

> *"There was Dave Smith in Penticton,"* says Dick Laidman who was one of the postwar optimists, and ultimately became president of P.W.A., *"Dave had a little flying school and charter business. There was Carl Agar and Alf Stringer in Kelowna of the South Okanagan Flying Club, later to become Okanagan Helicopters, ourselves with L & M Air Services in Vernon and, in Kamloops, Harry Taylor and Pete Cornwall with Taylor Cornwall Air Services plus Harry Bray's Kamloops Air Services. Then Russ Baker came in with Central B.C. Airways and we were all scrapping over the business which was not enough for even one to live upon.*

CMFT Collection #338.53 Joe Lalonde collection

Filby and Smith Airways began operations with a Piper Cub similar to this one.

"Russ Baker had formed Central B.C. Airways in Fort St. James a couple of years before he came to Kamloops, but he had been fortunate to secure the forestry protection contract from the B.C. government, which we had all bid upon. Russ managed to procure it with real hard work and a lot of lobbying. This is where he forced his way into Kamloops and forced poor old Harry Bray out of business. Central B.C. was going to emerge as the newcomer. (And went on to become the dominant third-level operator in B.C. evolving into Pacific Western Airlines)."

The smallest of the Okanagan operations was Filby and Smith Airways, which was started by Dave Smith, a Penticton fruit grower with an enthusiasm for aviation. Smith acquired a Piper Cub and commenced a small flying training and charter operation in Penticton, talking ex-RCAF pilot Dan McIvor into working for him as an instructor.

"I was attempting, unsuccessfully, to become a fruit grower under the Veterans Land Act when Dave Smith came to see me," says Dan McIvor. *"He needed an instruc-*

tor and wanted me to get my rating and come to work for him. At first I turned him down on the proposal, but the next morning I went out to the airport and agreed to it.

"The test officer had been in Penticton but had gone to Grand Forks; so Dave said, 'The inspector is down at Grand Forks. If you take the patter book and read it on the way down, I'll fly you down for the test.' So we got in the airplane, I read the book on the way down, took the test on arrival and got my instructor's rating.

"I instructed for Dave for a while. I ran a school at Revelstoke, and, on my way up, I would fly into Vernon and gas up there. Dick Laidman offered me $200 a month to come and work for L & M, and all I had to do was fly an airplane, do the maintenance and accounting. So I moved up."

After McIvor's departure, Smith, who had obtained his instructor's rating in the meantime, operated the business by himself, but he was killed in a flying accident in 1948 which also ended Filby and Smith Air Services.

The company to which McIvor moved in 1947, Dick Laidman's L & M Air Services, had originated in Yellowknife in the latter days of World War II. Vernon-born

Dan McIvor June, 1990.

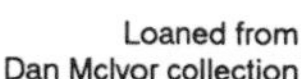

Loaned from
Dan McIvor collection

Laidman had left the Okanagan in 1938 to work as an air engineer for Starrett Airways and Transportation Ltd. in Hudson, Ontario. In 1942, Starrett amalgamated with nine other companies to form Canadian Pacific Air Lines. Laidman was moved to Yellowknife with the opening of the Northwest Staging Route, but, by the end of the war, found that a deteriorating relationship was developing between him and his employer.

"The superintendent of the Mackenzie Division, 'Wop' May, and I just didn't seem to see eye to eye," says Laidman. *"Boyles Brothers Drilling asked me to supervise a machine shop servicing their drilling camps, because mining had opened wide in the Yellowknife area. I had a couple of small aircraft myself, a Hornet Moth and a Tiger Moth, which I used to carry parts back and forth and service the fourteen camps spread out over the Northwest Territory; so was into a sort of gyppo charter business as well.*

"Having spent a number of years in the bush, with the snow and the cold, a return to the Okanagan looked pretty good; so I applied for a licence for a flying school and charter service in Vernon. I had a lawyer in Yellowknife set up the company. A friend of mine, by the name of Freddy Miller, was the base manager at Yellowknife; so we used his and my initials in the title; so that was the original L & M.

"After I moved out, Freddy stayed in Yellowknife for a while then he went back east. I then began referring to the company as Land and Marine, because it sounded pretty good. We were operating from both land and water. When Hugh Mann joined the company, a lot of people thought it was Laidman and Mann; so we let it ride at that. So that was how the whole thing stayed.

"When I came out of Yellowknife and had a licence to operate in Vernon, I found that the airport was not going to be licenced by the Airways Branch of the Department of Transport because the runway was too short. It was only

1,950 feet long and the minimum they would allow was 2,500 feet. There was 600 feet available at the west end of the runway but it had to be procured. The existing aldermen and the mayor of Vernon had tried dealing with the Indian band which owned the land but had come to a complete impasse.

"I had grown up in the area and knew some of the relatives of Pierre Jack, the chief; so I thought that there might be a way of getting the matter settled. It took me four months of sitting on fence posts, rolling cigarettes and talking, but, finally, they had a band council meeting and agreed to a deal. The Vernon council was able to lease the land and I was able to start operating.

"I had a couple of partners, Peter Deck and Jimmy Engels, and a little later, Hugh Mann. We had a nice little flying school, a little charter business, and, eventually, even a little scheduled run from Kamloops through to Penticton, making connection with CP Air Lines' trans-B.C. run.

"We started with the original Hornet Moth that I had bought from Consolidated Mining and Smelting while at Yellowknife, and I had the Tiger Moth that I procured from War Assets and rebuilt at the end of the war. It became very evident that right to the south of us in Rutland, which was the Kelowna Airport at the time, Carl Agar and a couple of his cohorts had a little flying school and had become Cessna dealers. Cessna had come out with their first postwar, two-place aeroplane. It was pretty obvious that it was the most economical aeroplane to operate. The Hornet Moth was great for the bush, but not for back in civilization.

"With a little persuasion at the bank and the little money that we could all scrape together, we got a Cessna 140. Then we bought a Stinson 108 which we operated on floats in summer and skis in the winter.

"We followed those up with an Anson from Western Aircraft Sales, the sales arm of Queen Charlotte Airlines.

Loaned from Dick Laidman collection

Dick Laidman with his DH Hornet Moth CF-BBE at Lumby, BC, 1945. L & M began operating with a 'BBE and a Tiger Moth.

They had bought a whole lot of war surplus Anson Vs and were converting them to civil use in Vancouver. We bought one semi-finished and completed it to use as a feeder airplane and for the larger charters. In late 1948, we decided we wanted something more sophisticated than the Anson; so we got a Twin Beechcraft. We used it on wheels in the wintertime and on floats in the summer.

"Our Class 2 service licence allowed us to operate from Kamloops to Vernon to Kelowna to Penticton. The Beechcraft on floats enabled us to operate, more or less, from right downtown. We were able to land on the river in Kamloops, right at the foot of the city. In Vernon we landed right at Okanagan Landing. At Kelowna we landed at the foot of Pandosy Street and, in Penticton, right at the foot of Main Street. It was a commuter type of service, but, unfor-

CMFT Collection #352.24 Ron Williams collection

A Twin Beechcraft like the one on the right was a mainstay of L & M Air Services. The aircraft on the left is a Fairchild 71.

tunately, the population in those little towns wasn't big enough to support that type of operation. At the end of the war, everybody could see a great future for aviation, a beautiful horizon which went black pretty fast.

"It was the big flood in 1948 which kept us going for a couple of years longer. It was a tragedy to many people, but to the little struggling airlines it was a chance to prove what could be done. We put the old Anson to work. It had been sitting, not doing too much until that flood came along; then we started a service from Vernon to Vancouver on a daily basis, making about four trips a day because there was no other connection, neither rail nor road.

"When the flood first started, we were called upon to see if we would haul asparagus out of Kamloops. We did that until about two days later when, on the last trip, we were

taking off with water on the airport. We came back to Vernon and they started trucking the asparagus to Vernon for us to fly from there. It was all in baskets and, when it arrived, it was the most limp looking grass I had ever seen. The asparagus had wilted in the heat! We decided that if we flew high enough and opened up all the vents, maybe it would get cool enough for the asparagus to stiffen up. It turned out the idea worked. By the time it arrived in Vancouver, it was beautiful. I don't know what it was like when it got to the store, but it was all right when we delivered it.

"During the flood, we hauled all types of things both to and from the Okanagan. It was a boon to us as an air carrier, but, unfortunately, a lot of people suffered. We had people stranded up on the North Thompson with their cars under water, and we had to take them out by floatplane."

The flood was a bonus to L & M, but afterwards it was back to the usual struggle for existence, flying whenever and wherever the customer required.

"We were flying all over the southern part of the province and as far north as Prince George," relates Dan McIvor, who had joined L & M during 1947. *"I got to know the province pretty well. I knew all of it and if it was late in the evening, I wouldn't stop, I'd come home in the dark.*

"One day, I had gone down to Trail with a passenger and it was just grounding time when I took off to go back to Vernon. Our procedure for occasions like that was for someone to run a car out to the end of the runway and shine the lights down the strip in the direction of landing. We would come in over the car and land using the aircraft landing lights. On this occasion, I had an old car with a generator that didn't charge and Dick (Laidman) parked the car, shut the engine off and left. The lights soon went out.

"I came around and saw a car with its lights on so came on down over it—wrong car! I climbed up and flew around

and found another car. I came down over it but it wasn't the right car either. I pulled up again and circled around. Then the lights came on in a house across the road from the airport and I could see the lights in the hangar, so I knew the position of the airport. A car drove out from the house and parked at the end of the strip. It was Normie Brown, a neighbor, who had realized my predicament and helped out. With the car in position I was able to land without difficulty.

"We didn't land that way very often, but we would do it whenever it was necessary, providing the weather was clear and we could see the lights of the town."

An interested onlooker of the somewhat unusual night landing was John Hatch of Queen Charlotte Airlines who had earlier flown in with a Beaver. He strolled over to McIvor, shook his hand and asked, "You do this often?" "Only when necessary," replied McIvor modestly. "My boy," said Hatch, "any time you want a job with us, just ask."

Regardless of the efforts made, however, there was only a limited amount of business available for L & M, and, by the end of 1949, the company was feeling the effects of hard times.

Laidman says of the final days: *"We had a real hard winter and a lot of fruit growers suffered hard times; so there was little flying training to be done. There was some charter business but very little. Gradually, we decided to close the operation. It was obvious that we couldn't continue; so we disbanded and sold off the equipment, ending up about level. The initial investment, which wasn't that great, was lost.*

CMFT Collection #260.5 Margery Kite collection

Q.C.A.'s Avro Anson over Vancouver, circa 1945.

17

THE STRUGGLE FOR SURVIVAL

Commercial aviation in the Kamloops area

In the late 1920s, the Canadian government introduced a scheme to provide assistance to Aero Clubs throughout the country. Shortly after the Aero Club of British Columbia commenced operations in 1929, a promotional visit by Paddy Burke led to the establishment of a Kamloops branch. Unfortunately, this was just a paper organization and did not become operational. It was not until Humphrey (Hump) Madden flew up to Kamloops from Vancouver, late in 1930, that the first efforts to licence an airport at Kamloops took place. Hump did not come to Kamloops with the intention of building an airport or starting an airline, he just wanted to fly for a living.

"We went up to Kamloops. I didn't know where I was going to land, of course. But I circled around and found a field that I could just get into and landed there. Then I looked around and found another field that was a little better and flew over to it. I discovered it was on an Indian reservation; so I went to the Indians and said, 'Can I make a deal. Can I use your land?'

"They agreed, but the Department of Transport said that I would have to license this as an airport and gave me the rules for doing that. With the help of the municipality, I got a survey done on the field and eventually got it licenced. But I had to make an agreement with the Indians and get the agreement signed.

"I remember the lawyer, Mr. Black, getting everyone together, the Indian chief and the others. Then there was a misunderstanding. I got the impression they wanted me to buy the reservation but I told them where to go. It was a very unfortunate thing. I got a call from Ottawa, a wire actually, 'Get moving.' I didn't know quite where to go so I went further east and I ended up in Trail, where the Consolidated Mining and Smelting had quite a nice little field at Columbia Gardens about eight miles from Trail. I stayed there and I started building up a little business as a flying school."

Over a decade after Madden's shortlived attempt at running a flying school at Kamloops, Frank Gilbert moved his Gilbert's Flying Service from Vancouver into the airport at Kamloops. Here again it was as shortlived a venture as it was in 1942 and wartime conditions were making it difficult for a flying school to obtain fuel. Gilbert had moved from Vancouver only to complete the training of the few students who were still on his books, before putting his aircraft into storage for the duration of the war.

Immediately after World War II, Kamloops became a veritable hotbed of aviation, with Brisbane Aviation, Kamloops Flying Club, Kamloops Air Services, Taylor Cornwall Air Services and Central B.C. Airways all basing their activities there. Within five years, all but one of these operations had been forced out, by postwar economics. The sole survivor was Central B.C. Airways, the upstart from Fort St. James which had muscled into the area on the strength of a forestry contract, and was to build aggressively into a large airline, Pacific Western Airlines.

When Stan Sharp sought alternative work for his Vancouver based Brisbane Aviation immediately after the war, it seemed only natural to enter the flying school business to complement his school for aviation mechanics. Kamloops was just one of the towns where he attempted to start an operation.

"I made a deal to use the Kamloops Airport and run a flying school up there," says Sharp. *"I hired a local boy, a war hero, and put him in charge. One day I went up to see him, and, when I flew in, there were a number of people waiting around, but our airplane was just tied down.*

"When I asked, I found these people were waiting for my instructor, to fly with him. I borrowed a car and went downtown and found him drinking in the Legion. He was just not looking after the business; so I had to close that operation down."

The Kamloops Flying Club lived only slightly longer than Brisbane's Kamloops operation. Formed in 1945 to take advantage of the Canadian government's subsidy scheme, whereby ex-British Commonwealth Air Training Plan training aircraft were made available to flying clubs at very nominal prices, the club acquired two ex-RCAF Tiger Moths (CF-CIF and CF-CII) in January 1946.

The Kamloops Flying Club, in common with many other flying clubs, soon found that the ex-RCAF Tiger Moths were not the most reliable of aircraft. In late May, CF-CIF suffered an engine failure and landed in the trees. It was replaced by another (CF-CHV) which was resold to the Comox Aero Club later that year.

Since Taylor Cornwall Air Services had commenced operating a flying school at Kamloops, the town could be said to be overserved by flying schools. And business was not really good for either school.

This latter concern was run by two partners, Harry Taylor and Pete Cornwall. They had not rushed into the aviation business immediately after the war, but after working for others for a couple of years, they decided to try it on their own. Cornwall was a Toronto air traffic controller working part-time for Leavens Brothers as a flying instructor, when he met Harry who was also instructing for Leavens Brothers.

"We decided to seek our fame and fortune in aviation," says Pete Cornwall, *"and set off for Cranbrook to start up a flying school which we named Taylor Cornwall Air Services. There was another operator there already and he was after the licence there. We had a try but it didn't work out; so we moved to my home town of Kamloops in desperation.*

"The Kamloops Flying Club was getting going about the same time as we moved in there. We tried, several times, to get them to amalgamate with us, but that was a hopeless cause; so we had competition right from the start.

An Aeronca Chief similar to this one was one of the first aircraft operated by Tayor Cornwall Air Services at Cranbrook, B.C.

CMFT Collection #338.41
Joe Lalonde collection

"We started off operating two Aeroncas, a Champ and a Chief, and after awhile we added a Cessna 140. The business was great, at first, but eventually we ran out of money."

Before running out of money, however, Taylor Cornwall Air Services experimented with agricultural aviation. Harry Bray, whose Kamloops Air Services shared a hangar with them at Kamloops Airport, supported their efforts by flying their aircraft whenever they needed an extra pilot to help them out during a busy period. His charter business and their flying school did not directly compete; so they assisted each other on an 'I'll scratch your back if you scratch mine' basis.

"They started out with a small contract to put weedkiller onto some sagebrush around Merritt," recalls Bray. *"They got a small contract from some ranchers around there, then branched out into general agricultural flying.*

"One of the first good contracts they got was to stir up the air over Sid Smith's hop fields, just east of Kamloops. He didn't want them sprayed, he wanted the air stirred up for frost control. Of course this had to be done at night. We used to take the two Aeroncas out onto Highway 1 east of Kamloops. I don't remember ever asking anyone's permission, but we used to put barricades up with signs blocking off the section we wanted to use. We posted a man with a lantern at each end. The cars were stopped when we took off and again when we wanted to land. In between, we whirled over the hops, stirring up the air."

"It didn't really pay off," says Pete Cornwall. *"We couldn't get anything more than mosquito control which wasn't enough. Then Art Seller started spraying in the area and he had more equipment and more money behind him; so he ended up with most of the business."*

Since the business that remained was not enough to sustain a two-man operation, Cornwall and Taylor went onto a part-time operation. For one winter, Cornwall flew for Imperial Oil, while Taylor spent a season flying from Fort St. James for Russ Baker's Central B.C. Airways, but the company continued operating.

"We were there if anybody phoned us," says Cornwall. *"There was generally someone out there, either Harry Bray, Harry Taylor or myself. Somebody was generally around in case any business showed up.*

"After about five years, however, we gave it up. The Aeronca Champ got broken and, when we got paid for it, the money was used to pay Imperial Oil and miscellaneous other people whom we owed money. We sold the Champ and the Cessna 140. We couldn't see any future in continu-

ing it on; so we just called it quits and got out while we were still alive."

Harry Bray, who cooperated so closely with Taylor, and Cornwall, had started Kamloops Air Services when the dreams that he shared with three of his wartime friends were not fulfilled.

"When the war was winding down, we all got together and decided we were going to start a tourist lodge in B.C. One of us, a fellow by the name of Veitch, who had done some work with the tourist division of the B.C. government, suggested Chilko Lake. Our idea was to build a lodge on an isolated lake and fly in parties of hunters and fishermen. The others in the venture were Bob Marcoux and my bomb aimer, Pete Hunting. All four of us came to B.C. to start what would have been basically a hunting and fishing lodge.

"We went to the B.C. government full of these wonderful plans and they were most enthused. However, they advised us against doing it at Chilko Lake because there were plans to dam it for hydro-electric purposes. We looked around for somewhere else, and finally selected Chehalis Lake, but for various reasons we didn't get going there too well.

"One day, I was talking to Earl Brett out at Chilliwack and he said, 'Why don't you go to the Kamloops area. They're really gung ho for aviation.'

"So I took the night train to Kamloops and arrived there on the day they were having a conference on aviation. The town council had an aviation committee and they were looking for someone to start a charter service based at Kamloops; so it looked like a good place to go into with an air service. The town wanted us and offered us help in applying for the charter licence. In one sense, you could say that we never really picked Kamloops in which to start our business, they picked us.

"By that time, we had our first aircraft, an old Cirrus Moth on floats which had been used prewar by Harold

Turner and Lock Madill in Vancouver. Brisbane Aviation was in the process of rebuilding it. We didn't have our lodge, but Kamloops looked like a good place because there were hundreds of small lakes in the area, all with excellent hunting and fishing, and access to most of them was limited unless you had an aircraft."

Of the original four, three were still enthused about aviation when they made the move to Kamloops. It was Harry Bray, Pete Hunting and Bob Marcoux who set about building up Kamloops Air Services. It soon became apparent, however, that there just wasn't a living for all three in the air charter business. Bob Marcoux was the first to leave. He found a job in Vancouver that offered steadier income. Pete Hunting decided to return to England, which left Harry Bray to continue the business.

"Business was very slow," remarks Bray. *"In the late '40s there was a real depression on as far as aviation was concerned. I remember reading in the Legion magazine, about 1948, how ninety-odd percent of all veterans who had started up aviation businesses had gone bankrupt. Everybody was starving to death. I don't think it was too many people in the business, it was a case of the business not being around. The aircraft hadn't been developed to suit the public, most of the equipment was too small and as a result, our charges were too high. We were also very much restricted by the Air Transport Board.*

"I remember trying to build up some winter business by offering a cut rate. We had basically a four month season for flying, which was the tourist season, and the planes sat idle the rest of the time. I applied to the Air Transport Board to reduce my rates from $40 to $25 an hour for the winter, but it was absolutely denied. When I tried to explain that by law I was required to keep the business open twelve months a year, which entailed hangar heating costs and payroll costs, and that by charging $25 per hour I could generate a

little business, which would help to cover these costs, the response was, 'No. You will keep your rates at $40 per hour.' So, naturally, we didn't get much local business.

"We did get a few ranchers, looking for lost cattle, and the odd bit of timber work, but there were none of the big industrial projects about at that time. The only real money in the area, at that time, was the forestry contract and Central B.C. Airways had that."

Aircraft, too, were a problem. The Cirrus Moth on floats was limited to carrying one passenger. For a fledgling aviation company further aircraft of greater capacity were needed.

"We started with that Cirrus Moth because it was the only thing we could get. We tried to buy a Grumman Goose from War Assets but that was thwarted. We had been trying to get something from War Assets for some time when we learned of a Goose down in Western Air Command which was to be turned over to them. We got the serial number and all

CMFT Collection #275.77 Ingwold Wikene collection

A Republic Seabee similar to the above was the mainstay of Kamloops Air Service.

and wired it to Ottawa saying we were interested. The next day we went to the base to see it and we were sort of persona non grata. There were mechanics swarming all over it chopping it to pieces. At that point we gave up on being able to get anything worthwhile out of the War Assets Department.

"About that time the Republic Aircraft Corporation had started advertising the Seabee amphibian, and it looked like the answer to our problems. We bought the second one to come into Canada and the first in B.C. The price was $2,500. The Canadian dollar was at a ten percent premium back then so we got it delivered for the premium and it was in Kamloops for $2,500.

"We were very disappointed with it. It didn't pack the load it was supposed to carry and wasn't able to get where we had hoped it would go. But we were out of money, and it was all we had for equipment; so we just put on a brave front and kept operating. Later on, we found that a lot of the disappointment was due to our own faults and inexperience. There were a lot of little tricks you could use to get more performance out of the Seabee, but it took time to find them out.

"One obvious thing to do was to lighten the aircraft; so we stripped off quite a bit of unnecessary equipment. We heard that one operator in the States had removed the wheels and improved the performance so we did that. We ran it that way for about three months, then we had a visit from Carter Guest, the aviation inspector, and he wasn't very happy about it as it was not approved in Canada.

"At the time, he told us to put the wheels back on, but he didn't say when; so we kept operating that way. Eventually a bulletin came out permitting the modification, but we had to carry forty pounds of ballast in the nose to maintain the center of gravity in the correct position."

With the Seabee (eventually two Seabees) as the mainstay of its operations, Kamloops Air Services struggled along, flying supplies and people to hunting and fishing lodges in the region and getting some work from the local sawmills. When business was good, they would charter aircraft from Taylor Cornwall Air Services, Kamloops Flying Club or L & M Air Services of Vernon to take care of the excess business. When times were not so good Bray would fly for Taylor Cornwall Air Services to help them out.

> *"We were operating with Taylor Cornwall in a cooperative arrangement,"* says Bray. *"They had branched out into agricultural operations and I would be flying for Pete Cornwall if I wasn't busy and he would fly for me if things were slack for him. I don't think either of us would have survived without the other."*

In January of 1947, Kamloops Air Services had an urgent need for a ski-plane and Bray turned to the Aero Club for help, an event which he maintains helped ensure its financial survival for at least an extra year.

> *"A fellow came knocking on my door just after New Year's Day and said his brother was dying in the Azure Lake area. He asked me to fly in and pick him up. He said that the ice was probably pretty good up there by then; although, it hadn't been when he had left and walked out.*
>
> *"At the time, I didn't have any experience flying off skis and my Seabee was not equipped for skis; so I went across to the flying club where somebody found a set for their Tiger Moth and I got a very quick course of instruction on their use from somebody who had once flown off skis. They said that, when you land on those lakes at that time of year, the surface might consist of heavy snow on thin ice. Because of the heavy snow, there was likely to be a lot of the water on top of the ice, and if I were to break through the snow crust and get down into the slush, I would be in trouble. The trick, they said, was to fly down and bounce the plane on the surface a couple of time, then climb up and take a look. If*

there was nothing below but white I would be okay, but if there were dark patches then I should stay away. That was my total course on skis.

"I took the Aero Club's airplane and started north. We had a gas cache at Dunn Lake; so I landed there to refuel. It was a terribly rough experience. I thought that ski operations were not all that good. What I didn't realize was that the lake had frozen then broken up, then refrozen and it was like a sawtooth underneath. Being my first landing on skis, I thought that this must be fairly normal.

"We refuelled and set off north again. When we got to Azure Lake, I made a couple of passes and all looked good below; so I went in and landed. This one was beautifully smooth, totally different to the Dunn Lake operation. I was just thinking how nice skis really were, when I got this terrible sinking feeling and the aircraft went nose down through the ice. The wings held on the ice but the front cockpit where the passenger was filling with cold water and the passenger was yelling, 'We're goners, we're goners.' As he had the main handle for releasing the coupe top, we were goners unless he opened it; so I was shouting back, 'You're damn right, we're goners, unless you get that coupe top open.' We survived but the plane didn't, which helped the flying club somewhat since they got paid off in cash for the plane which they had originally acquired for almost nothing."

The Flying Club also managed to benefit financially from Harry Bray's charter service during the 1948 Fraser River flood when he had more business than he knew how to handle and was renting every available airplane to keep up with the demand.

"We got a call to bring a corpse out of Vavenby. There was one of the pilots with the flying club who had been doing a fair amount of bootleg charters and we had had words with him previously about this. Since we were using the

Flying Club's aeroplane on a temporary basis, we sent him off to do this job for us. Their plane was a little, Ercoupe side-by-side two-seater, quite small in the cockpit, and the pilot was rather large. The corpse wasn't exactly small either. I don't think he ever forgave us.

"The 1948 Fraser River flood was a wonderful bonanza. There I was down on my knees trying to get customers for all that time, then all of a sudden, I had so much business that I actually had to get the radio to announce, 'Please, don't phone Kamloops Air Services for aircraft because they don't have any more available.' People were standing in line to get aboard airplanes.

"We chartered L & M's Anson and ran it from Kamloops to Vancouver until we got flooded out. It was going day and night while the runway got shorter and shorter. That work probably kept L & M in business for about another year.

"We also chartered one of Queen Charlotte Airlines' Stranraers for a couple of trips. The flood was a wonderful bonanza. With the railway cut, flying was the only way to get from the coast to the interior. We just went from the crack of dawn until after dark every night."

After the flood, however, it was back to business as usual. As competition from Central B.C. Airways became intense, cooperation became the name of the game among those operators who saw themselves as their victims.

"The presence of L & M in Vernon did not really restrict our operations at Kamloops." says Bray, *"In fact they were allies against Central B.C. Airways when things got really rough. I was unable to hire a full time engineer; so L & M provided their engineer to work on our planes. I used to fly to Vernon to get the weekly checks done. One time, I ended up in hospital in the middle of summer. L & M were highly supportive and came up to Kamloops with their Stinson and carried on my contracts rather than have them fall into the hands of Central B.C.*

CMFT Collection #353.19 Neil Cameron collection

An Ercoupe like this one was borrowed from the Flying Club to transport a corpse from Vavenby.

"When they acquired their Anson, I ran it for a while. I had a licence for a service from Kamloops to Vancouver, and I used it for that service. I also obtained a licence for a service serving Kamloops, Vernon, Kelowna and Penticton. We ran that for a few days. On the inaugural run all the mayors were invited. For free, of course. They were just about the only passengers we had on that service. We may have had the odd travelling salesman and so forth, but the service was a financial disaster."

The help from Central B.C. Airways, however, took a different form. Russ Baker was following a vigorous program of expansion into the area and was always anxious to ease the "strain" on his competitors.

"When they got their biggest gun, which was a new Beaver, CF- FHB," says Bray, *"they would fly into some of my customers' camps. Usually it would be Hal Quin or Russ Baker that would pay the visit. They would look around and*

CMFT Collection #261.14 Mary Carstensen collection

Kamloops Air Service chartered a Q.C.A. Supermarine Stranraer, like these at Sullivan Bay, B.C., to cope with the extra business generated by the 1948 flood.

admire the camp and ask, 'Who do you have flying supplies in to you?' The answer of course would be, 'Harry Bray' to which their response would be, 'Gee, Harry Bray. He's one heck of a nice fellow, but he's really working too hard, and his equipment isn't in the best shape. It's not really well maintained because he's struggling so hard and hasn't got the finances to do it. You know, he's going to kill himself if he doesn't have someone take some of the load off him. We'd like to help him. Perhaps we could take some of this heavy freight that's really bothering him.'

"Then they would enquire about what I was charging, and if it was 6 cents a pound, offer to do it at 4 cents a pound. All they would need was some help to get a charter licence from the Air Transport Board.

"I had a lot of loyal customers who told me about things like this. They actually made sworn statements which helped me a lot when Central B.C. Airways applied to become the second charter operator out of Kamloops, which they were denied, but it didn't really make much difference as they held the forestry contract which was paying for their airplane. They still stole a lot of business from me, but after you have put in two dozen complaints to the Air Transport Board, there's no point complaining any more because no one is listening.

"One other ploy they tried was a kind of cat and mouse game. At one time I had only one Seabee in service. Whenever I left on a charter, Russ would have one of his stooges in town phone out to Kamloops Air Services for an immediate charter. Of course, the girl on the desk would have to tell them they would have to wait for a few hours. They would then wire the Air Transport Board complaining that we were not providing sufficient public service, giving details that on a certain day at a certain time, they had been unable to get an airplane.

"Just before the hearing on the second charter licence, one of the fellows involved developed a case of conscience. This fellow, God bless him, gave us a sworn statement about the affair then left town the day he was supposed to show up as a prime witness for Baker.

"By April 1, 1950, I was almost the only survivor left in central B.C., apart from Russ Baker's outfit. Willy Cooper was still going up in Terrace, but L & M and Taylor Cornwall had gone out of business. Bill Smith in Penticton had been killed and I'd bought the assets of the outfit in Trail the previous year. The charter business was pretty well dead. On April 1, 1950, I sold out to Central B.C. Airways. Part of the deal included a six-month contract with them as a pilot. My friends Dan McIvor and Dick Laidman assured me that in six months and a day I would be out of a job, but

it wasn't so. Russ Baker treated me well. I suppose I got much better pay, more security and certainly a lot fewer headaches.

"After I moved to Central B.C. Airways, I found that Russ Baker had no more financing behind him than I did. I suppose I should have hung on a little bit longer, but Baker had a much greater gift of the gab and better connections.

"When I started Kamloops Air Services, Bob Marcoux, Pete Hunting and I put our wartime credits into the business, something around $10,000. Bob Marcoux had a friend in Montreal who put in $15,000. Four and a half years later, we owned two Seabees, a panel truck, quite a bit of ground equipment, spare engines and so forth, for which we were paid $10,000. The people who put up the $15,000 didn't get a nickel, Marcoux didn't get a nickel, I didn't get a nickel and Pete Hunting didn't get a nickel. I just went around and paid up part of our debts. That was what we got out of Kamloops Air Services."

Although Central B.C. Airways was the victor in the air service war around the Kamloops and central B.C. area, most of the losers in the skirmish eventually benefitted from their loss. Almost all went to work for their victorious rival which developed (as Pacific Western Airlines) into Canada's third largest airline, and, as the company grew, these "losers" rose in seniority. When Harry Bray retired from PWA, he was the senior captain on the line, while Dick Laidman rose to become the company president for seven years in the 1960s.

PWA acquired Canadian Pacific Air Lines in the '80s, then in the same decade absorbed Wardair, to emerge as the international air carrier giant known as Canadian Airlines International.

18

MALIBU SEAAERO

The start of Vancouver's corporate flying

Perhaps British Columbia's most unusual flying service in the immediate postwar era was Malibu SeaAero. Set up in 1945 and only the second company to obtain a charter licence under the new postwar regulations, it maintained an aerial link to the Malibu Lodge on Princess Louisa Inlet.

Owned by Thomas Hamilton, founder of the Hamilton Aircraft Propellor Company, the Malibu Lodge was established as a high-class resort, with guests having the option of flying in on Malibu SeaAero's Grumman Goose or travelling on the company's yacht, a converted, ex-naval "Fairmile" patrol boat. In addition to serving their own lodge, Malibu SeaAero undertook charters for other customers, which led ex-RCAF flier, George Williamson, onto the company's payroll.

"In 1948, the Powell River Company acquired three Grumman Goose Aircraft and commenced operating one in the Queen Charlottes," says Williamson. *"The B.C. Electric Company had arranged for one to be shared by their construction arm, Northern Construction Company and by the Powell River Company. But Powell River was not in a position to charge for use of the aircraft, not having a charter licence. They got around that by having the aircraft operated by Malibu SeaAero on a management contract basis. I was hired by Malibu to fly this aircraft.*

"The Malibu Club operated unsuccessfully. Tom Hamilton, being a yachting enthusiast, had discovered Princess Louisa Inlet and thought he would like to share it with other people. He developed this lodge, at great expense, right at the entrance to the inlet. It was going to be an exclusive resort for all the wealthy people from Hollywood. The concept was there but, unfortunately, the clientele was not."

"Transportation to the lodge was by air and by sea, which accounts for the name SeaAero. When I went to work for them I was actually employed by B.C. Electric but more often than not I was off flying the Malibu aircraft. I was so busy that I might fly up to Malibu at seven o'clock at night, stay overnight and bring a load back in the morning. When I got to Vancouver, which was about a forty-five minute run, the other airplane would be loaded up waiting for me to take it up to the dam site at Bridge River. I would spend the day there then fly back about five o'clock, then get in the Malibu aircraft and fly back to the lodge for the night.

"Often, there would be supplies on the flights to the lodge, but Hamilton would not authorize flights unless there were paying passengers to go along. There was a spare room at

George F. Williamson with Cessna Citation.

CMFT Collection #303.1
George F. Williamson collection

the airport where they would store the freight, and I have seen that room full of stuff that they were crying for up at the lodge but he wouldn't allow us to fly it up. Then, when we got passengers, we might not have room for it.

"I recall one lady who went up. She had eleven suitcases. When we got all this stuff loaded, I had to climb in through the pilot's window. The bow was loaded. The aircraft was overloaded like you wouldn't believe. I taxied out to the runway and as I turned around out there I noticed nine black marks on the ground. I thought, 'Gee, that's funny;' so I opened the window and hopped out with difficulty and looked at my tailwheel. It was flat. It was shattered. I radioed back and they sent the mechanic out and he jacked the airplane up, installed a new tailwheel; then I lined up and took off. When I landed at Malibu, I thought the airplane was going straight to the bottom. The green water came over the bow. We didn't do that again!

"When I got back to Vancouver, I found out that we had no spare tailwheel. I made up a tailwheel out of an old block of wood laminated with a steel core. I got an old Seabee tire, cut the side out of it, nailed it on and used that to move the airplane around the hangar. In the morning I would take off with a serviceable tailwheel and come back and land and, if there was time, they would switch the tailwheel to the other airplane so I could fly it. If there wasn't time, I would take the airplane with the wooden wheel and taxi around to the seaplane ramp and take off on the water. It was almost a month before we were able to get a replacement tailwheel for that aircraft.

"My being utilized to fly the Malibu aircraft was not what B.C. Electric, Northern Construction and The Powell River Company wanted. More often than not, I was off flying the Malibu aircraft when the other aircraft was sitting idle.

"The service the companies were getting from Malibu was not satisfactory; so they decided to buy Malibu out. Er-

CMFT Collection #369.2 Inky Klett collection

B.N.P. Airways' Grumman Goose fleet in front of their hangar at Vancouver Airport, circa 1948.

roneously, they bought only the assets and not the shares of the company, and the Air Transport Board would not let them transfer the licence. All they basically bought was the aircraft and spares; so they ended up with the Malibu name but no charter. However, we continued as B.N.P. Airways, named with the initials of the three companies.

"We operated for several years without a charter. We applied for it but there were problems. Everybody in Vancouver was afraid of the wealth behind B.N.P. Airways. They were afraid we would blanket the coast with aircraft and put them all out of business, but that was never the intention. Eventually, we got a charter with restrictions. We were restricted to certain size airplanes which specifically spelled out the Grumman Goose and we were limited to two aircraft. The Malibu Lodge itself went under. It was unoccupied for a year or two, then it was sold to a non-denominational group called Young Life. As far as I know, it is still used by them as a summer camp. So the Malibu

CMFT Collection #338.38 Joe Lalonde collection

Malibu SeaAero's Grumman Goose CF-BHL. Note logo on nose.

SeaAero charter actually ended up in B.N.P. Airways hands and Malibu ceased to function as either a resort or an aircraft company."

As a footnote, it is of interest that Thomas Hamilton, the founder of Hamilton Standard, Hamilton Metalplane, Malibu Lodge, Malibu SeaAero, etc., is the same U.S. gentleman from Chapter 2, who built the Hamilton biplane in Vancouver during World War I.

CMFT Collection #338.41 Joe Lalonde collection

Vancouver's U-Fly Aeronca Chief, CF-BTR, in front of the Malibu SeaAero hangar at Vancouver Airport, circa 1946.

19

ENTHUSIASM AND HIGH INTEREST

The rise and fall of Associated Air Taxi

Unlike the majority of those who set up aviation related businesses at the end of World War II, Bob Gayer had not been in the Air Force, nor had he any prewar flying experience.

"I was a mining engineer and had made my living in the United States for a number of years," Gayer says. *"I came back to Canada during the war and I ended up walking all over B.C., mostly up and down, carrying a pack and looking at prospect holes. The net result of all this physical activity was that I decided there had to be a better way of doing things, and, with all the Air Force planes passing overhead, it didn't take too much imagination to figure out that better way.*

"Towards the end of the war, I had the opportunity to option a property from a prospector in the Nelson area. I had competitors interested in the options; so to get there first, I chartered an aircraft from Spilsbury and Hepburn, a twin engine Cessna Crane. At that time, Jim Spilsbury didn't have any regular pilots; so he hired Len Milne from the Aero Club of B.C. to fly the plane for me.

"Len and I became pretty friendly on the trip, and as we went back he said, 'You know Bob, this trip is costing you quite a few dollars. You could have learned to fly, rented an airplane and made this trip by yourself for a lot less than what this one charter is costing you.'

"I was certainly going to be making more trips by air so, as soon as I got home, my wife and I went out and took flying lessons.

"I didn't intend to start a flying business at that time, but Len Milne came to me with a proposition.

Loaned from Arnold M. Feast collection

No 11 Civil Flying Instructors Refresher Course, Brantford, Ontario, May-June, 1957. A. M. Feast second from left, bottom. Len Milne sixth from left, bottom

"'Bob,' he said, 'I'd like to borrow some money to start an aircraft charter business.' It wasn't a large amount of money, about $2,500. He was going to buy an aeroplane to charter out, but he would continue working at the Aero Club to have a regular source of income. It sounded all right to me so I put a few dollars in and became a minor shareholder.

"Len put the whole thing together as a fairly loose joint venture with one of his students, Dennis Pierce, and with

Bill Purcello. It started as a 'hip pocket' operation out at the airport. All we had was a card table with a phone on it and a chair to sit on in a small room about half the size of a living room. We had no money and probably had trouble paying the phone bill. I had plenty of time on my hands so went down to the airport to see what potential the business had and it was quite apparent that it had one hell of a future.

"As well as using our plane, we were borrowing airplanes when the need arose. We started out using a Fleet Canuck on floats, CF-DYT, and had a loose lease arrangement with Duncan Bell-Irving which enabled us to use his Fleet Fawn, CF-BQB. In addition, we chartered Queen Charlotte Airlines' Cessna Crane a few times. It was a great little airplane, twin-engined, and could carry a pilot and about half a passenger with a full load of gas—to be legal, that is. We had to fudge a little to get a worthwhile load into it.

Duncan Bell-Irving and Mrs. Bell-Irving with Fleet Fawn, CF-BQB.

Loaned from D. G. Bell-Irving collection

"We had to obtain more aircraft to keep abreast of the demands. Sometimes we purchased used aircraft and sometimes new ones. We could have kept our expenses down by buying RCAF surplus, but it was not as attractive as it appeared on the surface. You also bought yourself a lot of

CMFT Collection #468.7 Cecil Long collection

A Fleet Canuck with floats like this one was Associated Air Taxi's first aircraft.

work before your aircraft were ready to earn you any money. The biggest problem with buying the newer equipment was financing. Some of our aircraft were bought on lease-to-purchase arrangements at interest rates as high as forty-five percent. We had to try to earn the value of the aircraft in the first year and a half that we used it, otherwise we were dead.

"The largest of the other operators on the coast was Queen Charlotte Airlines, and, in reality, we were in competition with them although Spilsbury didn't seem to notice it. Jim was trying to run a 'Gentleman's Airline,' becoming a first class scheduled operation. We were a rougher sort of outfit. Jim had a big advantage. Running a scheduled service with large aircraft, his prices were much lower per seat. Where we had the advantage was that he was running to a schedule whereas we went upon demand. Up in the logging camps, there were always a few loggers who were in a hurry

to get to town when they had a few days off and didn't mind paying for the quickest way.

"When it was time to go back to camp, very often they had no money; so they would show up to get the cheapest seat, which was Q.C.A.s, but they wanted the seat on account. With Queen Charlotte, it had to be cash on the barrel head. When Jim wouldn't carry them on credit, they came to us. The guy had to get to work to earn the money for his next binge so he would ask us to charge it up for him—and charge we did. If we'd have had a one passenger airplane we could have got him to his job for $200 but were operating larger planes by then and one man in a four passenger plane would cost $800; so that's what we would have to charge.

"Operationally, it was the pilots who made our company. We were fortunate in some of our early choices, and it

CMFT Collection #275.26 Ingwold Wikene collection

Associated Air Taxi Grumman Widgeon at Vancouver Airport, summer, 1953.

became a sort of a club that grew. It was like joining a gentleman's club. You didn't get hired unless the other pilots accepted you. This led to the thing of which I was really proud. We operated a floatplane school. This wasn't a floatplane school for ab initio pilots but a school for pilots who already had their commercial licenses.

"We had found that the weather and water conditions on the west coast were totally unlike the conditions in the Arctic or north of Winnipeg. Out here you had to be able to land a small plane in high seas, get your passenger aboard, and get off again without wrecking the plane or breaking the floats.

"It was a different flying environment to that found anywhere else, and we decided it required special training. "By this time we had amalgamated with Port Alberni Airways, which had been started by Jack Moul in 1946. Their charter business was restricted by the poor weather conditions but they had always had a hankering to run a seaplane school; so we put an Aeronca 7AC on floats and based it at Port Alberni, where 'Slim' Crossen and Jack Moul gave the instruction. They taught our pilots to do almost everything that was possible with floats. We didn't teach pilots to land on glaciers with floats because it was too risky, but we had pilots who did it.

"Once we started the school, we refused to hire anybody who wouldn't go through our course. We were hiring a lot of pilots in those days and there were some who objected strenuously to the concept.

"I particularly remember one chap who was adamant that he wouldn't take the course. Kenny Kirk was just about to take a Cessna Crane on floats up to Halfmoon Bay under very severe southeaster conditions. He was only picking up one passenger; so I thought 'Here's my chance. I'll put this new guy in the co-pilot's seat and he'll maybe pick up something about flying in rough water conditions.'

"Kenny was alerted about this, and I suppose he might have pushed it a bit. From what I later heard, Kenny arrived at Halfmoon Bay and the co-pilot looked down and said, 'You can't land there.' Kenny just showed no concern and said, 'Oh certainly. It's a piece of cake,' and went ahead and put the plane down in the water. He had some difficulty taxiing to the dock without shattering the props due to the wave action, but he managed it safely, got his passenger aboard and took off for Vancouver, all blase about it. Upon arrival at Vancouver, this new guy got out of the plane and all he said was, 'How do I get over to Port Alberni to take that course?'

"In addition to training our own pilots, we did offer the course to outsiders. We would only accept commercial pilots, and we did put a premium price on it. It was tying up our best pilots and putting the equipment through a tremendous pounding; so it had to have a premium price.

"We started out as a charter operator offering what was virtually a taxi service, but the airplane is the poorest taxi ever built. As a charter operator there were disadvantages because you have to charge on a per-flight basis while there is often a lot of business available if you can charge on a per-seat basis. So after a while we also got into Class 2 scheduled operations.

"There were two things developing. One was the summer home traffic to the Gulf Islands and the other was the logging business. The boats were too slow for a lot of people. They took about four hours, whereas a flight with us only took about twenty minutes. That business rapidly grew to the point where we would have so many aircraft in the air that they were shuttling back and forth like yo-yos. On a holiday like the 1st of July, we would get so much business that we couldn't handle it; so we would charter Q.C.A.'s Stranraers and load them up with passengers, and they'd shuttle back and forth for us.

"Gradually, as the roads went in and better ferry services came in, this traffic dried up on us. But that was around the time that we sold out to Central B.C. Airways, which later became Pacific Western Airlines. We went through a very long, dry economic spell, a combination of long, hot summers shutting down logging operations for extended periods, followed by extremely cold winters. We had a lot of airplanes on lease-to-purchase at very high interest rates. The obvious course was to sell out when Russ Baker needed the licenses. In order to get established in Vancouver, he had to have a fixed base operation there. The Air Transport Board and the Department of Transport had gone as far as they were prepared to go with Central B.C. Airways unless Russ could acquire somebody else's existing licenses. So he commenced negotiations with us.

"After we had established our price, their negotiators came back saying that it was too high, explaining that our accounts receivable were not collectable, our aircraft were all a pile of junk and so on, and the only thing we had of any value were our licenses. They were wrong on all three counts. They kept whittling the price down; so we kept holding various bits and pieces. All Baker really wanted was the licenses; so, finally, that was all he bought.

"We were able to collect most of the accounts receivable which we had retained, and which turned out to be a lot more valuable than Russ Baker's accountants had thought. Then we sold off the aircraft and paid off the mortgage holder.

"After we settled with Central B.C. Airways, they virtually ignored the company they had purchased. They even gave up the telephone number, so 'Slim' Knights and Louise, who were both out of their jobs, got together and got the telephone number, calling themselves 'Associated Air Travels.' They were able to get a great number of calls for air charters, which came in on our well known number.

They provided airplanes for these customers by leasing and borrowing from other people. For a while they had a modestly successful business, more or less a charter brokerage outfit."

CMFT Collection #377.2 Joe Antonelli collection

Fairchild 82A, CF-AXE, was a heavy hauler for Associated Air Taxi in 1951-52.

Loaned from Lock Madill

With the advent of WWII civilian flying was suspended. Homebuilt airplanes like this Gibson/Milne Special shown at the opening of Vancouver Airport in 1934 were grounded. The homebuilt movement did not see a resurgence until the late 1950s.

20

A VANCOUVER SUCCESS STORY

From Vancouver's U-Fly to West Coast Air Services

When postwar civilian flying resumed at Vancouver Airport, it was virtually a fresh start as far as the small flying schools were concerned. Most of the prewar operators had departed and a new group of optimists moved in to fill the void. One prewar company that did, however, briefly reappear, was Gilbert's Flying Service, albeit with new owners.

"In 1937, my brother, Lloyd, learned to fly from Frank Gilbert," says Al Michaud, one of the two brothers who re-opened the school. *"Lloyd bought a small airplane, a little 38-horsepower Aeronca and used to leave it with Frank, who would rent it out when he was busy.*

"Gilbert had a partner named Bell who went to Trans Canada Airlines in 1939. Lloyd then bought Bell's interest in the partnership and became an instructor and a partner of Frank's. Later, they incorporated as Gilbert's Flying Service.

"In 1941, civil flying stopped in Vancouver. There were two problems. They were worried about the Japanese and there were restrictions on fuel. It was deemed that the only way to get fuel was on an essential basis, and this was hard, even though the flying service was doing a job. Mostly, they wanted to move the airplanes out of the coastal area. So the school moved to Kamloops for a short time to finish off some students, then was closed down.

"Frank wanted to get his money out; so Lloyd and I bought the airplanes even though they were not where we were able to use them. They were stored, until '45, in the interior where it was dry. We had a couple at Ashcroft and one at Cranbrook. In August of '45, we got permission to come back onto the airport, although the war was not quite over. We got fuel allotments and re-opened the school.

"As the business had been incorporated, we operated for the first several months under the old name Gilbert's Flying Service then renamed ourselves Vancouver's U-Fly, largely because we intended to keep training, although we were doing some charter. In '46, we became distributors for Cessna aircraft; so we got involved in the sales and servicing business.

"We operated out of a car at the start and, very awkwardly, without a telephone. To some extent, that was because telephones were not available. We eventually negotiated a little office which we had to share with B.C. Airlines—two competitors in an office that was about ten by twenty. At that time, we were able to negotiate a joint phone; so we had one phone and two carriers in competition."

If operating from a shared office was awkward for Vancouver's U-Fly, Bill Sylvester's B.C. Airlines also had their problems with the arrangement. One of U-Fly's first employees was the former ace salesman for the prewar Foggin Flying Service, Neil Cameron, and his duties as office manager were much the same as before, getting customers and making the bookings. B.C. Airlines found Cameron a thorn in their side even prior to moving into the shared premises.

"There was rivalry between Vancouver's U-Fly and B.C. Airlines during 1945, 1946 and maybe into 1947," says George Williamson, who flew for B.C. Airlines during this period. *"We had no offices and we operated from our respective automobiles. Neil Cameron would arrive early,*

CMFT Collection #468.3 Cecil Long collection

Left to Right: "Roly," Cecil Long, Neil Cameron, and Lloyd Michaud with Cessna 140 at Vancouver Airport, December, 1947.

on his little motorcycle, set up his office in this little phone booth, and he would hand out little cards or brochures on the advantage of going up for a ride, $3 for a fifteen-minute ride around the city.

"He'd see you talking to a potential passenger and come sidling up and put in his two bits worth. Pretty soon, he was doing the talking and you were sort of an interested bystander. The next thing you'd know, the passenger was being led out to the airplane. He would open the gate and invite them to go out and sit in the airplane. He'd get them in the airplane and then, 'Well, I could have the pilot here in a second and off you'd go on a ride.' He was a foxy man.

"Templeton, the airport manager, took pity on us and found this old building somewhere. They dragged it over on skids and stuck it up by the fence and permitted us to share it. Vancouver's U-Fly had a little desk in one corner and we had a desk in the other. Well, can you appreciate passengers

coming in with two people assailing them, to offer rides. It was kind of crude, and, in 1946, when you were trying to be private and talk on the phone, it was impossible. So U-Fly built their own office, and B.C. Airlines took over the old office and had it remodelled."

By 1948, the two rivals had developed in separate ways and the rivalry had somewhat decreased. While B.C. Airlines concentrated on charter business, Vancouver's U-Fly was more heavily involved in flying training and aircraft sales, although it was to eventually enter the charter field as a major operator.

B.C. Airlines was an early competitor at Vancouver Airport.

CMFT Collection #468.1
Cecil Long collection

"When we started," says Al Michaud, *"the only people operating a charter service out of Vancouver were Spilsbury and Hepburn, who later changed the name to Queen Charlotte Airlines, which became a rather dominant carrier on the coast itself. Then Bill Sylvester's operation, B.C. Airlines, was doing the majority of the charter out of Vancouver, but it kept growing.*

"The real breakthrough for us came when Cessna brought out the Cessna 180. They were priced quite a bit under the Beaver, which was on the market by that time.

B.C. Airlines' Cessna 180. West Coast Air Services, as distributors for Cessna, could also sell aircraft to competitors.

CMFT Collection #419.2
Lee Banting collection

The Beaver was a good airplane, and we later operated a lot of them, but it was a bigger airplane and cost a lot more money.

"The 180 was an inexpensive airplane that could perform with four people aboard, getting on and off the water without a struggle. That got us heavily into the charter business. We were selling these airplanes, and they were a hot item in those days. People wanted them because they were performers. That gave us the initiative to expand. We had the advantage of being able to buy these airplanes, keep them, then sell them after a year and always have a new airplane. Although our aircraft sales were a very marginal operation, it allowed us to replace our equipment annually or every second year; so our equipment was always nice and new, which was a basic advantage; so it remained a key part of the business.

"In the early '50s, the charter business was growing faster than the flight school business; so we eventually changed the name to West Coast Air Services to better incorporate what we thought was a general aviation business.

"We made the name change in 1954. It was at that time that we had started doing more dollar volume on charter flying than school flying. The school was doing about ten

thousand hours a year flying at that time, but we were limited on price. We kept our rates a little above the Aero Club, but it was a competitive situation; so it was marginal. We continued to run a flight school until 1963, but it became a less important part of our operation.

"We eventually started buying Beavers about '57. Pacific Western Airlines, which was built up from Russ Baker's Central B.C. Airways after it bought out Associated Air Taxi and moved to Vancouver, eventually bought out Queen Charlotte Airlines. As it grew, it became less interested in the charter business. They got right out of the seaplane business. Since we always got along very well with them, we took over some of their charter business, buying their bases at Kamloops and Nelson, and we bought their Beavers, three at that time, and some other equipment, parts, and accessories.

CMFT Collection #36.57 Mrs. H. Steenblok collection

West Coast Air Services' Beaver at Port Alberni, B.C.

"With the opening of the Pitt Meadows Airport, in 1963, the Department of Transport encouraged us to move our flying school there, but we elected to sell the training equipment and get out of the flying school business. Moving would have meant that we had to set up two separate bases, and the lack of management control concerned us. So we sold our remaining training planes to Skyway Air Services, on the basis that they would take over our students who were partially through.

"In the late '60s, Pacific Western Airlines became more interested in big airplanes than in the Mallards operating their smaller scheduled services on the coast; so they sold us those planes and the licences were transferred to West Coast Air Services. That got us into the scheduled carrier business, operating along the west coast to Tofino and Tahsis, and the north coast to Ocean Falls, Bella Bella, and Namu. That grew quite rapidly after we bought it.

"Pacific Western had been more interested in the big airplanes than those small runs. They had maintained that service but had not really worked at it. We ended up with as many as six Mallards at one time. Although, we were really basically only operating four. We had a pretty high rate on those routes because of the nature of being amphibious, but there was no other way to get there except by boat, and that was a long slow deal. Those Mallards did their job on the coast. They made a lot of sense. They were sturdy; they could stand the heavy water. They did a job. The nice thing about the Mallards is that we never bought a Mallard that we didn't sell for more money than we paid for it. They had an accelerating value at that time."

By the late 1970s, West Coast Air Services had become a major operator along the B.C. coast. However, changes were in store.

"In 1979, my brother and I," Al Michaud recalls, *"were approached by a group of investors. My brother had really*

wanted to get out for several years, and I was in the age group where I had to be practical about it and say, 'Well, maybe it's a good time.' So we sold our interest in West Coast Air Services.

"At that time, Dick Laidman had the vision of putting a number of charter companies together and developing an airline. He interested Jim Pattison in the idea. They bought Air West Airlines and four other companies, then, in early '80, bought West Coast Air Services from the group that had bought it from us and merged all these companies into what is today Air B.C."

21

FINDING A SPECIAL NICHE IN THE WOODS

The success of Skyway Air Services

The growth of Skyway Air Services from an ex-serviceman's one-plane flying school to a major Canadian aviation company resulted from a determination to succeed, a willingness to move into new ventures and the ability to gather together reliable people.

In 1945, Art Seller bought a Tiger Moth and started the Royal City Flying Club at Vancouver Airport, hoping to cash in on the fabled "postwar aviation boom."

"There were quite a few flying schools there," says Seller, *"and competition was pretty tough. We used to come out to Langley, where Trans Canada Airlines had an emergency strip. In late 1947 I decided to move my operation there. It was about that time that I renamed the business Skyway Air Services.*

"There were no facilities at Langley. Fortunately, the field had been a farm field and the old outside privies were still there. These I used, one as an office and the other as a fuel storage shed."

Shortly after the move to Langley, Seller met the business licence inspector for Langley, Ed Batchelor, and discovered that he was a former RAF Sunderland pilot and flying instructor and, in addition, was a qualified aircraft mechanic.

"I bumped into Arthur at just the right moment," says Batchelor, who was to become chief pilot for Skyway and

remain with them for thirty-five years. *"He needed an engineer and an instructor. I had managed to pick up both the engineer's ticket and a commercial licence, with an instructor's rating; so that's how we got together.*

CMFT Collection #277.5 Art Seller collection

Art Seller with Skyway Air Services Ltd. first office and first Tiger Moth at Langley Airport 1947.

"It took us quite a while to get the school really moving. Arthur got a little tear-drop trailer for an office and parked it by the side of the road. On rainy days we would go across the road to the old Blair farmhouse into the kitchen to keep warm.

"Our fleet grew a little bit. We added a couple of Fleet Canucks, then some Aeroncas, Luscombes and Piper Super Cruisers. Having all these odds and ends of airplanes often meant that we would have aircraft sitting idle in spite of having students wanting to fly. Often a student would phone but the type he flew was already booked while a plane of a

Skyway Air Services: Eleanor Jones, Dispatcher/Bookkeeper; Ed Batchelor, Instructor/Engineer, Langley, B.C.

CMFT Collection #277.4
Art Seller collection

different type was available. It was my dream to, one day, have a line of four airplanes all identical. Eventually, in 1953, we did achieve this. We got four Piper PA18s. By golly, that was wonderful.

"During this period we were the only operation using the field and did our own policing of flying discipline. Students were good; they used to pitch in. Whenever you needed manpower, you could nearly always find somebody willing to help."

While Ed Batchelor concentrated on building up the flying school end of things, Seller sought to build up the business in other ways.

"The event that made me decide to broaden the scope of my activities," recalls Seller, *"was an infestation of aphids in the pea crop in Ladner, in 1947. The farmers were threatened with total crop loss; so some Americans were called in with sprayplanes. They went home with more money than Royal City Flying Club made in a year. I decided to convert a Tiger Moth for crop dusting.*

"We started out with Tiger Moths, then got Stearmans with 450-horsepower Pratt and Whitney motors, which did a much better job. They were set up to take either dust or liquid sprays; so we could use the same airplane as a duster

or sprayer. Finally, we got Grumman Avengers. We used those on the 'Project Budworm' and as fire bombers."

Although the spraying and dusting operations were to provide the cornerstone of the company's fortunes in future years, initially it was a struggle to educate the farmers in the capabilities of agricultural aircraft and to obtain sufficient business in a given area to make the spraying worthwhile.

CMFT Collection #277.2 Art Seller collection

Dusting potatoes on the Savage farm, Ladner, B.C. circa 1948.

"We had complaints," says John Anderson, who commenced his commercial aviation career spraying for Skyway. *"There were some types of farmers who would get quite a kick out of telling you that you weren't flying low enough. They'd say, 'Get down, get lower and lower.' We'd come back in with potato tops hanging from the undercarriage, figuring that was low enough.*

"The flying was quite different in a lot of ways. You could call it a challenge. The business was relatively new and we had to feel our own way. Art and I were doing spraying and dusting in formation, which worked out very well, although I wouldn't recommend it for all people. We got so that our patterns were pretty much the same, and we knew what the other guy was going to do all the time. It had the advantage that you could see where the other chap's spray material was going and adjust yourself to the proper spacing.

"When we worked in the interior we worked down to pretty small acreages, even one or two acres. We wouldn't go into an area for less than a total of a hundred acres, but we'd ask one of the local farmers to organize a hundred acres and then we'd go in and pick off all these small acreages which made up the total. I used to carry a little motorized scooter which I'd strap to the wing of the Tiger Moth so that I'd have transportation on the ground, otherwise I'd have a long walk into town."

Skyway's entry into spraying and dusting set the company on the road to success. Seller's timing could not have been better because he was set up for dusting just in time to take advantage of some major opportunities.

"I would say it was the 1948 flood of the Fraser Valley that really got us going," says Seller. *"The whole Fraser Valley was flooded and the mosquitos were very bad. We got the job of spreading DDT. Johnny Anderson and I were throwing DDT dust from sun up to sunset. It didn't matter if it was windy or not because they wanted the dust to spread. We sprayed the whole Fraser Valley with DDT. If they did that today they'd throw everybody in jail.*

"Another good project was the Alcan Kitimat-Kemano construction project. When that commenced, they had a bad mosquito infestation, so we put a Tiger Moth sprayer on floats. I flew it up there averaging about $700 per hour, a $10,000 contract. That really helped us out. Between that

and the 1948 flood we managed to get on our feet because the flying school was long hours for little money.

" 'Project Budworm' is what really got us going. There was a Spruce Budworm infestation in New Brunswick. They wanted all the Canadian Stearman spray planes they could get; so I sent five out and put trusty Ed Batchelor in charge. He navigated them out."

Moving a fleet of aircraft from one side of the country to the other was a major undertaking. From 1952-55, Batchelor shepherded the Skyway's fleet of Stearmans eastward across the country each spring and back in the fall.

"The old Stearman did a wonderful job," says Batchelor. *"The hardest part of the whole thing was the journey there and back. We'd be airborne at first light, fly all day and make about 600 or 700 miles, because we had to be on the ground every hour and a half to refuel."*

Eventually, however, larger aircraft were needed and Skyway purchased some surplus Grumman Avengers (TBMs) from the Royal Canadian Navy to fill the need, but only after Seller had had a chance to see what they could do.

Skyway's Stearman sprayer pioneered the New Brunswick Budworm project. Later replaced by Grumman Avengers.

CMFT Collection #277.8
Art Seller collection

o

"There was an infestation of Spruce Budworm on Vancouver Island," says Seller. *"We called in three Americans with TBMs to handle the job. They carried 700 gallons of oil and DDT and proved to be excellent machines.*

"The next year, when the Canadian government declared eighteen of them surplus, I bid on them. We didn't have any money, but I bid on them anyway. I got seventeen for prices ranging from $1,700 to $7,000. They were beautiful machines, the RCN had kept them in first-rate condition. We got Fairey Aviation to do the spray plane conversion and then eventually into fire bombers. The TBMs were the machine that got us into fire bombing and sold the fire service on using our services.

"We actually started experimenting with the Stearmans. Ed Batchelor, Johnny Anderson, Les Kerr, and myself used to bomb fires with the Stearmans carrying 100 gallons of benthonite in the tanks. Unless the fire was just a very small smoker 100 gallons going down into the forest wasn't very effective.

"When we got the Avengers going, in 1958, it enabled us to do a real selling job on fire bombing. We showed that it was an effective way of fighting fires. Of course, to stop a fire you really have to go to the fire when it should be fought, while it is just a smoker. Surrounding it with chemical then stops it from spreading. The Avenger carried enough chemical to enable us to have a good chance of doing that."

While Skyway was growing into Canada's largest fire bombing and spray operation, the flying school had been kept going to supplement these activities. When Batchelor and the other experienced instructors headed off to New Brunswick each summer, Seller had other instructors willing to step into the breach.

"Our good friend and very reliable instructor, Harry Warman, used to help out," remarks Seller. *"He worked for Standard Oil. In those days we used to be able to tell a*

student, 'Well, we'll have a booking open tonight.' And after working at Standard Oil, Harry would come out and look after the flying school. He started instructing for us part time, weekends, evenings and summers, until eventually it got to the point where we needed staff and he came on full time."

At its biggest, Skyway Air Services grew to about 100 people and seventy airplanes of which twenty-five were in the flying-school fleet. The opening of Pitt Meadows Airport and the concurrent eviction of flight training from Vancouver Airport provided a boost to the flying school.

"Our school immediately started to grow," says Batchelor, *"Vancouver's U-Fly went out of business as far as flying training was concerned, and Arthur picked up most of their Cessna 140s. We picked up quite a lot of their students, too; so the school took quite a boost."*

In the mid '60s, Skyway had become a very large business. By seizing opportunities as they arose, the company had grown from a small flying school into the country's largest crop spraying and water bombing company with operations spread out from its home on the west coast right across to the east coast. For its founder, however, the business had grown too big.

"The pressure was there. People were getting killed and the pressure got to me," explains Seller. *"I decided that I'd better get out of this thing or I wasn't going to be here. So I sold off the spraying and fire bombing side of the business to Les Kerr, who set up ConAir, in 1969, to handle it. We had taught Les to fly and he was working for us at the time. I'm very pleased that I sold to the right person who kept it going and made it grow.*

"I came back to the flying school at Langley from the fire bombing and crop spraying base, which was at Abbotsford by then, and relaxed. I was a little tired of the noise and people so started a commercial glider school. I just wanted

to enjoy the thrill of sailplaning. It certainly didn't pay. I operated that for two to two and a half years.

"I was also developing a seaplane base at Fort Langley. When my son David bought Skyway Air Services from me in the early '70s, I decided to retire, but retirement didn't suit me very well; so I went back to my old haunt, Fort Langley, and have been developing a small airstrip there ever since."

Skyway Air Services has survived the departure of its founding father and thrives as a flying school at Langley Airport, while ConAir Aviation Ltd. has built the former Skyway water bombing operations into a worldwide operation and is now a world leader in this field. The crop spraying side of the business was sold by ConAir in the late 1970s.

From the small beginning as Royal City Flying Club, Art Seller's willingness to enter new fields of endeavour led to the development of a major company which has had major influence on the progress of aviation in British Columbia.

CMFT Collection #63.1 Art Seller collection

Tiger Moth spraying mosquitos near the Fraser River. Note spray booms under the wing.

22

B.C.'S WORLD-RENOWNED INNOVATOR

The pioneering Okanagan Helicopters

The vast majority of uses for aircraft have been pioneered outside of British Columbia and copied by entrepreneurs who have built their small companies up into major enterprises. One B.C.-based enterprise, however, can legitimately claim to have been a true innovator in its field. At the end of World War II, Carl Agar moved to the Okanagan to operate the South Okanagan Flying Club. Shortly afterwards, with three partners, he established Okanagan Flying Services in Kelowna. Seeking new fields of endeavour, the partners purchased one of the first helicopters to enter B.C., intending to use it for crop spraying. It proved unsuited to this task and Carl Agar was forced to find alternative work for the machine and in doing so became a true innovator.

Carl Agar has been widely recognized as being the father of mountain flying in helicopters. His drive and determination enabled helicopters to revolutionize the mining industry and brought substantial benefits to the B.C. economy in the mid-50s as Okanagan Helicopters flew high into the mountains speeding up survey and construction projects. From its humble beginnings, Okanagan Helicopters has grown to become one of the largest helicopter operators in the world.

One of Agar's partners was Alf Stringer, who had served as an aircraft mechanic in the British Commonwealth Air

Training Plan during the war. He worked with Agar throughout the formative years of Okanagan Helicopters and was a director of the company until 1963. Stringer saw all the major innovations which Okanagan Helicopters brought to the helicopter industry, which was just in its infancy in the late 1940s.

"The first winter after the war I spent working in a garage in downtown Vancouver, because I couldn't find any work in the aviation business," relates Stringer. *"Then I heard that the South Okanagan Flying Club was going to start up in Penticton and that my friend, Carl Agar, was one of the founders. He came to Vancouver and we went out and had a couple of cups of coffee together. Then he let me know that they'd decided to hire me as the maintenance engineer to go to Penticton and look after the Tiger Moth.*

"We had our difficulties in keeping this little show on the road, but we managed to keep it going. We went down to Osoyoos and to various and sundry little airstrips where we could do some training, hunting for students. We spent, maybe, four days a week in Penticton and then went someplace else for two or three more days a week to try and pick up a student or two.

"We eventually ended up with two Tiger Moths doing training. Then Carl Agar, Barney Bent, Andy Duncan and myself put our heads together. We decided that the Tiger Moth was not the thing for elementary training because Cessna were then producing a little high-wing aircraft that was being well accepted in the United States as a trainer. It was more modern and so was more appealing. We decided that we would apply for our own charter for a commercial flying school. We eventually received our licence and bought a Cessna. That got us started as a partnership, doing elementary flying training up in the Okanagan Valley. We did some training in Penticton and some in Rutland up in the Kelowna area. That was 1946.

"In the late summer of '46, Carl read an aviation magazine item about Central Aircraft doing tests on some Bell helicopters in Yakima, fitting spray gear to them to try and get it approved by the Federal Aviation Authority. We decided that we'd get in a car and go down to Yakima and have a look at the helicopter, talk to the people in Central Aircraft, who'd been involved with fixed wing for years, and see why they were thinking of transitioning to helicopters for spraying and dusting.

"They were very receptive to us, and we picked up a good deal of information from them. On the way back from Yakima we decided that we would dedicate our winter to going around to the orchardists and seeing if we could raise enough interest to buy a helicopter. In the spring of 1947, Okanagan Air Service was established, and the money was there to order a helicopter.

"Carl and myself went down to Yakima for training. I took a mechanics course and Carl started his flight training. Carl went back to Penticton and did some more training with the Cessna, then came back down to Yakima in time to pick up a few more hours in the helicopter, then ferried Okanagan's machine back to Penticton in the fall of 1947, just in time to do some minor spraying.

"We were pressed into service pretty quickly because the Department of Entomology in Summerland wanted to get some test-spraying done just to see what the machine would do. They brought various pieces of equipment down and set them out on the airport at Penticton, and we flew spray-patterns, changing the jets and different things, until we got the droplet size they wanted. Then we went up to Kelowna, to the Rutland area, and started to do the first spraying.

"It was in one of the first fields that Carl ran into a power line. After we got the machine packed up and shipped away, we discovered that there was a machine in Vancouver doing very little. It was owned by a Winnipeg outfit called Skyway.

Paul Ostrander brought it up to Kelowna, that first fall, and we worked with them for a while to finish our commitments.

Loaned from Ingwold Wikene collection

Bell 47, CF-FZN, at Sullivan Station, Surrey, B.C., summer, 1947.

"I spent that first winter in Yakima rebuilding our machine, getting it back to something that was flyable. In the meantime, Bell had brought out various and sundry modifications, which we incorporated to update the machine as much as possible.

"We had got the helicopter because we were convinced, after our visit to Yakima, that it had a great future for spraying and dusting in the Okanagan Valley, but we found out otherwise pretty early. Because of the size of the orchards in the Okanagan, the helicopter was just not compatible with spraying. An orchardist might have a thirty-acre orchard, but it would be broken down into ten acres of peaches and ten acres of pears and seven acres of apples

and so on, each section needing different sprays at different times of the year. If you got the drift-off from one section onto a neighbouring crop you could get into some big problems. Because we saw the spray field narrowing down, we had to start looking somewhere else for work.

"The second summer, 1948, was a year that they had a major flood in the Fraser Valley. After this flood, there were a lot of low swampy areas left that were ideal breeding grounds for mosquitos, and the mosquito infestation was just tremendous.

"We were asked to come down and spray some 2-4-D and to kill mosquitos. We sprayed all kinds of things on them. We sprayed mixtures of anything that would emulsify. You'd never get away, today, with the type of applications of sprays that went on at that time.

"We also got some work in the Kootenays spraying Hemlock Looper. This was bigger acreages, ten or eleven thousand acres, and was something for which the helicopter was just excellent, because it could follow the terrain better than a fixed-wing aircraft and land in any little field to be refilled. It worked out very well.

"That first fall we got the first survey job doing topographic surveys in the Cheam Range out from Hope. That's when Carl started to develop his mountain flying techniques for which he became very famous. Landing at those heights with that little power in a helicopter just hadn't been done before. Carl used to say, 'Every landing was a controlled crash. You just looked at the spot where you wanted to land and you were there. You didn't do any hovering. You had to be right the first time or you were going to bend things.'

Getting off was equally spectacular because he always tried to land near a lip or some type of ridge so he could leap off, stick the nose down and head down into a valley or ravine to build up enough speed to get away.

CMFT Collection #145.1 Textron Inc. collection

Carl Agar and Bell 47G on mountain pad.

"Because the machine was so underpowered, it was very restricted in the things it could do, and it was difficult to convince people that the machine had the capabilities to do different jobs. It wasn't so hard to convince people who'd really been out in the bush, climbing around on foot for years. Once they got into the helicopter and discovered it could go places in thirty minutes that had taken them three days previously, they didn't need additional convincing, but when you went in to talk to some mining company or forestry people that had been used to timber cruising by walking through bush and looking up at the trees, it took a lot of selling. Topographic surveys were quite different. They accepted the helicopter initially and they were all for it.

"In the fall of 1949, Carl Agar flew Professor Heslop from the University of British Columbia in the Kitimat area. That's when the routes for the powerline from Kemano over to Kitimat were surveyed. That was the initial step in the big Alcan project, which turned out to be a major milestone for

Okanagan. We were in on the ground floor. Okanagan was there for many, many years during the construction of that whole project, and then afterwards.

"Because the spraying business in the Okanagan was not economic, we had to develop other work. Since we were getting calls from the Fraser Valley and Vancouver area, we decided we should move to Vancouver. In 1949, we moved down and we worked out of a little space leased in the B.N.P. Airways hangar.

"There were no other helicopter operators in Vancouver at that time. Skyway (the Winnipeg company) had folded, but their machine had been sitting, damaged, in Vancouver for some time. We took it over and repaired it. Then we had two machines; so we then had to get another pilot. Bill McLeod was the first pilot that was actually hired by Okanagan, as such, to be on the permanent payroll."

McLeod had learned to fly with Len Foggin (Foggin's Flying Service) before World War II, then served in the RCAF. After the war, he flew with B.C. Airlines and Queen Charlotte Airlines but was seeking new opportunities.

"I was renewing my instructor's category and had a couple of offers of jobs." says McLeod. *"One day Alf Stringer got a hold of me. He said, 'Carl wants to see you in the coffee shop.' So I went over. Carl looked at me and said, 'How would you like to learn to fly a helicopter?' I said, 'I've never even seen one.'*

"He said, 'I've got a job to do with one. How about coming along with me. You'll be able to see one and see what you can do.'

"The job was to fly up alongside a smokestack in Marpole, hook a hook onto it and throw a continuous rope down for the steeplejacks.

"It was a beautiful day, with a steady westerly wind blowing about twenty-five mph, which was ideal. I had to

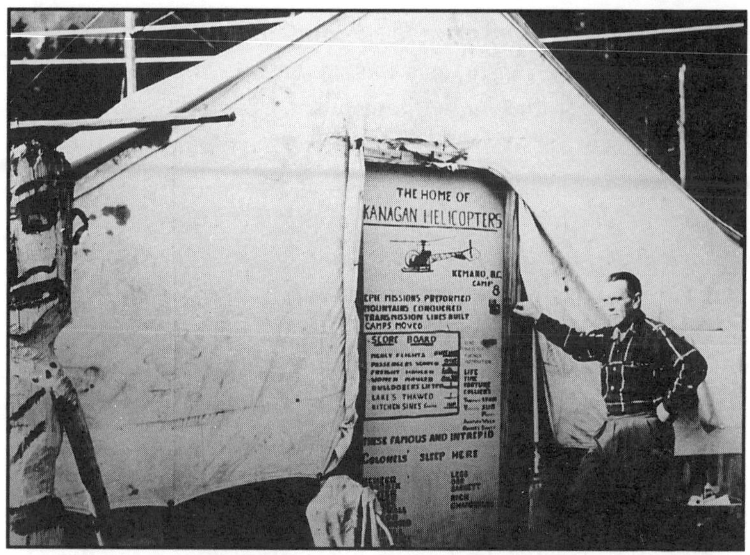

THE HOME OF
KANAGAN HELICOPTERS
KEMANO, B.C.
CAMP 8
MOUNTAINS CONQUERED
TRANSMISSION LINES BUILT
CAMPS MOVED
SCORE BOARD
LAKES THAWED
THESE FAMOUS AND INTREPID
COLONELS' SLEEP HERE

CMFT Collection # 330.39 Lock Madill collection

Okanagan Helicopters Camp 8, Kemano, B.C. at the beginning of the Alcan project, circa 1950.

undo my belt, climb out, put one foot out on the wheel leg and fix the hook onto the stack. I got back into my seat then realized that this long hook was against my stomach. I got back out, got one foot against the chimney, leaned over and pushed the airplane away until we cleared the hook. I gave him the sign. As we went away I thought, 'If you can do that, then I'm going to learn to fly it.'

"That's how it all started. I was the first person Carl ever trained on a helicopter.

"Carl had done a little mountain work and taught me what he knew. That first season, I kept learning by scaring the devil out of myself and surviving. Every time you scared yourself bad enough, you figured out another way of doing it so you wouldn't scare yourself quite so bad the second time. I learned a tremendous amount that first year and developed procedures that are still in use today.

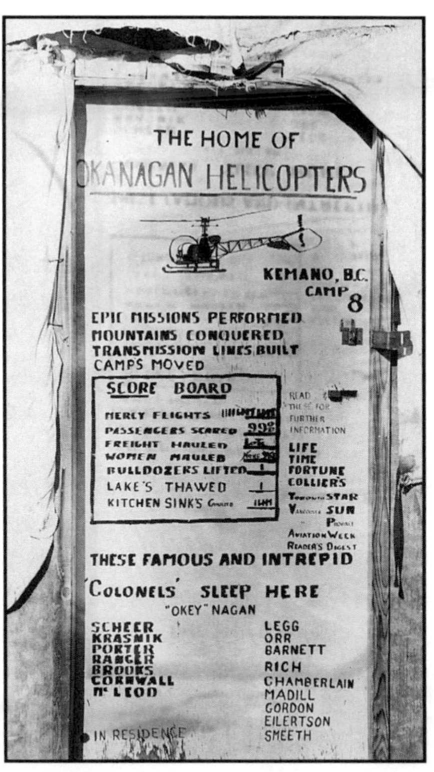

THE HOME OF
OKANAGAN HELICOPTERS
KEMANO, B.C.
CAMP 8
EPIC MISSIONS PERFORMED
MOUNTAINS CONQUERED
TRANSMISSION LINES BUILT
CAMPS MOVED
SCORE BOARD
MERCY FLIGHTS
PASSENGERS SCARED 99%
FREIGHT HAULED
WOMEN HAULED
BULLDOZERS LIFTED 1
LAKE'S THAWED 1
KITCHEN SINK'S
READ THESE FOR FURTHER INFORMATION
LIFE
TIME
FORTUNE
COLLIER'S
STAR
SUN
AVIATION WEEK
READER'S DIGEST
THESE FAMOUS AND INTREPID
'COLONELS' SLEEP HERE
"OKEY" NAGAN
SCHEER
KRASNIK
PORTER
RANGER
BROOKS
CORNWALL
MCLEOD
LEGG
ORR
BARNETT
RICH
CHAMBERLAIN
MADILL
GORDON
EILERTSON
SMEETH
IN RESIDENCE

Detail of sign on Camp 8 tent. Note that several names have been added.

Loaned from Lock Madill collection

"We had a very underpowered helicopter and it was fairly heavy. One thing we hadn't learned right away was that, when you landed at high altitude, you landed immediately adjacent to an edge, because you didn't have enough power to get off. You literally threw yourself over the edge and lost height.

"Probably my worst scare was when I landed about thirty feet from an edge, facing the edge. When I took off I realized, just as I went over the edge, that I was going to go over but the tail wasn't. I booted on hard rudder and shoved the stick ahead and cartwheeled it over. I cleared the tail and scared the hell out of myself and my passenger, but I got away with it.

"After scares like that, you put your thinking cap on and say, 'Well, obviously you can't get away with that as standard practice.' So you figure out another way of doing it. After that, I always attempted to land sideways to the drop off, if possible, and then, as the body of the aeroplane went over, the tail of the aeroplane went over with it.

"Every year there was something new. Nothing ecstatic, but I don't think I got complacent about a helicopter until I had about ten years on them, because there was always something new coming up. Somebody always wanted me to pack a heavier load or go to a higher altitude or something that I hadn't tried before.

"The Alcan project was the real start of major civil use of helicopters. When I went up in February, 1951, the idea was to go up and meet the survey crew to give them a two-week lead time on the construction crew which was following. When the construction crew came up, they started using the helicopter as well as the surveyors. We were only supposed to be there for six weeks, but at the end of six weeks you couldn't get that machine away from them for anything, they found it so useful.

"We put another machine in. Okanagan didn't have the resources to buy machines, and Alcan bought the Sikorsky S55s and more Bell 47s. Okanagan operated them on a lease basis and wound up purchasing them at the end."

Alf Stringer was also heavily involved with the Alcan project and sees it as one of the most important milestones in the path to commercial acceptance for helicopters.

"The Alcan project was a big, big project," says Stringer, *"and the helicopter played a major supporting role for moving personnel and equipment, something that hadn't been done to that extent before on anything that size.*

"When we first went in there, they just had a tent camp set up, and that's the way the crews lived the first winter. The helicopter was out in the open, and there was all kinds

Loaned from Lock Madill collection

Okanagan Helicopters crew at Kemano, BC, about 1953 or 1954. Left to Right: Lock Madill, Frank Ranger, Jock Graham, Bill Smith, and George Chamberlain.

of snow removal and de-icing to be done. It was quite a program to keep the machine serviceable through the winter months.

"Initially we didn't know what the demands were going to be, and I'm not convinced that Alcan didn't either. To them, the machine was a relatively unknown quantity. They learned what it would do as they went along. As they learned they would say, 'Well, we need another machine if we are going to do this.' So we'd get another machine organized for them and it just grew from there—out of strict necessity as far as we were concerned.

"We used Bell 47s for a while and then got the first Sikorsky S55. They discovered it would haul enough, in the way of people and equipment, to be just what they needed.

It hauled weights of materials in for them that moved their project on considerably faster than they could have moved it any other way."

CMFT Collection #330.7 Lock Madill collection

Okanagan Helicopters' Sikorsky S55 at Kemano, B.C., 1953-54.

Okanagan's pioneering work in mountain flying not only opened new ground for the helicopter; it influenced the development of the machine itself.

"We were still operating with wheels," relates Stringer. *"It was a little while before they came along with the skid gear. Carl and I had spent quite a bit of time talking to Bell about a different type of landing gear, because the wheels were heavy, ungainly and not very successful in landing in rough terrain in the mountains. We were trying to convince them that, because the helicopter could land vertically, they didn't need wheels on the thing. They eventually built a skid gear, which was the best thing that ever happened, as far as we were concerned.*

CMFT Collection #330.11 Lock Madill collection

Bell 47 and Sikorsky S55 at West Tahtsa Lake, approximately 1953 to 1955.

"We had a job over on the west coast. An outfit wanted to move a couple of small drills into a site near Ahousat. We went over there and set up a base camp near an ocean site and hauled their material to the top of the mountain. That got the mining companies talking about helicopters being the way to go as far as hauling camps in to remote areas and servicing the camps after they were in there. They had been using fixed-wing aircraft for many years hauling their food supplies into a lake then backpacking their equipment up the mountain. So then the helicopter took off from the lake where the aircraft left the stuff and hauled it right to where they wanted it.

"We gradually got into forestry. With the mining companies using it and Alcan using it, there was a great deal of public information about the helicopter and its versatility. The B.C. Forest Service had accepted the machine for doing

forestry patrols and various sundry things. The forest companies gradually saw the light and decided that these machines actually had some application for them in hunting for new roads in the bush, hauling crews in to do certain jobs, and hauling in fallers.

"We expanded eastward. We moved into Toronto Island Airport when we took over what was then Canadian Helicopters. Vancouver was the head office for all of Canada, but the machines that were working out of eastern Canada were maintained at Toronto Island Airport, although the major overhauls were done at Vancouver.

"When we were first into Toronto they were starting to do some of the initial supply into the far north for what turned out to be Mid-Canada Line. So we started some of the initial survey work. Helicopters were working with their snowcat trains, following these trains along and picking out routes where they could best travel. They were using the helicopter as a sort of seeing eye dog to pick their way through these areas.

"The Mid-Canada Line turned out to be a very important part of the company's growth, because we inherited ten Sikorsky S55s to maintain and operate. We were on the western end of the Mid-Canada Line. Our easternmost point was Winisk. We used a good many of the crews that we already had and some crews from Canadian Helicopters that had S55 experience. We were able to start with company crews, but we had to hire some more maintenance personnel and get them trained down at Sikorsky.

"In the late '50s, we were looking more at the expansion of numbers of helicopters than new types of work, because of increased numbers of customers. Okanagan was expanding across Canada and, at one stage, did a short jaunt over into Europe to try and get into the off-shore oil business. They were successful for a short period of time, but then politics pushed us out; so they were back into Canada again.

CMFT Collection #330.35 Lock Madill collection

One of the ten RCAF Sikorsky S55's Okanagan Helicopters maintained and operated on the Mid-Canada D.E.W. (Distant Early Warning) line contract.

"The Canadian helicopter industry was certainly starting to show signs that it would be desirable to go international, to be able to get more utilization out of the machines. In Canada, your major work is in a five-month period in the summer time, maybe even less than that. So you have a lot of unused time potential on the helicopter. It helps if you can find some source of supply to use that time, and operating internationally certainly helps. But we found that, very frequently, while it may be good for a short period of time, when you get into an international project, they want the machines year around; so you are not going to get the machine back to Canada for your summer work. You are just going to be adding machines to your fleet rather than increasing the utilization of some of those you already have.

"When we got into the '60s, there started to be some problems. As the Mid-Canada Line work tapered off, we had to lay off a good many personnel who'd been with the

CMFT Collection #330.23 Lock Madill collection

Acceptance of Okanagan's first S58 at Teterboro Airport, N.J., circa 1958.

company for a number of years. That was a heart breaking thing. Okanagan really had to fall back to regroup at that stage.

"At that time Carl Agar had developed emphysema; so his contribution, of necessity, had to become less and less. I started to become disenchanted with the operation due to some politics that had come into the company. It finally got to the point where I figured, 'Well, I'm still young enough to make a change; so I'm going to do it.' Carl was not well enough, because of this emphysema, to fight this circle any longer and had to back off because of his health. So about that time, in 1963, I decided that I'd come over to Victoria and manage Vancouver Island Helicopters."

Since 1963 Okanagan Helicopters has metamorphosed and has been renamed, but has remained one of the giants in the helicopter world with operations now being conducted worldwide.

Vancouver Island Helicopters, the small company to which Alf Stringer moved, grew under his managership for the next twenty-two years until he retired in 1985, and is yet another B.C. success story.

23

FIGHTING THE FIRES IN A BIG WAY

The Martin Mars of Forest Industries Flying Tankers

by Arnold Feast

Innovation, being the adaptation of existing equipment to new uses, is seldom easily achieved. In the twentieth century, innovation in aviation is rarely the work of an individual or a single organization, and many innovations have occurred simultaneously in several places. So it was with "water bombing."

Both in Canada and in the U.S.A., there had been experiments in water bombing. In the 1950s, the Province of Ontario was in the forefront of the efforts to develop water bombing systems, thanks largely to the advent of the ubiquitous de Havilland Beaver. This rugged single-engine machine and the subsequent larger equivalent, the DH Otter, paved the way for the first meaningful fire-suppression techniques. B.C.'s Al Michaud of West Coast Air Services was the first to adopt the Ontario Air Service's unique rotating water tanks on his Beavers to combat forest fires. West Coast Air was quickly followed by Pacific Western Airlines, Skyway Air Services and virtually every operator with suitable aircraft.

However, even their most sanguine supporters had to concede the limitations of such aircraft. Their load capacity, range, and speed were all too frequently inadequate to stem major forest conflagrations common to B.C.'s vast forest preserves. W. (Bill) F. Waddington, manager and senior pilot of Forest Industries Flying

Tankers, for many years until his retirement in the early eighties, spelled it out:

"Given dry, tindery forest conditions, a newly ignited fire can spread over an area of five acres in fifteen minutes. If not contained very early at this critical point, the blaze can become a raging inferno beyond any immediate efforts to check it."

As the flames and heat grow, even mature trees in the path of the fire will "candle," the trunks bursting instantaneously into flame from treetop to bole. Others "crown", their topmost branches igniting first then casting fiery tendrils downwind, far ahead of the advancing perimeter of the fire. As the oxygen over the burning area is consumed, the surrounding air rushes in with an ever-increasing velocity to fill the vacuum and fan the inferno with gale-like winds.

The concept of fighting forest fires by bombing the flames with water was first broached shortly after World War I. Almost as soon as the aeroplane had been developed into a practical if somewhat unreliable means of transport, suggestions were being made for its use as an aerial fire fighter. Even as early as 1920, when aircraft were still a novelty, the Canadian Air Board received proposals for so employing aircraft.

"Whilst I was operating at Victoria Beach," states Air Vice Marshall Leigh Stevenson, who flew the early HS2L and F3 flying boats, *"we got a set of elaborate blueprints showing how to carry water in an aircraft, the idea of a water bomber. Using our old F3 flying boat as a rough pattern, the designer had devised some big swing doors for the bottom of the hull. When you landed on the water, you were to open the doors to fill the hull with water which could be dropped on fires.*

"At that time, it was a little ridiculous because we had a hard time getting off the water with full tanks of gasoline. I

can remember having to pump fuel into Lake Winnipeg in order to get off of smooth water. Those machines were pretty sadly underpowered."

If this proposal was impractical at that time, aircraft still had their place in the arsenal of equipment which could be used to fight forest fires. In 1928, Cecil Coates got his introduction to aircraft when Dominion Airways obtained a contract to fly fire patrols in the Nelson area.

"Ted Dobbin came in with a Cirrus Moth on floats, and he suggested that I learn to fly with his school in Vancouver, which I did." says Coates, *"The next year I flew to Nelson as a co-pilot and observer with Ted Dobbin on forestry patrol in the Cirrus Moth on floats.*

"We would take off in the morning about, six o'clock, fly up the Kootenay Lake, across the Lardeau, go down the Arrow Lakes and back to Nelson. We would fly this circle twice a day at about 10,000 feet, if we could get that high, looking for forest fires, which are very hard to spot. If we spotted one we would report it, and they would get men up there as fast as they could."

The planes of the '20s may not have been much more than aerial lookouts, but, to some observers, the aeroplane offered the potential of becoming a true fire fighter. Dan McIvor, later to become instrumental in promoting the large water bomber concept, recalls his early impressions.

"When I was about eight years old," relates McIvor, *"mother and I were down at the beach near our cabin. An aeroplane went over, the first I had seen, and she told me what it was and that there were men up in it looking for forest fires. I knew in my own mind that when they found one, they would drop something on it and put it out. It was years before I realized that they didn't have anything to drop on it to put it out."*

By the late 1940s, McIvor was flying for Queen Charlotte Airlines on the B.C. coast. He spent a year at Zeballos and it was while there that he developed his intense interest in aerial fire fighting.

> *"They had a bad fire on the Tahsis Canal up on a steep sidehill, and they had no way at all of fighting it. They couldn't get equipment up; men couldn't handle it. A water bomber would have just cut it right off. Gordon Gibson and I talked for quite a while about getting a Stranraer from the company and turning it into a water bomber. But it came to nothing, and eventually I was transferred back to Vancouver.*

McIvor's idea of using large aircraft as water bombers to fight B.C.'s forest fires was to remain dormant for several more years, while he went to work for Pacific Western Airlines, with whom he flew the B.C. Forest Service contract for five seasons, working on just about every major fire during that period. The turning point came following his joining MacMillan & Bloedel, where he flew executive aircraft for another five years.

> "Once again I was involved with fires and I couldn't understand why nobody in B.C. was interested in using aircraft to drop water onto fires. Eventually, Ontario tried a system of dropping water-filled, paper bags and claimed some success. We decided to give the system a try and 'Inky' Klett organized a method whereby we could drop the bags from the company's Grumman Goose."

Ingvar (Inky) Klett, who, as a mechanic for B.N.P. Airways, maintained the Grumman Goose owned by West Coast Transport, MacMillan & Bloedel's aviation wing, recalls McIvor.

> *"In our area, out here, it seemed as if the only person interested in really fighting fires from the air was Dan. It might have been a result of all the fire patrols he would do. He would do two hour flights every night during the summer and would see how the little fires would spread overnight, and it didn't seem to matter how much the people on the ground would do trying to control it; they just weren't doing*

it. He felt they should do something about this, get lots of water to put on it.

"There must have been people in Ontario working on the program because we were able to get drawings for some of their schemes. We installed two sets of rollers in the Goose to take paper bags full of water. It was a cumbersome system. We had to fill these stout paper bags with water, seal them and then have them all sitting on the floor, The Goose would fly over the fire and with the two doors off, the bags would be put on the rollers and pushed out of the plane. It was not the world's best way of doing it. I always said, 'Couldn't you use a bag made out of something that didn't burn?' "

Despite the crudity of the system, McIvor was able to demonstrate to local fire fighters that water-filled bags dropped from the air, rendered aircraft capable of becoming more than just firespotters.

"We went out to a lightning strike and dropped about forty bags on it, five at a time," remembers McIvor *"I could hardly believe it when the ground crew sent in to mop up reported that we had controlled it. There was not a sign of the fire left. The idea of attacking a forest fire with bags of water is ridiculous, but in this case it had worked.*

"The next step came when Ontario devised some rotating tanks to fit under the wings of Beavers and Otters. The Beaver could only carry eighty gallons and the Otter 160, but they achieved some successes fighting small fires.

"I was a member of the Fire Protection Committee and it was our duty to find ways of fighting fires. We decided that if one operator would fit these tanks into a Beaver or Otter, and if the B.C. Forest Service would charter that airplane to fight a fire, then pretty soon we would have airplanes available all over the place.

"Al Michaud of West Coast Air Services was the smart one, he put a set of tanks on one of his Beavers. He got them

installed at ten o'clock one night and the very next morning that plane was off fighting a lightning strike around Sechelt. The Forest Service chartered that plane for ten hours that day and almost immediately Pacific Western Airlines, Skyway Air Services and everybody else was equipping their aeroplanes with tanks."

These small, externally fitted tanks made some impact on fires, but they were far from ideal. However, as a major forestry company, MacMillan & Bloedel could not afford to ignore the potential of this weapon in the war against forest fires and had a set of the tanks installed on its Grumman Goose, the aircraft which McIvor flew.

"The tanks were put on the side of the Goose," says Inky Klett, who did the installation work, *"which I don't think was a very good place to put them. They had filling tubes which extended into the water, but the plane could only carry ninety gallons at the most, and a lot of that spilled out on take off. However, they did prove the point that a fire could be cooled down by water bombing. Dan took that plane over to Sproat Lake and made about twenty-one round trips, picking up and dropping, on a fire that had been specially set for the purpose. Those drops got the fire put down or cooled down."*

The use of small airplanes to fight fires proved that the concept was practical. However, the amount of water they could drop was only effective on small fires. McIvor was not satisfied with the results being achieved; he wanted something more effective.

"We operated that whole summer using Beavers and Avengers. It was like dumping on bonfires with a cup of water. We could put out the small fires, but for a bigger fire we needed more water. It was that simple. For the big timber in the Vancouver Forest District, we needed a bigger plane.

"I started looking for a large flying boat because it was obvious that it had to be an aircraft capable of picking up

water on the lakes or sea. I looked for every flying boat I'd ever heard about, the old China Clipper, the Short Sunderland, the Canso and the Martin Mariner. Either they weren't around any more or they weren't available. I remembered reading about a great big airplane some years before. It was so big that a man could stand up inside the wing, actually walk out along the wing, open a door and service the engines in flight. I went to the airport one day and enquired about this plane and Bobby Bourne told me it was the Martin Mars. He also told me that they were being sold by the U.S. Navy as surplus.

"It was too late to buy them directly from the U.S. Navy, but I was able to find out who had bought them and what they had paid for them. A proposal was submitted to the management of MacMillan Bloedel, pointing out that the aircraft were capable of putting 6,000 gallons of water on a fire. This got us permission for Harold Rodgers of B.N.P. Airways, two engineers from Fairey Aviation and myself to go to Alameda to inspect the machines. They were in beautiful shape. They had been flying up until two years previously and much of the equipment was like new. We came back with the recommendation that the four machines be bought and one converted for trial as a water bomber.

"I was convinced that the Mars was just the aircraft we needed, but the directors turned us down. I was very unhappy with their decision until a friend pointed out that most things get rejected the first time and that you don't quit, you just keep trying.

"I went to vice president Ernie Shorter and told him that this thing was too good to let drop. He suggested that I get a report prepared that the directors couldn't turn down; so Duncan MacFayden and I spent about ten very full days preparing a report that they would accept."

While all this was going on, the salvage merchant who had bought the Mars flying boats had a problem of his own.

He was aware that he had a potential sale for the aircraft, but one of the terms of the Navy's sale was that he remove the first aircraft from the base at Alameda within ninety days and one every thirty days thereafter. If he sold them, they could be flown out. Otherwise he would have to start dismantling them. He overcame this problem by towing one across the water to San Francisco Municipal Airport and beaching it there. By the time the deadline for the second machine arrived, the aircraft had been purchased by the consortium of B.C. forest companies who were to form Forest Industries Flying Tankers Limited.

The Martin Mars JRM-1 is a high-wing, all-metal, four-engine flying boat whose hull features two decks, the lower one with watertight bulkheads extending the full length of its thirteen foot wide flight deck. It is 120 feet long with a wing span of 200 feet and is powered by four Curtiss Wright R-3350-8 radial engines rated at 2,400-horsepower Four bladed Curtiss Electric propellers measuring sixteen feet, eight inches in diameter drive this aerial giant. While in service with U.S. Navy squadron VR-2, the Mars fleet established distance and weight lifting records.

In recognition of their role as transport aircraft in the South Pacific, the Mars were christened after the islands they were to visit and serve: Marianna, Philippine, Hawaii, Caroline, and Marshall Mars. Caroline Mars, the last of the series to be produced, was fitted with Pratt & Whitney R-4360-24 engines to enhance performance. These 3,000-horsepower radials improved the gross take off weight to 82.5 tons compared to 72.5 tons of the JRM-1. Of the five Mars aircraft built by the Glenn L. Martin Company for the U.S. Navy, the Marshall Mars was the only one lost in service. It went down on April 5, 1950 off Honolulu after an in-flight fire.

Following their relatively short career in U.S. Navy service, it appeared that these behemoths of the air were destined for the scrap heap. This, however, was not to be. The efforts of Dan McIvor, with the help of a few believers like Ernie Shorter, Leigh Stevenson and Duncan MacFayden, were winning support at the M & B board level. Time, however, was fast running out on the purchase option granted by Mars Metal to M & B, when at last on July 29, 1959, with but minutes to spare, M & B forwarded a telegram advising agreement to exercise the option and purchase the four remaining Mars aircraft.

In late 1959, MacMillan & Bloedel was joined by five other major B.C. forest companies to form a new corporation, Forest Industries Flying Tankers Limited (often referred to simply as FIFT) to operate the aircraft. The six sponsoring companies became shareholders,[1] with shares allocated based on their respective holdings. M & B was the major shareholder and agreed to provide administrative management for FIFT, while British Columbia Forest Products Limited (BCFP), Canadian Forest Products Ltd. (Canfor), Powell River Company Limited, Tahsis Co. Ltd., and Western Forest Industries Limited each appointed a director to the new FIFT board.

---

1 Membership in FIFT changed over the years, some companies withdrawing, others joining as shareholders while mergers and consolidations changed the names of many of the original member companies. Canadian Forest Products withdrew in 1962 following the loss of Marianna's Mars; Pacific Logging Company joined in 1963, while Western Forest Industries withdrew in 1980. The holdings of the Powell River Company were acquired by MacMillan Bloedel in 1960, while Pacific Logging and Tahsis were consolidated as part of Canadian Pacific Forest Products in 1988, and finally, in 1988, the shares of B.C. Forest Products were transferred to Fletcher Challenge (Canada) Ltd.

On the February 23, 1960 ownership of the Mars was formally transferred by M & B to the new company.

In retrospect, the U.S. $100,000 purchase price for the four planes was a bargain when one considers that they cost the American taxpayers $3.5 million each when delivered in the mid-1940s to VR-2 Squadron of the U.S. Navy. However, it was a big gamble for the FIFT shareholders and showed remarkable courage and foresight on their part. Much more would have to be spent to convert them to their new role and there was no guarantee they could do the job. Mr. H. F. Forster of Mars Metal Corporation hadn't done badly on the transaction. His winning bid for the aircraft at an earlier open tender was $23,650 and this had been posted using borrowed money.

During the month of July, 1959, Dan McIvor became a familiar figure around Alameda Air Station as he scurried

With permission from Forest Industries Flying Tankers Limited collection

Dan McIvor in door of a Mars, 1959.

to and fro striving to solve the myriad problems associated with readying four strange and awesome aircraft for ferry to B.C. He had been singularly fortunate in securing the services of a senior ex-Mars captain and a flight engineer. McIvor still managed to find time to relieve Alameda Station, with the friendly connivance of the supply officer, of several million dollars worth of surplus Mars stores and equipment. The price, a friendly $3,500.

On August 8, the Marianna Mars made the ferry flight to Pat Bay. She was followed by the Caroline Mars on August 27, the Philippine on September 5, and the Hawaii on September 12. A tense episode occurred on the September 5 run when a Canadian engineer in training inadvertently cut off all fuel flow and the Philippine Mars plunged nearly 10,000 feet to wave height before control was re-established.

With permission from Forest Industries Flying Tankers Limited collection

FIFT cookhouse scene, Sproat Lake, 1960. Dan McIvor at left, facing camera. Bill Waddington second from right.

As the concept of using such a large aeroplane as a water bomber was not yet proven, (the U.S. Forestry Service had turned down the Mars) approval of the FIFT directors was only given for one of them to be converted by Fairey Aviation. Early in 1960, before the commencement of the fire season, this was completed.

"During that summer we didn't have any fires," recalls McIvor, *"and there was no conclusive test of the aeroplane at all. We had unserviceability, we had the props going out, we had engine failures, we had probes breaking off. Everything went wrong, but we managed to keep operating.*

"The next spring, just as fire season was approaching, I lost my medical rating. I was moved into the position of manager of the project and my co-pilot took over the job of captain of the aircraft. This was unfortunate, because he did not yet have enough experience in fighting fires. When

With permission of Forest Industries Flying Tankers Limited collection

The first water drop from a Mars, 1960.

you are fighting fires you should never go into the smoke and you should never go uphill. You must always come downhill. If anything happens, all you have to do is go up and you are in the clear. He chose to fight a fire by coming around the side of the hill into a saucer, barely clearing the tree tops and flew right into the hill, starting a bigger fire than the one he was fighting. All the crew were killed."

This accident was almost a fatal blow to the fledgling venture, as the Mars had not yet proven its worth in the fire fighting role.

"We had been operating on a month-to-month basis with this aircraft," continues McIvor, *"and it was touch and go whether we could get approval to get another converted. Ernie Shorter, the vice-president of operations for M & B came over from Vancouver to ask what had gone wrong. I had flown over the wreck, I had talked to people on the ground. The evidence was quite conclusive. I told Ernie.*

"There was nothing wrong with that aeroplane. There is nothing wrong with the concept. It was pilot error, nothing else but pilot error."

Ernie agreed with my conclusion and reported back to the directors and, within a week, we had approval to get the second aircraft converted. We still hadn't proved anything. We still didn't know whether the airplane could put fires out or not. Work started on the Caroline Mars.

"The next summer's fire season had just started when there was a fire down on Cowichan Lake. It was on a steep hillside and it was really smoking. It had burned about halfway up the hill. Bill Waddington and I were flying the Mars—I had my licence back by then—and we made the drop right across the top of the fire. We made eight drops, went down and picked up a ninth load, but when we got back to the site of the fire it was out. There wasn't any smoke, and the ground crew which came in to mop up reported that it was completely out.

"A few days later, we had another big fire in over-mature cedar up by Ramsay Arm on Bute Inlet. We put twenty-two drops on it in about two hours. When we made the first drop you could see the fire burning in the windfalls under the canopy of the trees, by the sixth load the fire was no longer visible and we were able to place the subsequent loads from as low as we could get. After the twenty-second, there was no more smoke and no more fire. The ground crews didn't have to do anything more than watch.

"With those two fires we proved the concept of the big water bomber. With two scoops just behind the step, the Mars could land on the water at seventy-four knots, skim along the surface at seventy-two knots, filling the tank with 6,000 gallons in twenty-six seconds and become airborne almost immediately afterwards. Being able to hit the fires with loads like that in rapid succession is what makes the Mars the best fire bomber in the world."

But the difficulties of FIFT were not yet over. During the rampaging night of October 12, 1962, Hurricane Freida caught the Caroline Mars atop her beaching gear on Pat Bay airport. Despite being securely anchored to tie-down clamps by 1/2 inch steel cables, the hawsers snapped and dawn disclosed the JRM-2 wrecked beyond repair. Sadly, the Directors of FIFT ordered Caroline Mars scrapped for salvage of all usable parts and components, which were then added to the stock of spares.

In December 1963, the company's Directors, with some trepidation, embarked on yet another gamble by authorizing conversion of Hawaii Mars. Thus, in July 1964, the only two remaining Mars aircraft in the world were once again together, destined to continue flying side-by-side in their new role as water bombers.

To provide a home for the last two Martin Mars flying boats in existence, the company in 1964 established its permanent operations base on Sproat Lake, There, during the summer months, one can still see the two mighty giants riding at anchor on the Lake or flying in and out on their missions. Each year, when the fire season is over, they are moved ashore where their maintenance crews go over them from stem to stern, like doctors performing a check-up, looking for corrosion or any other problem ailments.

To prolong the life of the Mars and add yet another tool to its arsenal for fighting forest fires, the company added three helicopters to its fleet in 1974. These machines, together with the Mars and the faithful Grumman Goose "bird-dog," combine to provide a complete fire-suppression service that is hard to beat.

At the close of the 1986 fire season the statistics were obligingly toted up by the company. Number of major fires quelled since the formation of the company, 373 – involving 6,479 drops. Total operational hours flown, 2,160 – in the course of which some 33,826,700 imperial gallons were dropped. Value of timber saved? Even a conservative estimate begins with multi-millions of dollars.

Conair Grumman TBM Avenger.

CMFT Collection #274.1
Conair collection

If the Martin Mars are viewed as the heavy sabres in the ongoing forest fire duels, surely ConAir's aircraft must be deemed the ruffling blades in the fray. Home based at Abbotsford Airport, the twenty-one year old air fire fighting company fields an impressive fleet of wheeled heavy and medium bombers, which it deploys with a surgical precision made possible by their unique water and retardant tank construction. ConAir ranges far afield on fire suppression in B.C. and beyond, buttressing its fixed-wing squadrons with the thirty-two helicopters and helitankers of its rotary-wing subsidiary, Frontier Helicopters Ltd.

Les Kerr, 1989.

CMFT Collection #274.3
Conair collection

ConAir Avitation Ltd. was formed in 1969 when Les Kerr, a staff pilot with Skyway Air Services, bought out Skyway's combined fire fighting and spraying operation. He was joined by fellow Skyway pilots Barry Marsden and Slim Knights. The company started up with thirty-five employees and a mix of fourteen aircraft consisting of Stearmans, Grumman Avengers and Douglas A-26 Invaders. In 1970 they disposed of the spray machines and concentrated on fire fighters solely. Twenty years later, ConAir operates the largest private fleet of fire fighting aircraft in the world.

An early fire contract with the province of British Columbia was followed by one with Alberta, the Yukon and the Northwest Territories. Their expertise was acknowledged internationally when they were retained by Australia, France, Mexico, Portugal and the United States.

In 1972 ConAir acquired the first of their Douglas DC-6B tankers, which now total ten. In 1978 they commenced adding ex-Canadian Armed Forces Grumman

ConAir Turbo Firecat prototype, 1988. ConAir built thirty-three Firecats (piston-engined) between 1978 and 1989.

CMFT Collection #274.2
Conair collection

Trackers, designated after conversion as the ConAir Firecat. They now own twelve Firecats. The acquisition of two Fokker F27's then followed, which after conversion are known as F27 Firefighters. In addition, ConAir operates and maintains on behalf of the federal government, four CL 215s, the amphibious aircraft specifically designed as a water bomber by Canadair Ltd. Rounding out ConAir's impressive fleet of fifty-one fixed-wing machines are seventeen Piper Aerostars functioning as "bird dog" machines, two Beechcraft King Air 200s, two Cessna 210s, one Cessna 337, all of which can double as communication or bird dog, plus one Harvard. The Avengers and A-26 Invaders were earlier phased out.

ConAir has been a pioneer in the field of design, development and installation of their innovative compartmentalized water/retardant tanks, now standard equipment on their fixed-wing and helitanker fleet. Parallel with this they have designed the key ground equipment and expertise necessary for fast reloading of the tanks permitting quick turnaround for the aircraft. The tank systems permit variable load release capability through the discharge doors of each compartment. The pilot preselects or alters the drop pattern while in flight to combat any constantly changing fire situation. The objective, a maximum dousing impact for a minimum load expenditure, is a key requirement for aircraft that may be required to fly a long distance to base for reloading.

The Abbotsford firm is now exporting its peaceful weapons systems and specialty services in fire fighting products, including modified aircraft, worldwide. Australia, France, Italy, Japan, Saudi Arabia, Spain and the United States are customers. It recently modified the Grumman Firecat to a turbine version, installing the P & W PT-6 engines. Three have since been sold to France. Its two companies now employ 540 personnel.

A latter-day pioneer in a specialized aviation technology, ConAir and its rotary-wing subsidiary are now world leaders in their field. Their reputation and attainments are a source of considerable pride to British Columbia.

24

THE LAST WORD – NATURALLY

The Flying Seven

by Elizabeth Caroline Gwilliam

This chapter, incorporating the history of British Columbia's "Flying Seven" was written by Mrs. E. C. Smith (nee Gwilliam) in late 1975. The passage of time has detracted not a whit from its relevance and interest. Sadly, the intervening years have seen the group's numbers reduced from seven to three. *The Editor*

Thanks to the brain wave Ms. Norris Preston had "in the middle of the night" the Victoria Status of Women Action Group (SWAG) were able to enjoy the official opening of the exhibit "Our Hidden Heritage" – Women in British Columbia History – on the second floor of the Provincial Museum in Victoria. The project has been piloted by Linda Gilligan, co-ordinator and research director, who spent many months searching through archives and libraries and interviewing "old-timers." On September 4, 1975, some of the real people stepped out of their picture frames in the exhibit at the official opening in the afternoon, in the form of the Flying Seven, five of the original group. At the evening gathering at the museum, after the introductory speeches and re-introduction of the five remaining Flying Seven, the question asked by the guests attending the function was, "How did you come together in a group?"

The Flying Seven ranged in age from eighteen to the fifties in 1936, when they met at the Vancouver Airport, each one having trained in their own way across Canada. Betsy Flaherty, Alma (Gaudreau) Gilbert, Rolie Moore, Jean Pike, and Tosca Trasolini had private pilot licences, while Margaret Fane and Elianne Roberge gained both private and commercial licences. The group held regular monthly meetings. One of the aims of this group was to promote aviation among the women in Canada, and they hoped other groups in Canadian cities would be inspired to form flying clubs for women. They held competitions and obtained trophies through several donors.

Vancouver Province Archives, via Margaret Rutledge

The Flying Seven line up in front of a fleet at Sea Island Airport. Left to Right: Jean Pike, Tosca Trasolini, Betsy Flaherty, Elianne Roberge, Alma (Gaudreau) Gilbert, Margaret Fane, and Rolie Moore.

Their first notable undertaking was a Dawn to Dusk Patrol in November, 1936, when all seven kept their planes in the air in a perpetual chain of take offs and landings on a foggy day, when wiser pilots shook their heads in dismay. It was a complete success and a "first" for women. Several members performed at Airshows in Vancouver and other British Columbia towns, usually where airports were opening. The Flying Seven hosted a number of social gatherings for celebrities in the aviation world and met world famous pilots at the airport on occasion. Several attended the ceremony at Vancouver Airport when the first Trans Canada Air Lines flight departed with Betsy Flaherty presenting the first ticket sold for her cross-Canada flight. The Aero Club of B.C. also appointed several members as directors.

The Flying Seven offered their services to the Department of National Defence in Ottawa at the beginning of World War II, feeling sure there were many women flyers who could be trained for national service. A formal acknowledgment reported "there were no regulations concerning women;" so they decided to support an Air Supremacy Drive on June 18, 1940. Three aircraft dropped 100,000 pamphlets over Vancouver, urging support for the boys who were training and those overseas.

Following a suggestion the "Female Air Bombardiers" would make good instructors, they sponsored the first training center for women in Canada, which opened in May, 1941, in Vancouver at the Model School, across the street from the present City Hall. To everyone's surprise a former pupil and graduate from this school was present at the evening presentation of the Flying Seven at the museum. Betsy, Rolie, Margaret, and Elianne were some of the organizers of the school. Technical flying theory, parachute packing, wireless classes, aircraft fabric, plus lectures on the RAF series were part of the four-month course. Sixty girl's names were drawn from a hatful of 300 registered applicants for the initial course.

Margaret Fane, the world's first woman radio operator, on duty with Ginger Coote Airways, Zeballos, B.C., 1938.

Loaned from Margaret Rutledge collection

Margaret Fane trained at the Aero Club in Edmonton and obtained her private pilot's licence in April, 1933. Her instructor was Captain Maurice Burbidge. She was the only woman pilot in a Dawn to Dusk Patrol in 1934. In July, 1935, she received her commercial licence. As Edmonton was a crossroads to the north, she met many famous pilots, such as "Punch" Dickens and "Wop" May. In 1935 Margaret's family moved to Vancouver where she met the girls who formed the Flying Seven. She had trained as the world's first woman radio operator and could replace a pilot or an airline radio operator. Her first husband, Gordon Scott, was Terminal Superintendent of Canadian Pacific Air Lines at the time of his death, and Margaret later became a Supervisor of Reservations of the same company. In November, 1956, she married William Keith Rutledge and currently resides in Richmond, B.C.

Betsy Flaherty came to Vancouver from Ontario and found work with David Spencer Ltd., later bought out by Eaton's Limited. She was appointed a buyer for children's wear and was one of the first buyers to fly east, but this was via Seattle and American Airlines. When she made a decision to take up flying, Hal Wilson was her instructor, and she received the second licence issued to a woman in Vancouver on December 16, 1931. She was the only woman pilot to fly from Vancouver to Vernon in an Aero Club machine on a British Columbia Air Tour, and on several occasions was the only woman competitor in the Aero Club competitions. In 1964, Betsy was a guest of Air Canada (formerly Trans Canada Air Lines) on a tour of Canada to commemorate the Twenty-fifth Anniversary of the first revenue flight. Air Canada also arranged a trip to Expo '67 so she could especially tour the Aviation exhibit. Her life came to a sudden end in 1968, just a week before the new jet terminal opened in Vancouver. She had expressed the wish to cut the ribbon at that event.

CMFT Collection #81.1 Beryl Armstrong collection

Left to Right: Beryl Armstrong, Margaret Ecker, Rolie Barrett, Pat Gray, Elianne Roberge, Betsy Flaherty, Wattie Fox, Han-Yin Cheng, Alma Gilbert, Betty Waller, and Miss Lee. Some of the original "Flying Seven" met in 1941 with others who later became part of the group.

Alma (Gaudreau) Gilbert was a petite, vivacious French girl who recalls the men seemed to think the women flyers were trying to make themselves equal to the men. She felt men treated the women pilots as more or less "one of the boys," and at times the women felt the respect and courtesy from them was lacking. Born in Quebec, Alma decided to go west in 1927. She became interested in aviation through friends and trained with Donald Lawson, receiving her private pilot's licence in 1933. She met the other girls who formed the Flying Seven and entered into flying competitions with them. In 1941 she obtained her commercial licence. She ferried single-engine Aeronca aircraft on two occasions from the eastern states in the early years of World War II for the training school she was with. She worked later with Boeing Aircraft and then in 1961 moved to Philadelphia, Pennsylvania. She later returned to Vancouver where she resides at present.

Rolie Moore (Mrs. Denis Pierce) was the aerobatic pilot of the Flying Seven, trained by Hal Wilson, and she obtained her private pilot's licence in 1935. She competed in England and the Western Zone Flying Competition at Saskatoon for the Webster Trophy, placing second. She obtained her commercial licence in July, 1939, and instructor's rating in 1946, the first B.C. woman to do so. She also acquired her public transport licence, having the second licence issued to a woman in Canada. Her first husband was killed overseas during World War II. At present she is interested in horses and riding clubs in the lower Fraser Valley where she resides.

Jean Pike received her private pilot's licence at a very early age, and was the youngest member of the Flying Seven. She took part in the Dawn to Dusk Patrol, but moved east the following April, and has not been contacted since.

Elianne Roberge, although born in British Columbia, received her early training in Quebec. Captain F. G. M. Sparks and Captain Dewar were her instructors at Ville LaSalle, and she obtained her private pilot's licence in October, 1930, and her commercial licence in October, 1932, the first western girl to do so. She returned to the west and met the girls in the Flying Seven group and took part in the Dawn to Dusk Patrol and Pamphlet Raid. In 1941 Elianne applied to Ottawa for a defence job, but ended up going to Washington D.C. to the Royal Air Force delegation as a secretary. In 1942 she had temporary leave to work in Edmonton for the late Grant McConachie, her former employer. Later she returned to Washington and was assigned to the British Air Commission, as Negotiator for Procurement of Aircraft Equipment for Lancaster Bombers and for the British Commonwealth Air Training Plan in the United States and Nassau, Bahamas. Elianne tried in vain to organize Canadian women pilots as a unit through the Canadian Department of National Defence. She intended to join the Overseas Contingent of United States and Rehabilitation for operation in China, but met her future husband, Fred Schlageter, and after being married, lived in San Francisco for a time before returning to Crescent Beach, where she later died.

Tosca Trasolini, a native daughter of Vancouver, trained in the Wells School of Aviation with Jack Wright as her instructor, one of the first pilots for Trans Canada Air Lines. She received her private pilot's licence on July 13, 1936, and joined the Flying Seven that year, taking part in the Dawn to Dusk Patrol. She won several competitions. Tosca obtained her American licence in 1958 and was secretary of the Flying Derby Club in southern California, where she resides. Tosca's husband, Leland Tenhoff, was in the United States Army, and formerly stationed in

Tosca Trasolini

Jean Pike

Elianne Roberge

Betsy Flaherty

Rolie Moore

Alma Gilbert

Thailand. She has now retired from her business career in the Los Angeles area.

A wartime flying role for women

While most roles for women during WWII were non-flying, an exception was the Air Transport Auxiliary (ATA) in the United Kingdom. The women's division of the ATA was composed of women pilots from all over the allied world. They ferried new airplanes from factories to airfields and flew damaged airplanes back to repair centers.

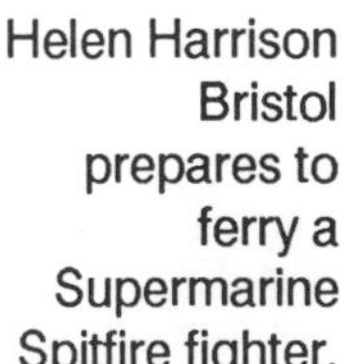

Helen Harrison Bristol prepares to ferry a Supermarine Spitfire fighter.

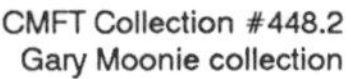

CMFT Collection #448.2
Gary Moonie collection

Helen Harrison Bristol was the first female Canadian pilot to serve in the Air Transport Auxiliary (ATA). She ferried all types of aircraft from fighters to heavy bombers.

CMFT Collection 87.60

The Canadian Museum of Flight and Transportation de Havilland Tiger Moth, Harvard, and Fleet Finch display.

25

FOR FUTURE GENERATIONS

Preserving Canada's aviation history

by Rose Zalesky, Canadian Museum of Flight and Transportation

Man has always dreamed of being able to fly, and his attempts to do so have ultimately produced the sophisticated aircraft and space vehicles which have changed our lives. In the context of time, the air and space ages are very young, and some of those who pioneered the use of aircraft in Canada are still living. It is only within the last few decades that serious moves were made to preserve examples of the machinery and paraphernalia that represents the growth of aviation in Canada, and to put to paper the stories and anecdotes of those who were there that best evoke an understanding of what it was like in those times.

During World War I the new fangled flying machines had proven their worth in battle and forever changed the face of war. When the fighting ceased, hundreds of men who were trained for aerial warfare tried to find ways of continuing their love affair with flying by inventing new reasons to fly.

The aeroplane and the people who operated them added a new dimension of speed and scope to exploration, mapping, mail service and the transportation of people and goods. Eventually a network of air routes was mapped and regular passenger and freight services became accepted as necessities.

Aircraft designers and manufacturers took up the challenge to produce more and better aircraft to carry out these tasks. The two decades preceding World War II and which spanned the great depression are now remembered as the Golden Age of Aviation.

World War II spawned accelerated advances in technology including the introduction of the jet and rocket ages. War's end brought a resurgence of peacetime aviation activity, and as each new advance in aircraft design and support equipment was made, it was "out with the old and in with the new," as commercial operators, the growing business aircraft sector and training schools strived to update and improve their fleets. Some recycling took place, but too many aircraft ended their days on the scrap heap.

While this book is a tribute to those who flew, maintained, or were a part of early air operations, it also recognizes the people who seek to capture the essence of early aviation for ensuing generations.

Canada's National Aviation Museum, after decades of collecting and restoring examples of aircraft and the trappings of flight, is now finally splendidly housed. New exhibits are being completed to better tell the story of aviation from a Canadian perspective.

The military has finally come on board, and new military museums are springing up on Armed Forces bases across the country.

We owe an enduring debt of gratitude to another group of people. These are the men and women who, in their spare time, scoured the hinterlands and farmyards of the nation for derelict or cast-off aircraft and artifacts, with no thought of reward, but simply to save as many of the rapidly disappearing airplanes as they could. There are approximately sixteen recognized aviation museums and collections across Canada today, most of which were spawned and are still operated by such volunteer collectors and restorers. Most are registered as non-profit organizations, with membership open to the public, and fill a niche for regional aviation museums. Sadly, with little or no support from governments, they face mounting housing problems and escalating costs.

The Canadian Museum of Flight and Transportation is a classic example of such an organization. Conceived in the early 1970s as the dream of aircraft parts dealer Ed Zalesky, and later joined by Captain Bill Thompson, G. Barry Jackson, Ron Stunden, and Rose Zalesky, the Museum was formalized as a society in 1977.

Not long after, the Pacific Aviation Museum, which had been formed a few years prior, was absorbed along with their small collection.

Volunteers utilized an information network to locate and retrieve wrecks, derelicts and the occasional intact aircraft. In some cases small sums of money were found to purchase the motley items, but in most cases, they were freely donated by concerned citizens or the Crown.

As the collection grew in size and scope, it began to attract better donations. A WWII Fleet Finch trainer, the first flying aircraft, was received in 1979. About this time, a book and photo library was taking shape, and storage for the growing collections was becoming a problem.

Collected items were stored mainly on the Zalesky family farm, spilling out of buildings erected to house them, and prompting many calls from Surrey's by-law squad. Continuous attempts to find a permanent home for the museum all failed, and finally, in 1985, the Zalesky property was expropriated for park purposes by Surrey municipality.

By this time, the museum was open to the public on a daily basis and was attracting visitors from around the world. Expertise and willing hands enjoined to create a smoothly operating organization, and more and more aircraft were placed on display.

CMFT Collection C87.42

The collection ranges from representative examples of WWI types through to homebuilts using state-of-the-art construction.

The five-year lease granted to the museum at the time of expropriation is being extended on a yearly basis, and attempts to find a new home site continue. The favoured location is a property purchased by Surrey in 1989 for the purpose.

The museum is now undergoing great change – in direction, in structure and in mandate. The original goal was to build a museum, and the method was to start at the beginning by building a collection. This has largely been accomplished, but the task of maintaining the exhibits and grounds now dictates daily activity. The next step is to provide structures and personnel to shelter, display and manage the collection on a new site. This is no easy task in the light of estimated costs exceeding $10,000,000 for a spartan facility.

Still, ways must be found to accomplish it, otherwise all the time, effort and money that has been invested by so

CMFT Collection 86.27.29

Volunteers, the backbone of the Museum, help to restore and maintain exhibits, and carry out myriad office and general maintenance tasks.

many people over nearly twenty years will have been in vain.

The hope always exists that the business community and governments will step in to give the volunteers a hand.

The collection now ranks amongst the best in Canada, and some one-of-a-kind types are included in the more than sixty aircraft on hand. An abbreviated list of the major aircraft in the collection is provided at the end of this chapter. Lacking covered display space, the viewing season is presently limited to the mid-May through mid-October season, where from twenty-five to thirty aircraft are exhibited in an outdoor park setting. The thousands of small items collected are in storage against the time that adequate exhibit facilities are built. There is an impressive aviation library, as well as a huge collection of photographs, all in the process of being cataloged on computer.

A board of directors elected annually from the general membership is the governing body. The list of over 1,800 members includes teenagers and great-grandmothers.

Museum aircraft are flown for special events and participate in air shows throughout the province and Washington state. Small exhibits and information displays are provided for community events.

There is an emphasis on education. In addition to providing special tours for school children, the Museum runs restoration seminars and other training projects.

Special events include the annual "Wings & Wheels" and car meets. These fun family events feature exhibits from other transportation oriented collections and draw visitors from all over the world.

The on-site gift shop/bookstore is an aviation buff's delight, and provides much of the funds required for daily operation.

The museum is a vibrant, interesting place, and work continues to create live, operating displays for the benefit of this and ensuing generations. While much has been accomplished, there is still much to do.

The dream to share the romance and treasures of our aviation past with future generations is the reason for its existence, and must not be lost.

ABBREVIATED LIST OF HOLDINGS

Canadian Museum of Flight and Transportation

WWI

- Sopwith Camel fighter (replica).

AEROBATIC AND SPORTPLANES

- Stampe biplane. French/Belgian primary aerobatic trainer.
- 1930 Waco INF biplane from the Golden Age of Flight, one of the oldest flying aircraft in Canada.

MILITARY

- 1941 de Havilland DH82C Tiger Moth. Canadian built primary trainer.
- 1941 Fleet 16B Finch. Canadian built primary trainer.
- Fairchild M62A Cornell. Primary trainer built by Fleet Aircraft Canada.
- CCF (Canadian Car and Foundry) Harvard Mk IV. Advanced trainer.
- Bristol Bolingbroke. Bomber/trainer.
- Westland Lysander. WWII Special Operations STOL airplane.
- Handley Page Hamden bomber. The only relatively complete example in existence.

JETS

- de Havilland Vampire. Second operational allied jet fighter.
- Canadair T-33. Canadian built trainer.
- Avro CF-100. Canadian designed and built all-weather fighter.

HOMEBUILTS

- SE5a. WWI fighter (replica).

- Mignet Pou-de-Ciel. 1920s design.
- Bowers Flybaby. Simple construction personal plane.
- Volmer Sportsman. Wooden construction amphibian.
- Rutan Quickie. Composite structure single place.

HELICOPTERS/ROTORCRAFT

- Piasecki HUP3. Search and Rescue.
- Benson Gyroglider and Gyrocopter.
- Sikorsky S55. Supply workhorse.
- Boeing Vertol H-21B. Heavy lift rescue/civilian freighter.

BUSHPLANES AND EARLY AIRLINERS

- Fairchild 71. 1930s bushplane.
- Noorduyn Norseman. One of the most famous bushplanes in Canada.
- Fairchild Husky. Canadian designed and built bushplane.
- Lockheed Lodestar. (Trans Canada Airlines) early airliner and once personal transport of Prime Minister Louis St. Laurent. One of the last remaining examples.
- Beech 18 (C-45). Mini airliner/corporate travel/RCAF.
- Republic Seabee amphibian. This type pioneered coastal charter.

GLIDERS AND SAILPLANES

- 1946 Bowlus (Nelson) Bumblebee/Dragonfly. One of two known in the world. Its wood construction is a work of art.
- Grunau Baby III German sport sailplane. A WWII war prize studied by the National Research Council of Canada.
- Dageling (Zogling). 1920s primary glider trainer.
- Corcoran Cinema TG-2. WWII primary glider trainer.

Index

Photo Credits

Alberni Valley Times
Ambrose, Jeanne
Antonelli, Joe
Armstrong, Beryl
Banting, Lee
Beavis, Mrs.
Bell, Graham
Bell-Irving, D. G.
Bertalino, Joe
Boeing Company
Boyd, Ewan
Burke, Brian
Callison, E. P. (Pat)
Cameron, Neil
Canadian Airways
Canadian Museum of Flight & Transportation
Carstenson, Mary
C.P.A. (via Gordon Croucher)
CP Air (via Wayne Cromie)
Coates, C. P.
ConAir
Fawkes, George
Feast, Arnold
Forest Industries Flying Tankers Ltd.
Gardham, Fred
Gerow, Earl
Hicks, Barbara
Imperial Oil Archives
Jordan, Joan
Jordan, K. E.
Klett, Inky
Kyte, Margery
Laidman, Dick
Lalonde, Joe
Lee, Jerri
Long, Cecil
McIvor, Dan
Madill, Lock
Michaud, Al & Lloyd
Mooney, Gary
Moore, Gordon
Morton, Margery
Moutray, John
Nicol, Marjorie
Peters, Gordon
Renfrew, Cliff
Rutledge, Margaret
Seller, Art
Seymour, Eldon
Spilsbury, Jim
Spires, Robert W.
Steenblok, Mrs. H.
Stevenson, Henry E.
Swartz, Ken
Tayler, Maxse M.
Textron, Inc.
Vancouver Province Archives (via Margaret Rutledge)
Vancouver Public Library
Wells, Billy
Wells, W. H.
Whittle, John
Wikene, Ingwold
Williams, Gordon S.
Williams, Ron
Williamson, George
Wilson, Charles W.